JOURNEY TO THE CENTER

CRISTINA DE MIDDEL

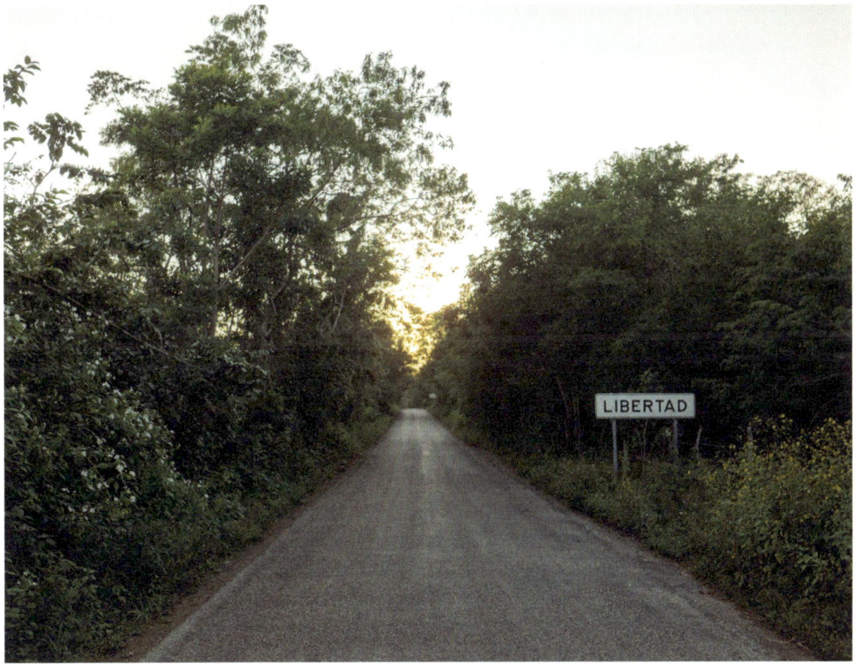
LIBERTAD

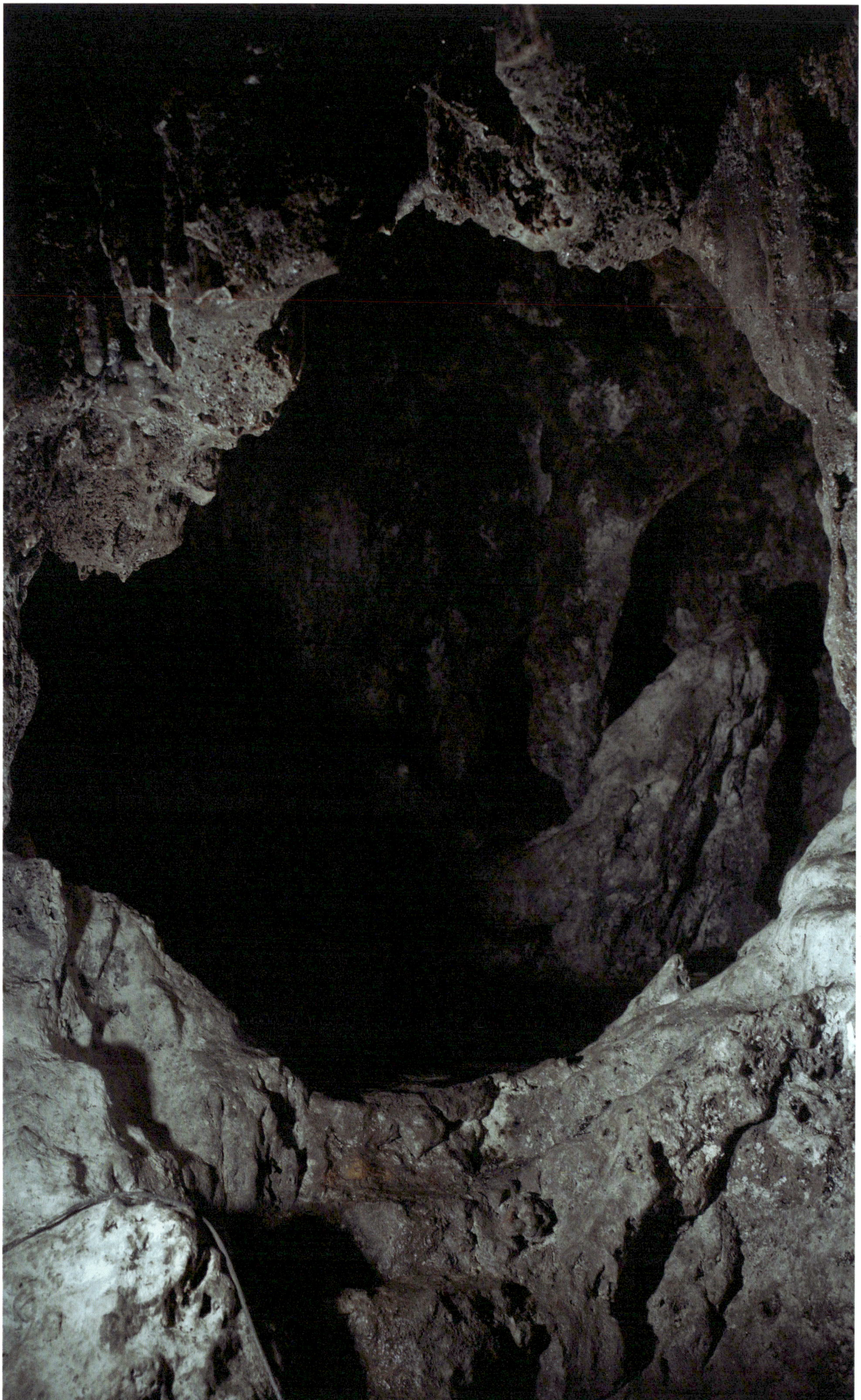

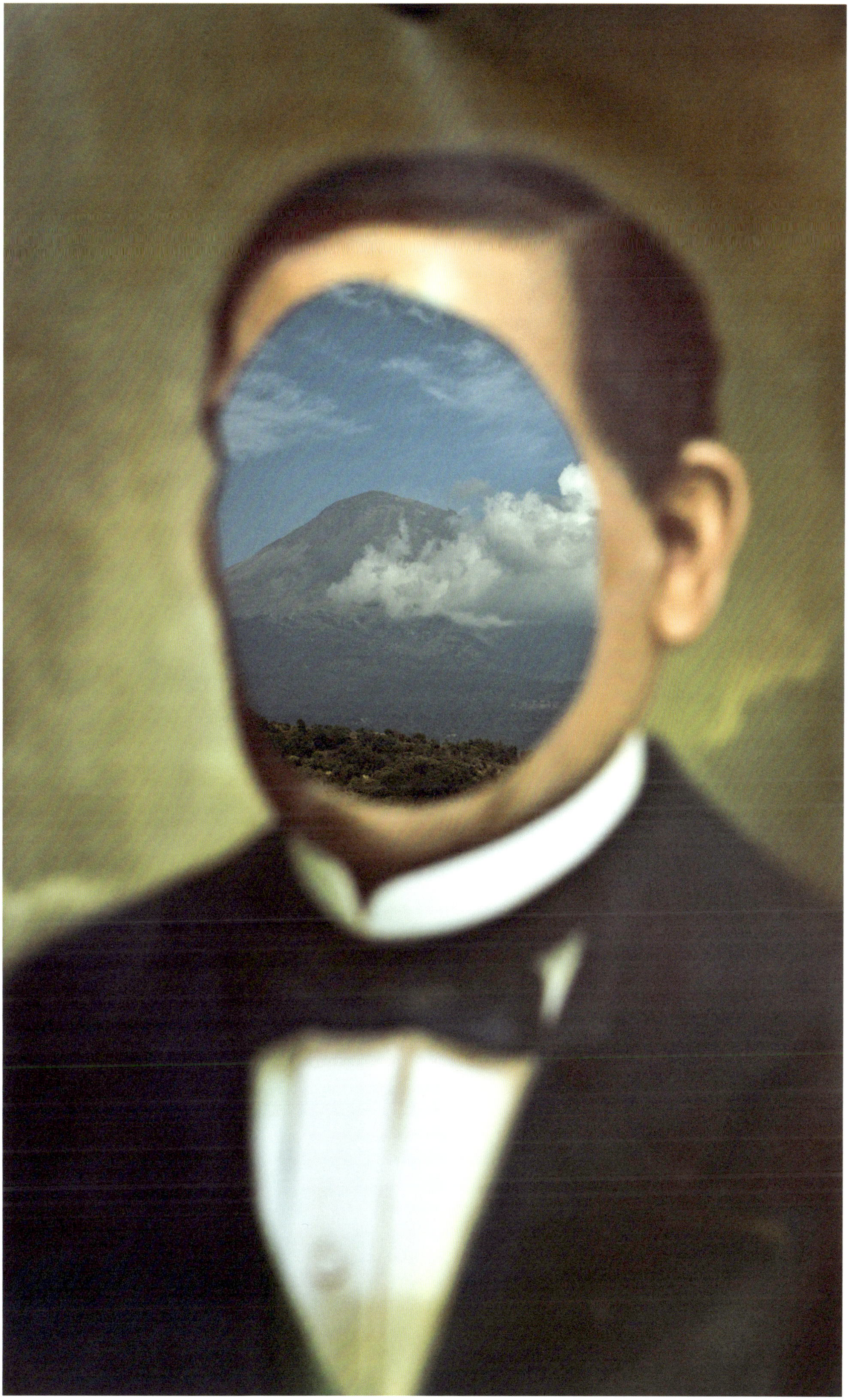

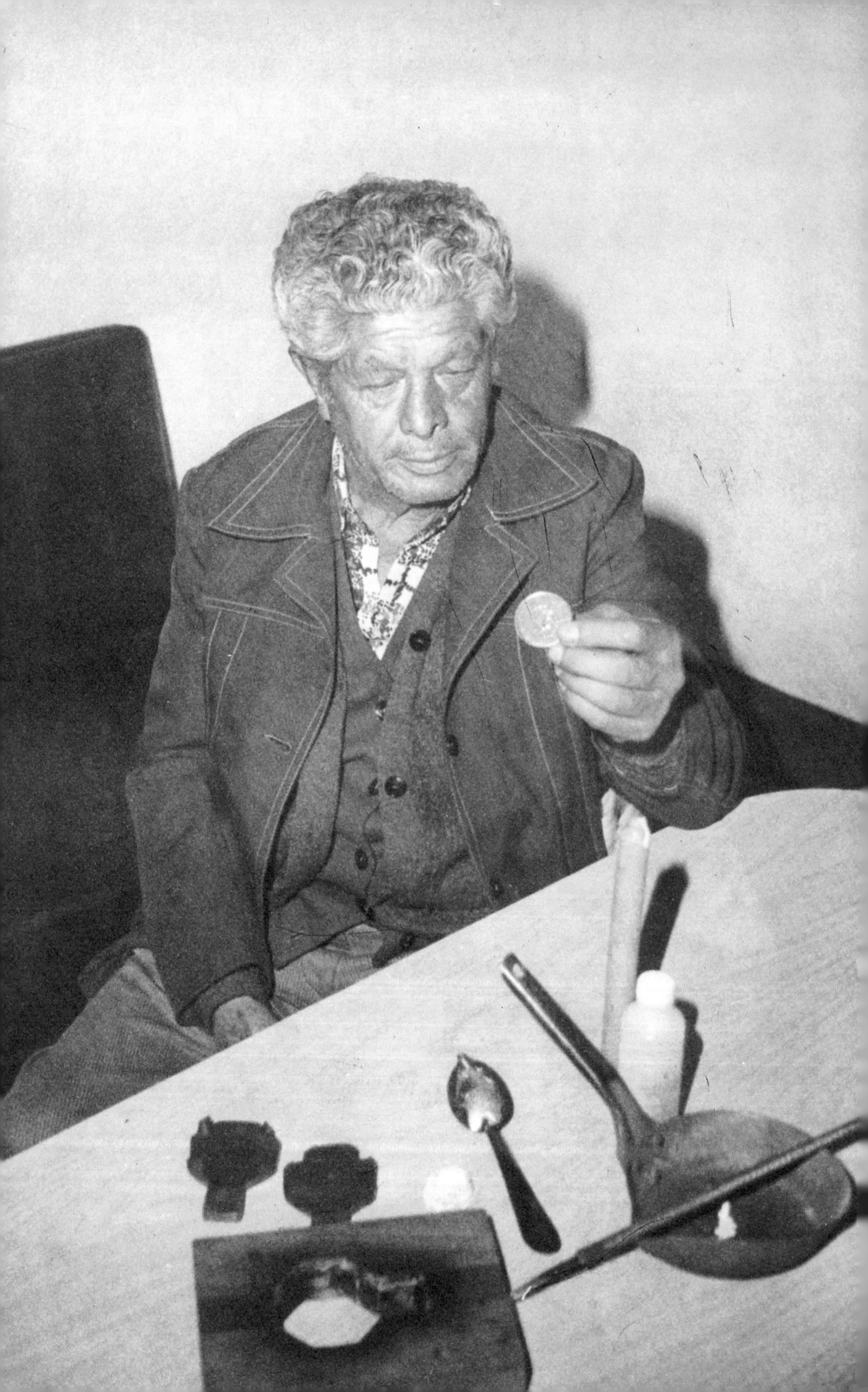

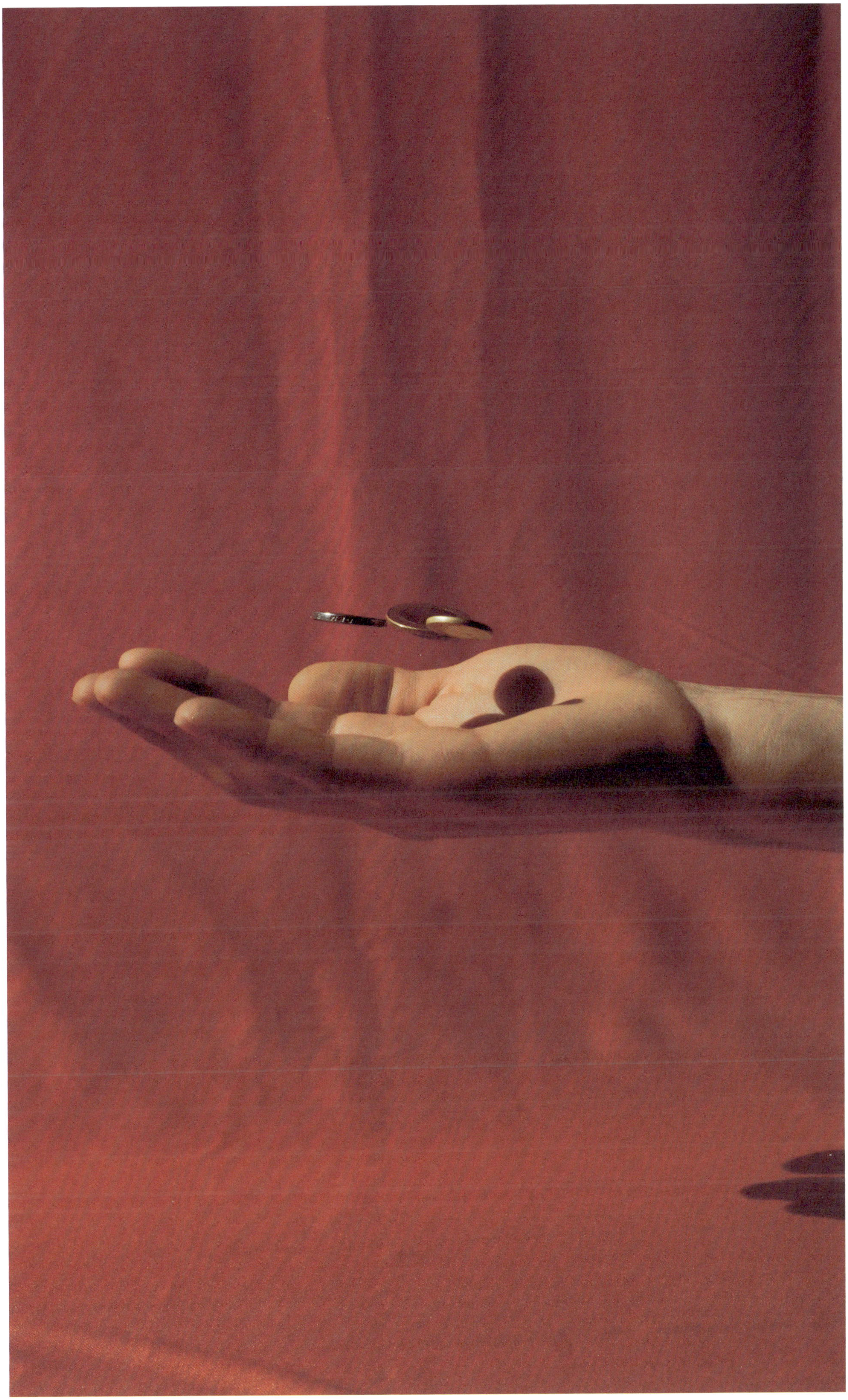

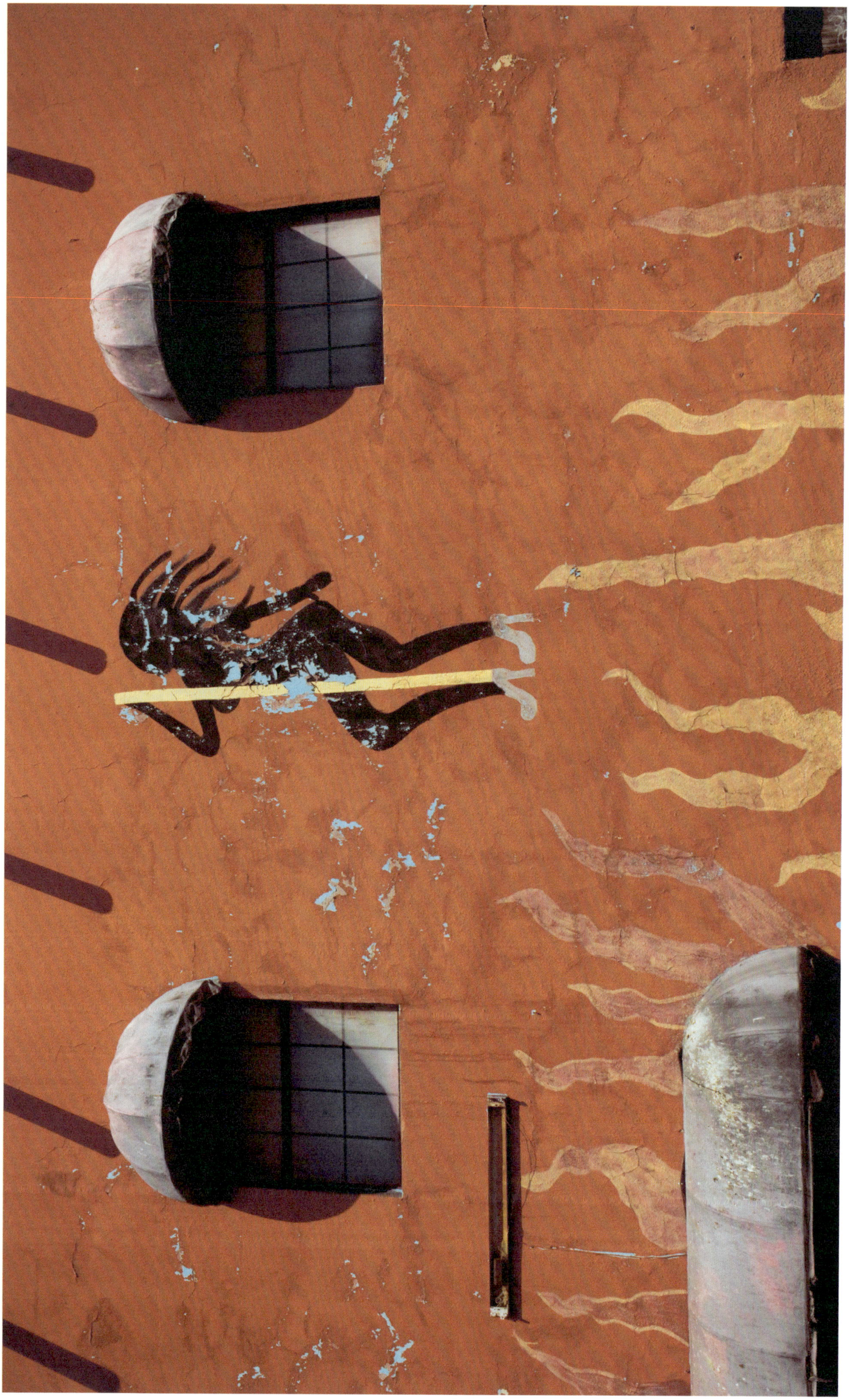

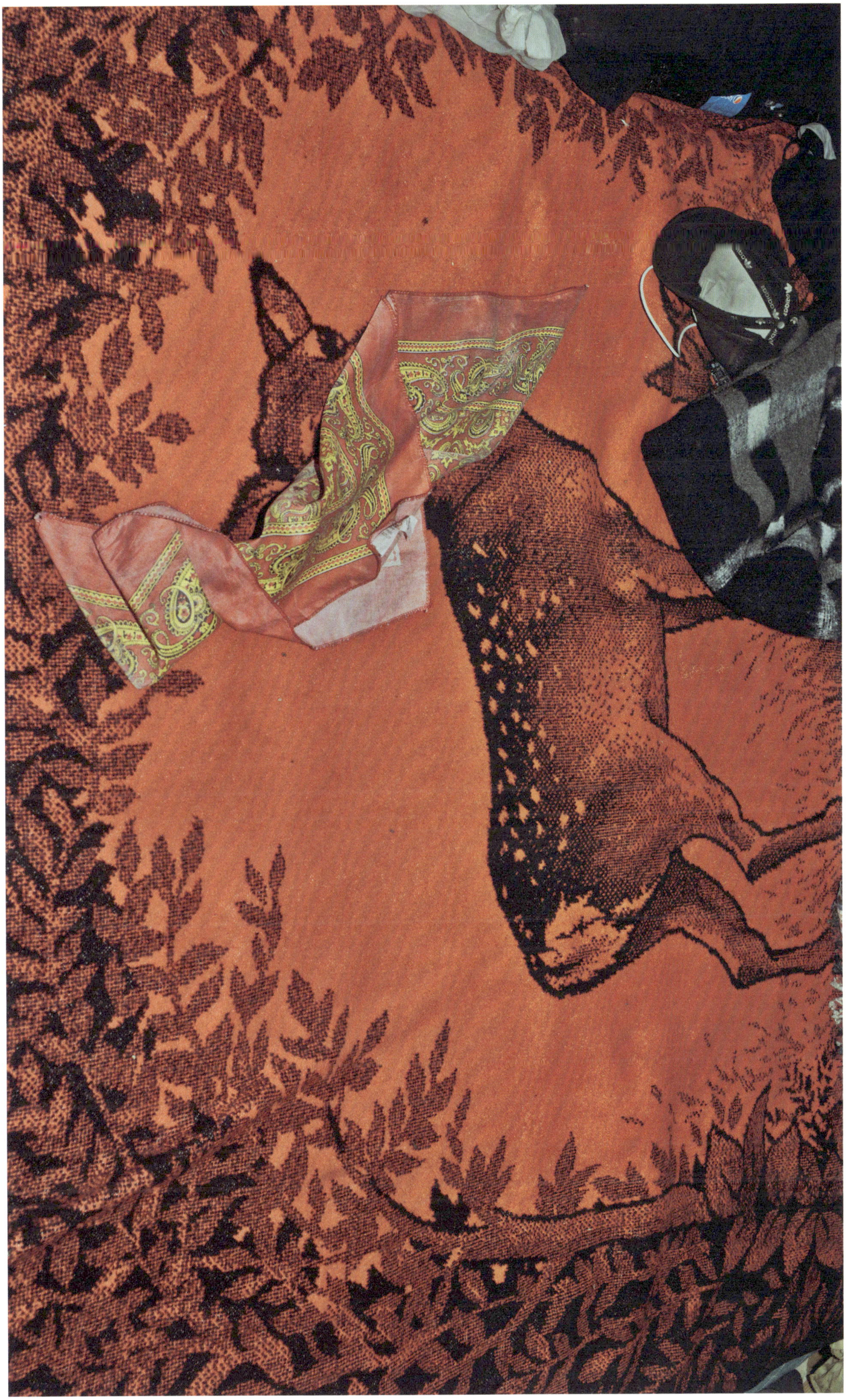

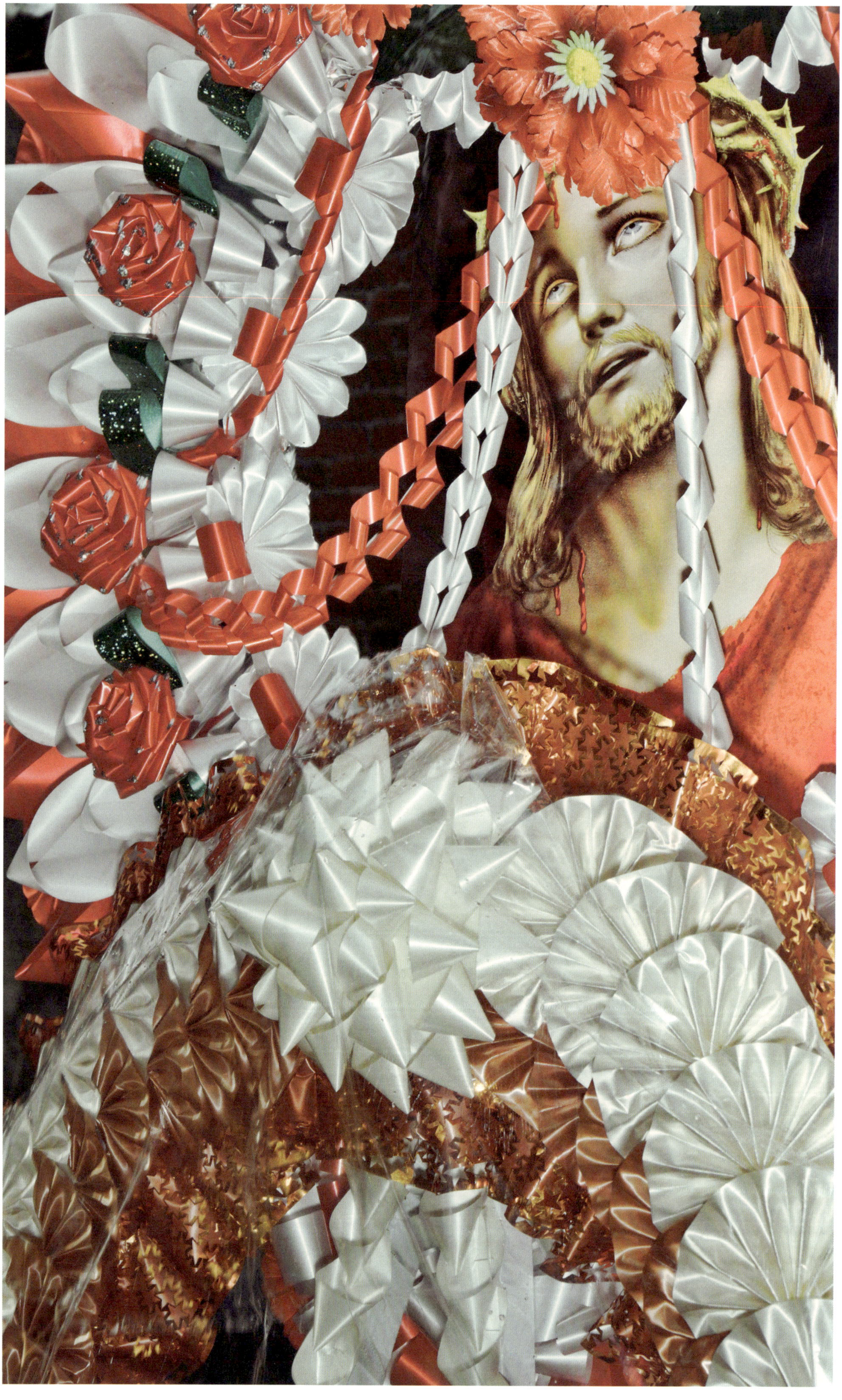

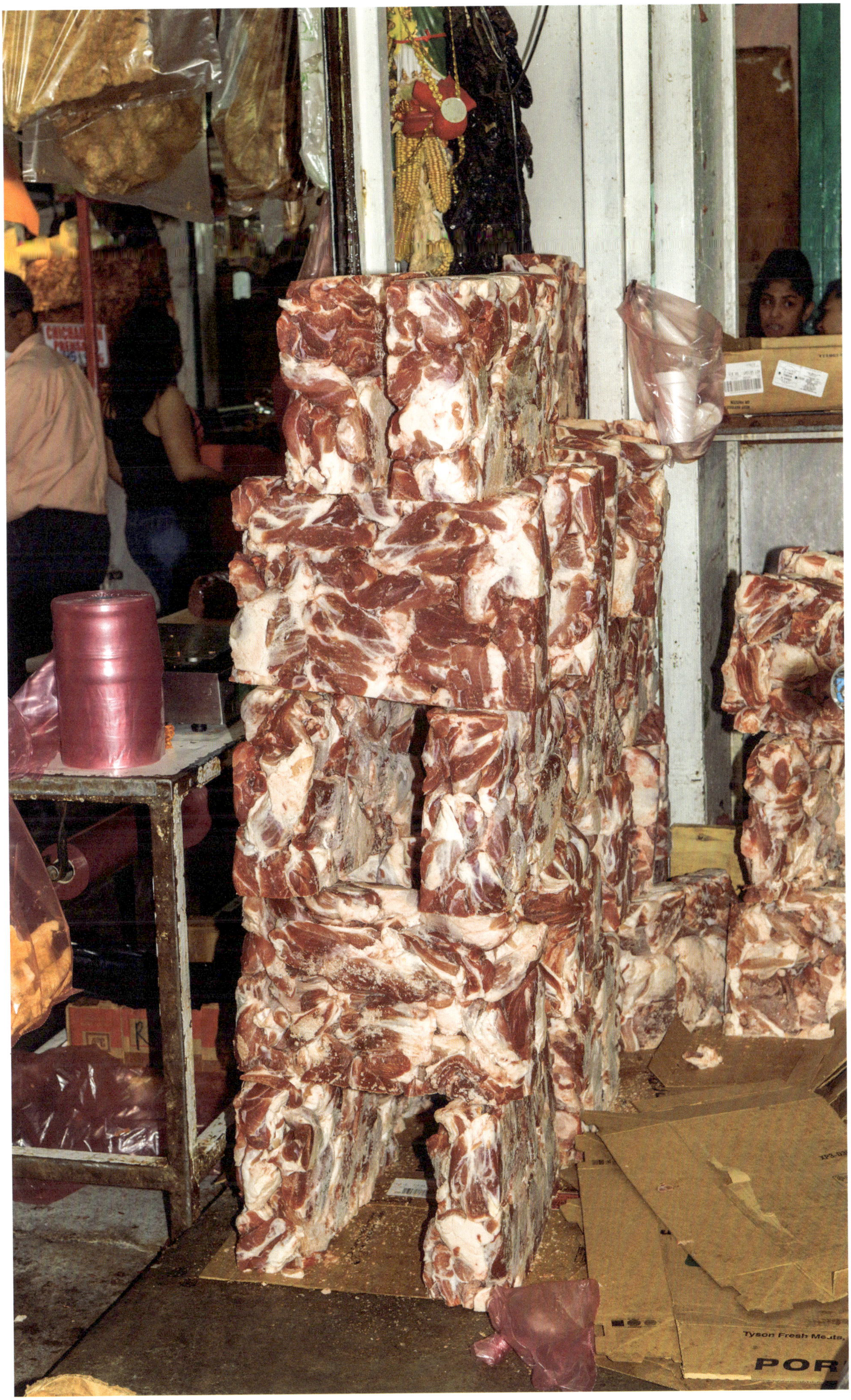
Tyson Fresh

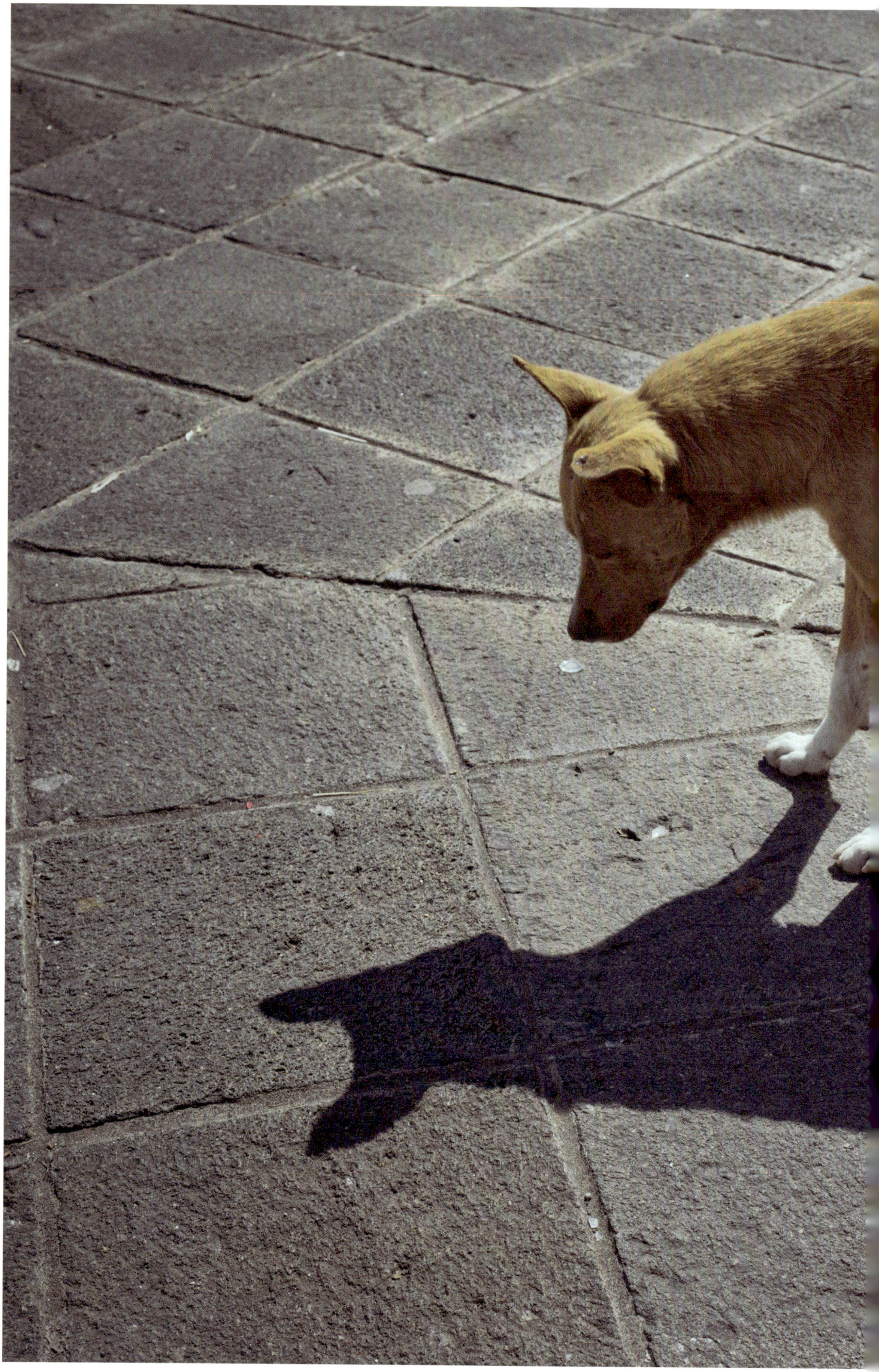

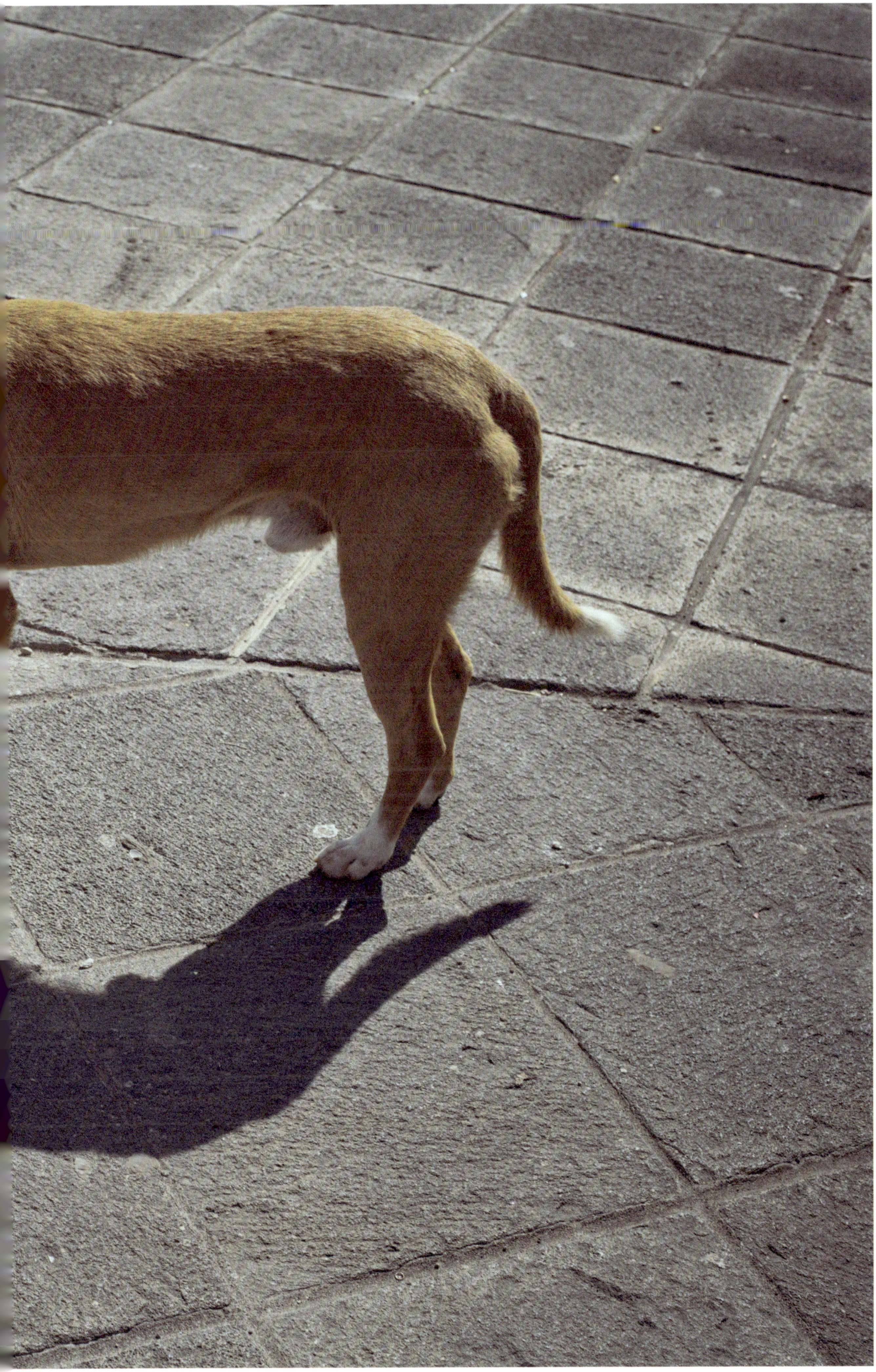

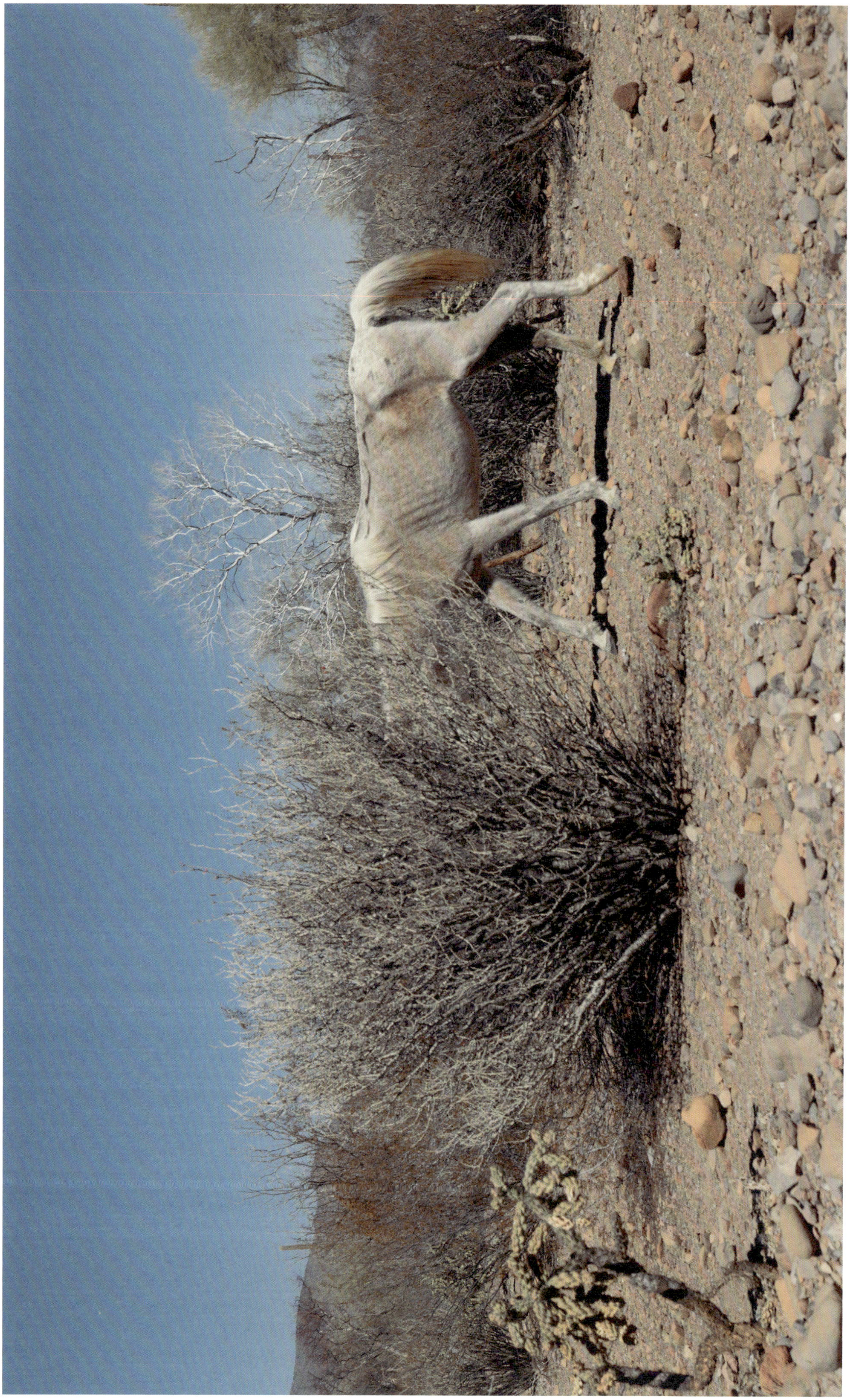

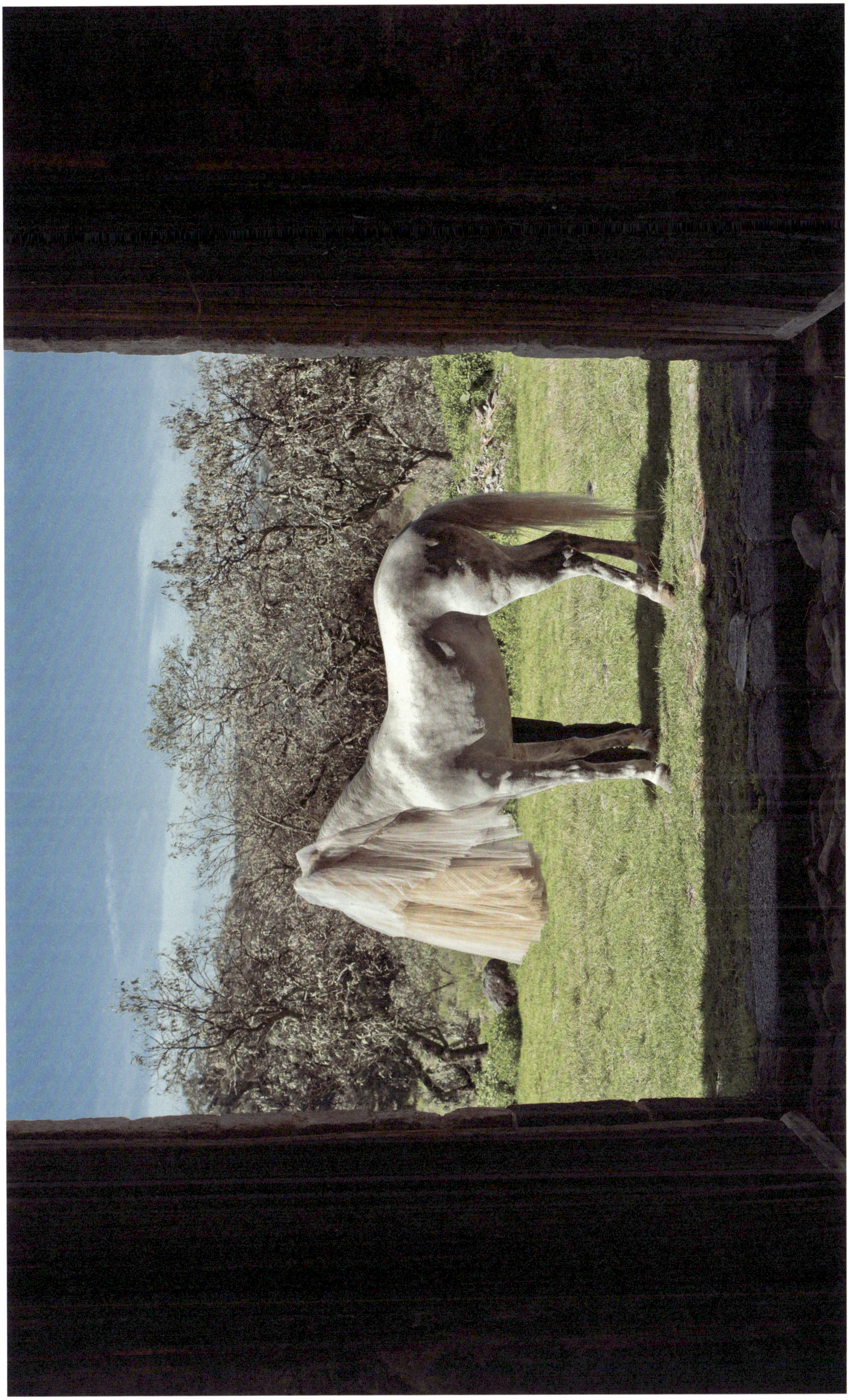

The fire of zeal kindled afresh in me! I forgot everything; the past perils of the journey, the future danger of our return.

Un feu intérieur se ranima dans ma poitrine ! J'oubliai tout, et les dangers du voyage, et les périls du retour.

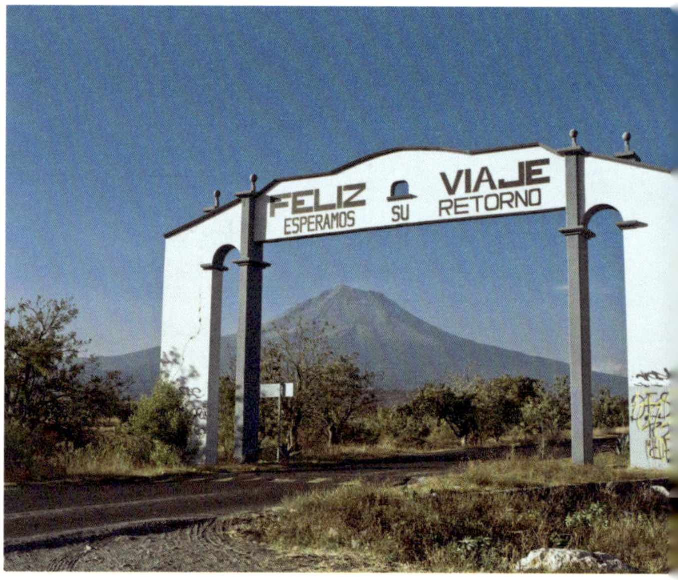

Journey to the Center of the Earth,
Jules Verne, 1864.

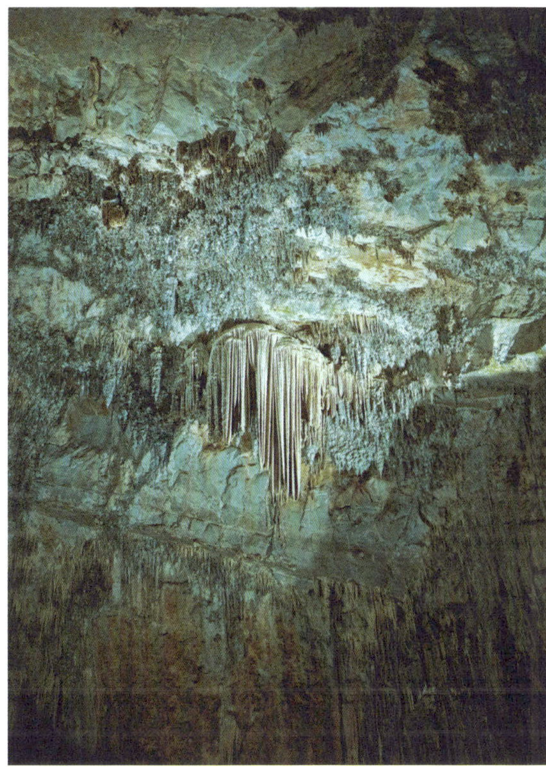

[4]

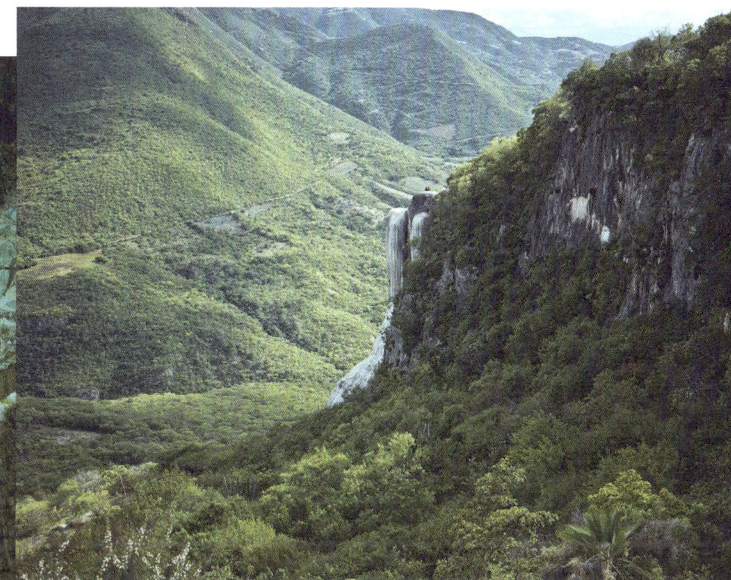

[5]

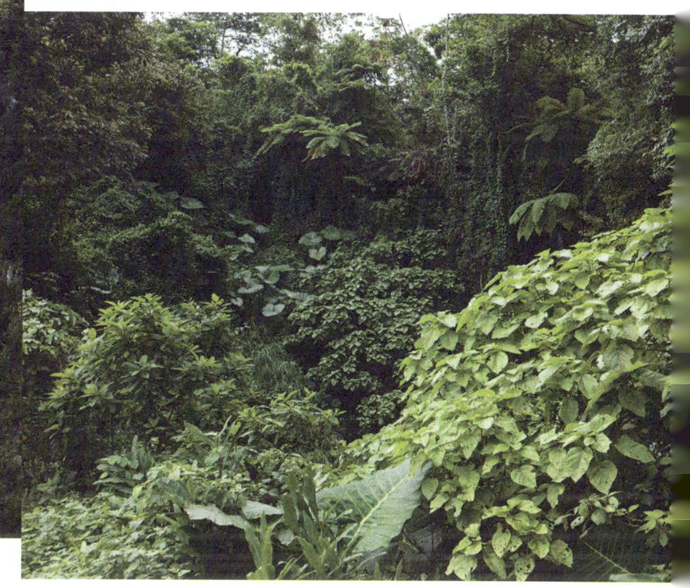

¡En mi pecho se reanimó el ardimiento! Olvidé todos los peligros del viaje, lo mismo que los que habíamos de afrontar al regreso.

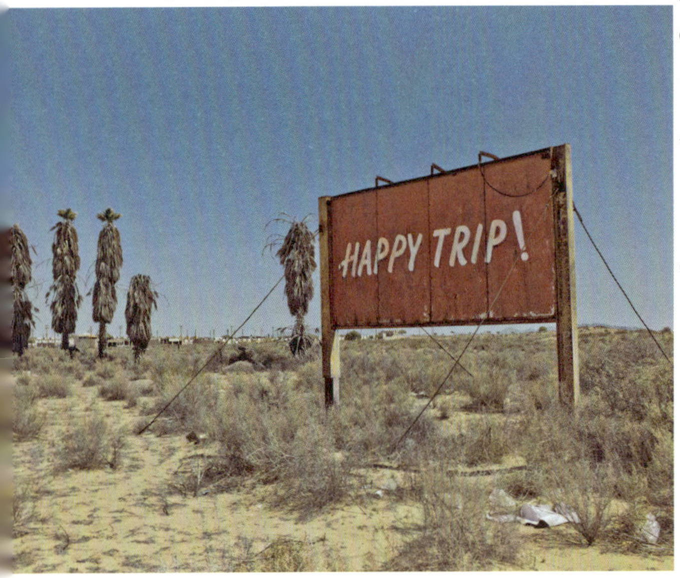

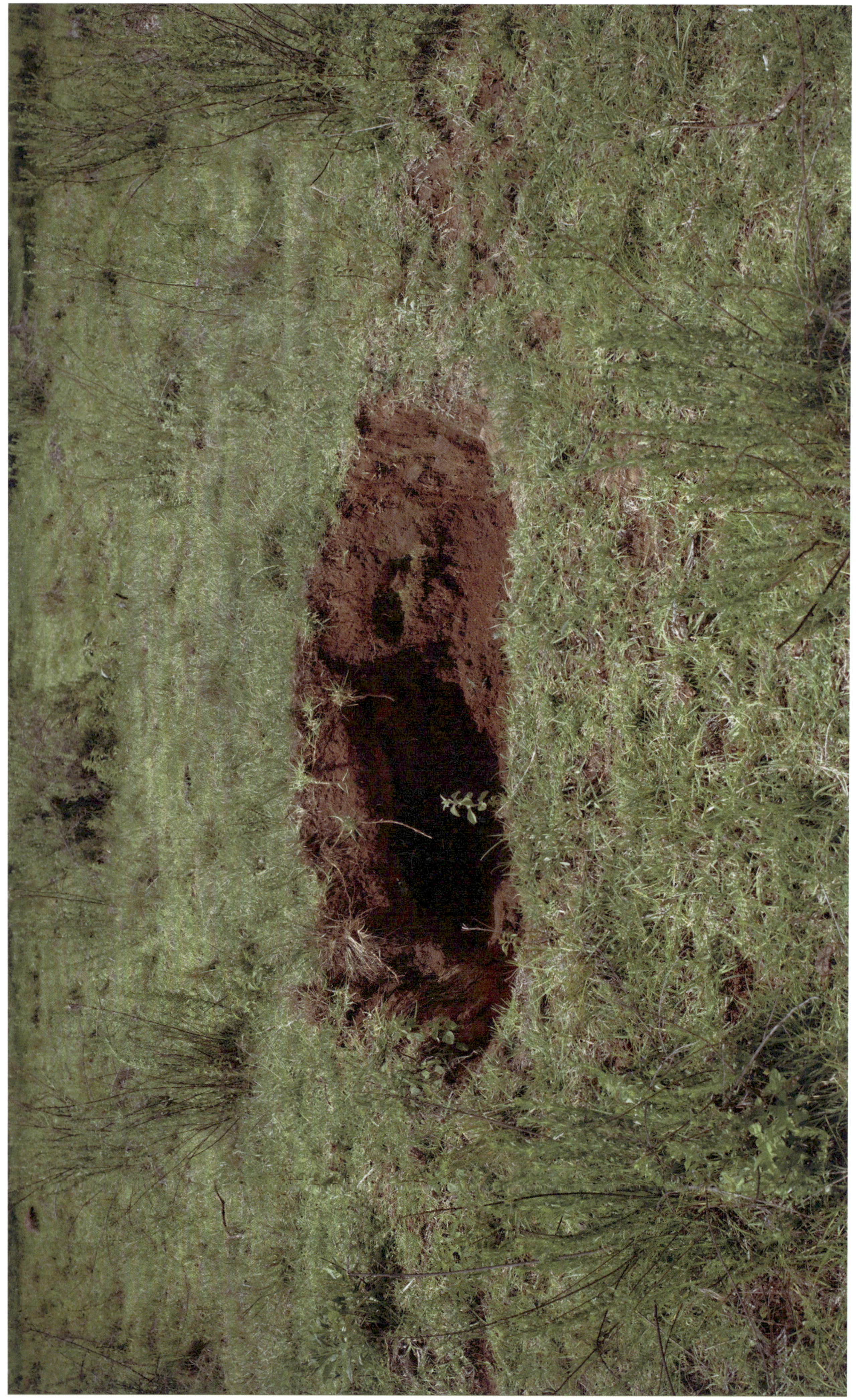

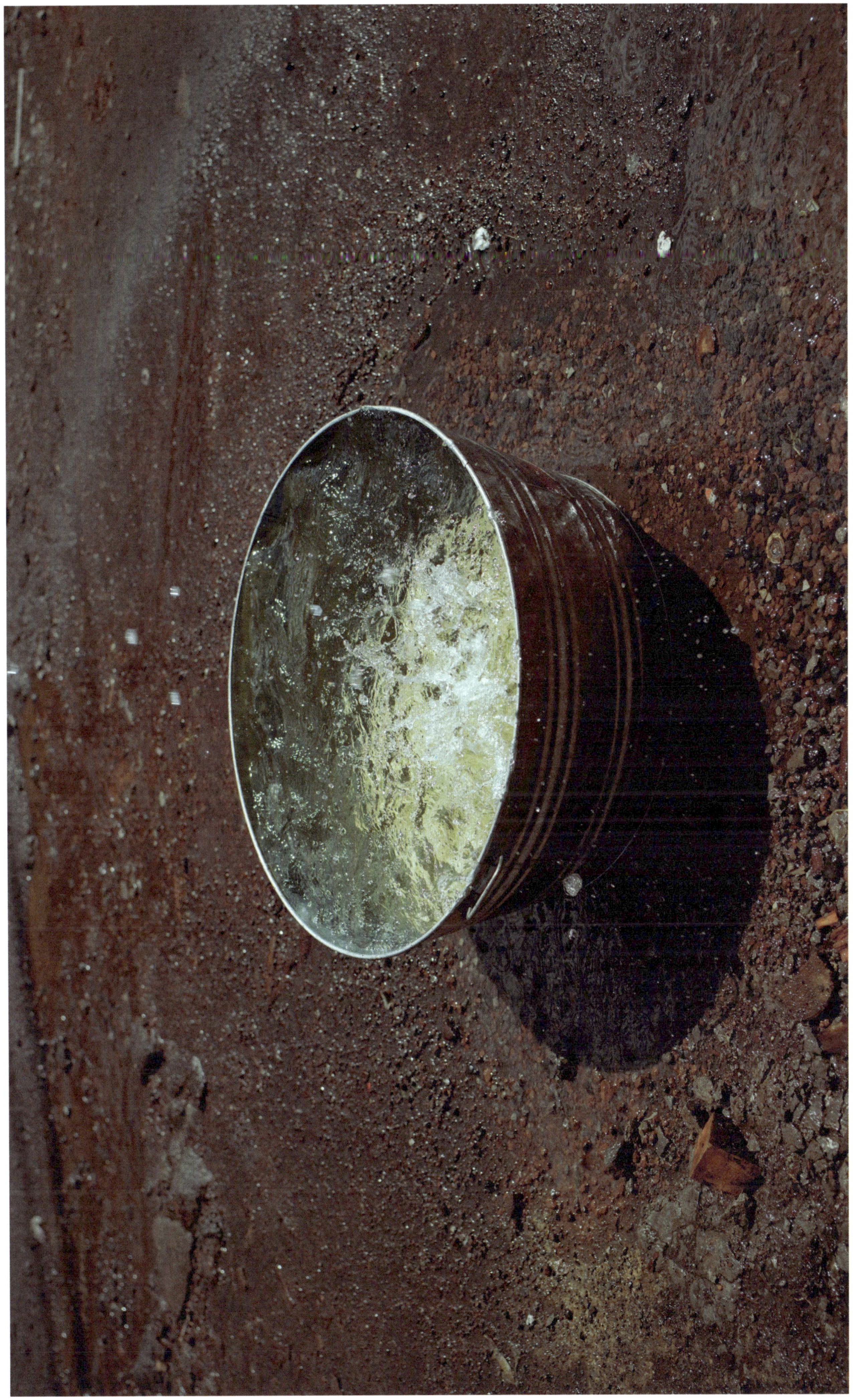

ELAD, CAMEROON

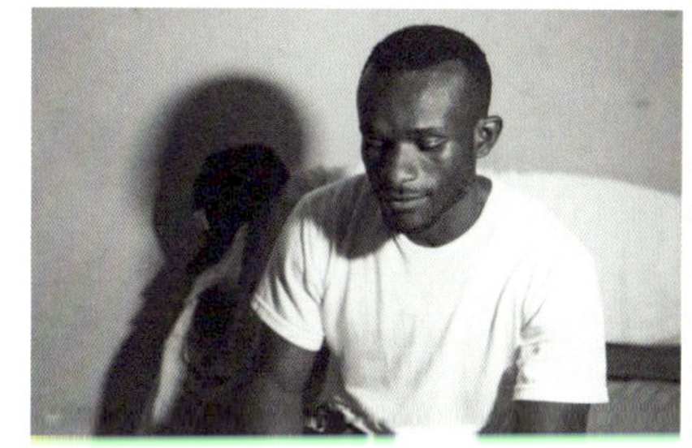

My name is Elad and I was born in the town of Kumba, where I also schooled and obtain the Advanced Level certificate. I later proceeded to the capital City of the South West region Buéa where I got admission to real Law. One year after I moved to Buéa my father passed on and I dropped out of school due to financial constrain. I am a Cameroonian by birth and my father is of francophone origin and mother anglophone. I have seven siblings who are still struggling in life. However, on the 29th of May of 2019 I had the chance to travel out of my country for the first time with the cooperation of my entire family.

Life normally after I dropped out of school was not easy, so I kept trying my hands on many different crafts and also worked as a laborer in different towns in my country, but it all went worst for me when the war broke out in my country Cameroon. I was victimized at some point by the war when I lost a friend by the bullets bought with taxpayer´s money. I also on several occasions was visited by members of the secessionist group asking me to join the fight. Initially they suggested the later I began receiving threats and I was going to be considered an informant of the government if I didn´t pick up arms. I was so confused and devastated by recent happenings in my life at the time to the extent that I lost my mind, and I was moved to the Eastern region of Cameroon which was not experiencing violence at the time. I was in the city of Bertoua in confinement and attended the therapist for over four months of my life. during this time, I was chained to the wall.

When I got better health wise, I was supported by my family to travel out of the country as we all thought it was best for me at the time. So, we began the preparations together with the only member of the family that lives abroad in USA for me to travel to be with her. It actually worked out for me and I got a chance on the 29th of May 2019 to leave the country along with one of my siblings. It took from the 29th of May to the 1st of July for me to arrive in Mexico going by plane, buses, motorbikes and on foot.

I started the American journey in Ecuador where I had a 90-day visa but only spent

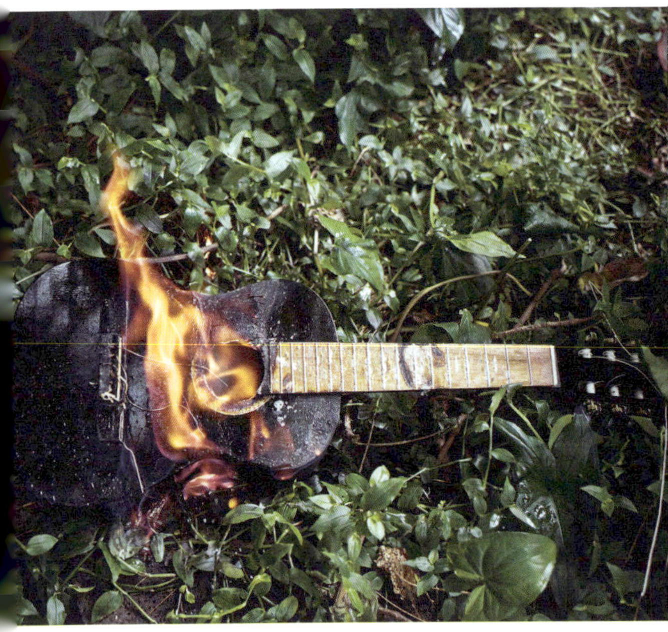

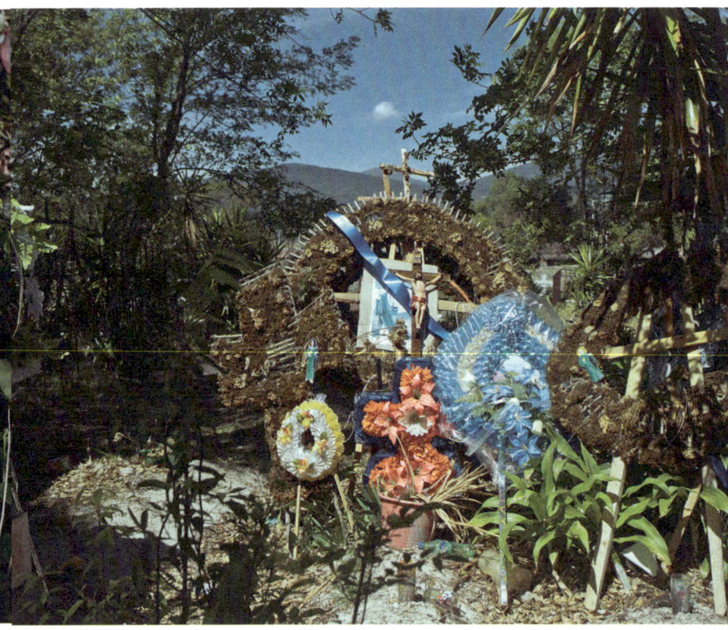

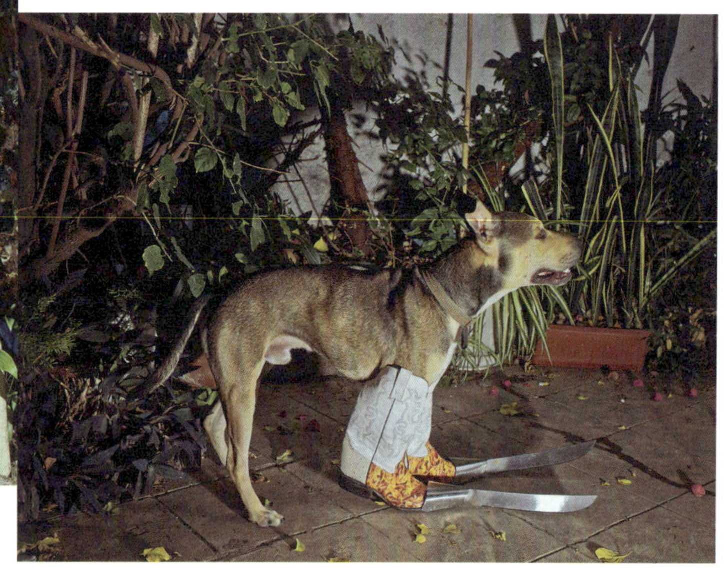

a night and was smuggled alongside other migrants with whom together formed a team of 5 and set out on the journey heading to Colombia. After a week in Colombia awaiting passes from the immigration, we took a bus that drove for two days reaching the Colombia Panama border city.

It took me and a group of 7 others, four days through the Panama jungle and one must there were the most challenging days of my life. The risk and insecurity one has to deal with goings through the route had their peak in the Panama jungle. No one that goes through the forest has adequate information about the route. We all rely on each other, our instincts to survive and God. We would walk eight hours and rest for thirty minutes just like that till we got to the Camp where United Nations offices would attend to us and separate us according to our nationality in different quarters. We received medical attention and food but minimal because of the size of the population. And from here we moved through to two other camps spending at least 12 days in each. The conditions vary per camp, but they all are generally poor.

In Costa Rica we needed to stay a week to be issued passes that permitted us to travel through the country. We suffered police harassment severally in fact even check points one had to strip naked for searches until we got to the border of Mexico and Guatemala.

I finally arrived in Mexico on the 1st of July 2019 alongside 5 others crossing through a river on floating tires. I have been in Mexico for one year already and still without papers and no job. Life here as a migrant is a huge challenge but I am encouraged by the difficulties I met on the road to survive the stress of Tapachula.

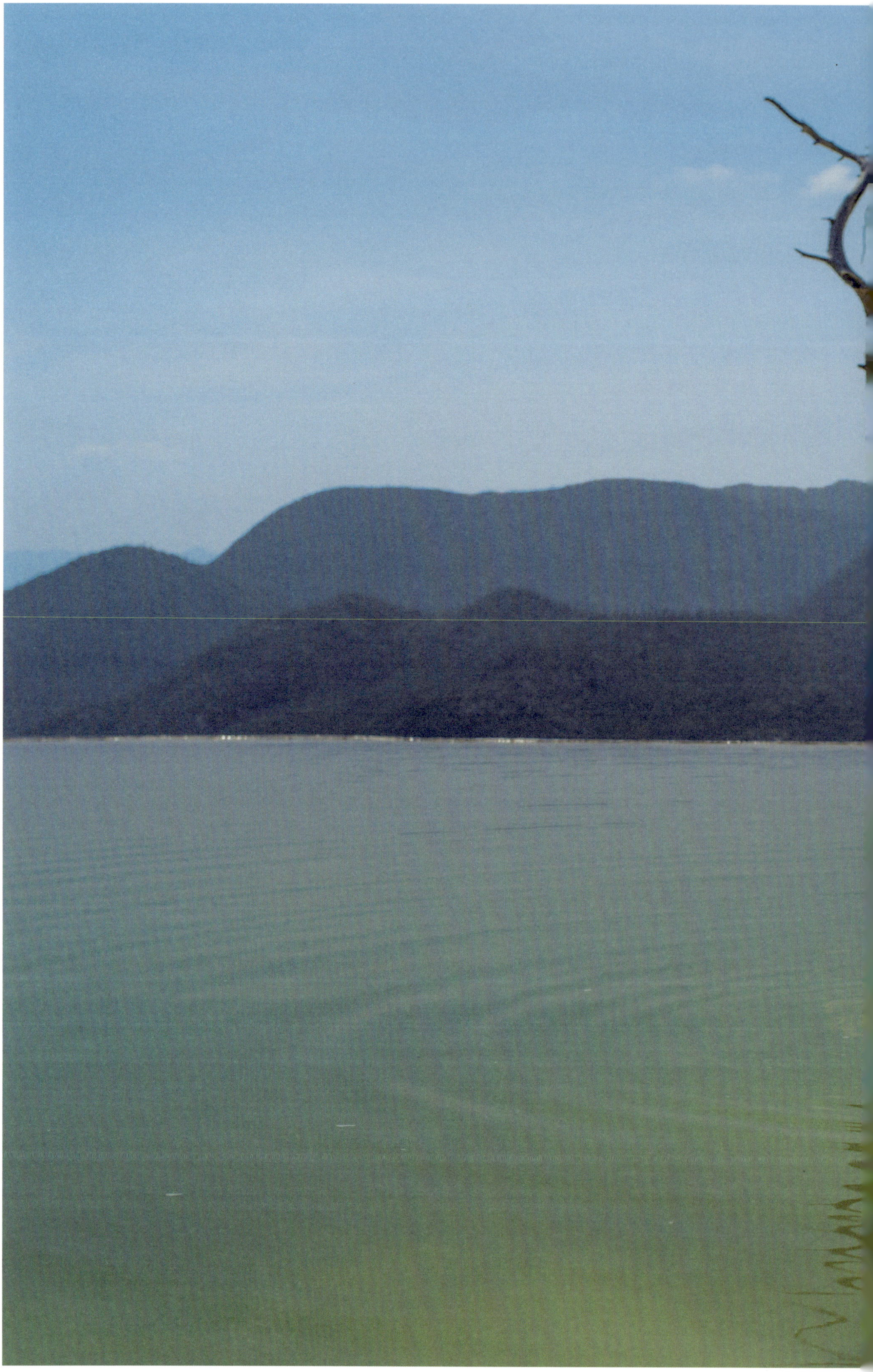

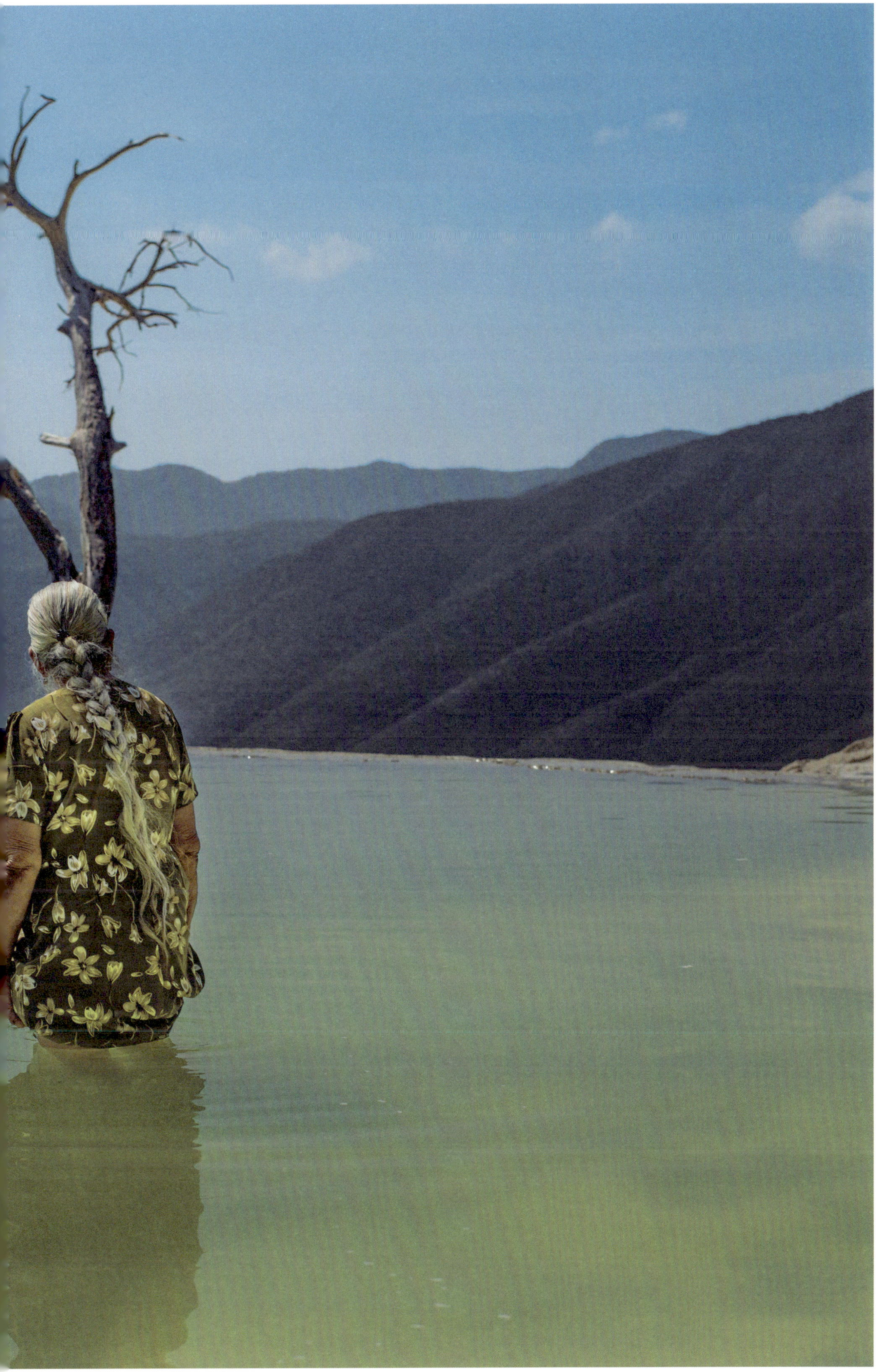

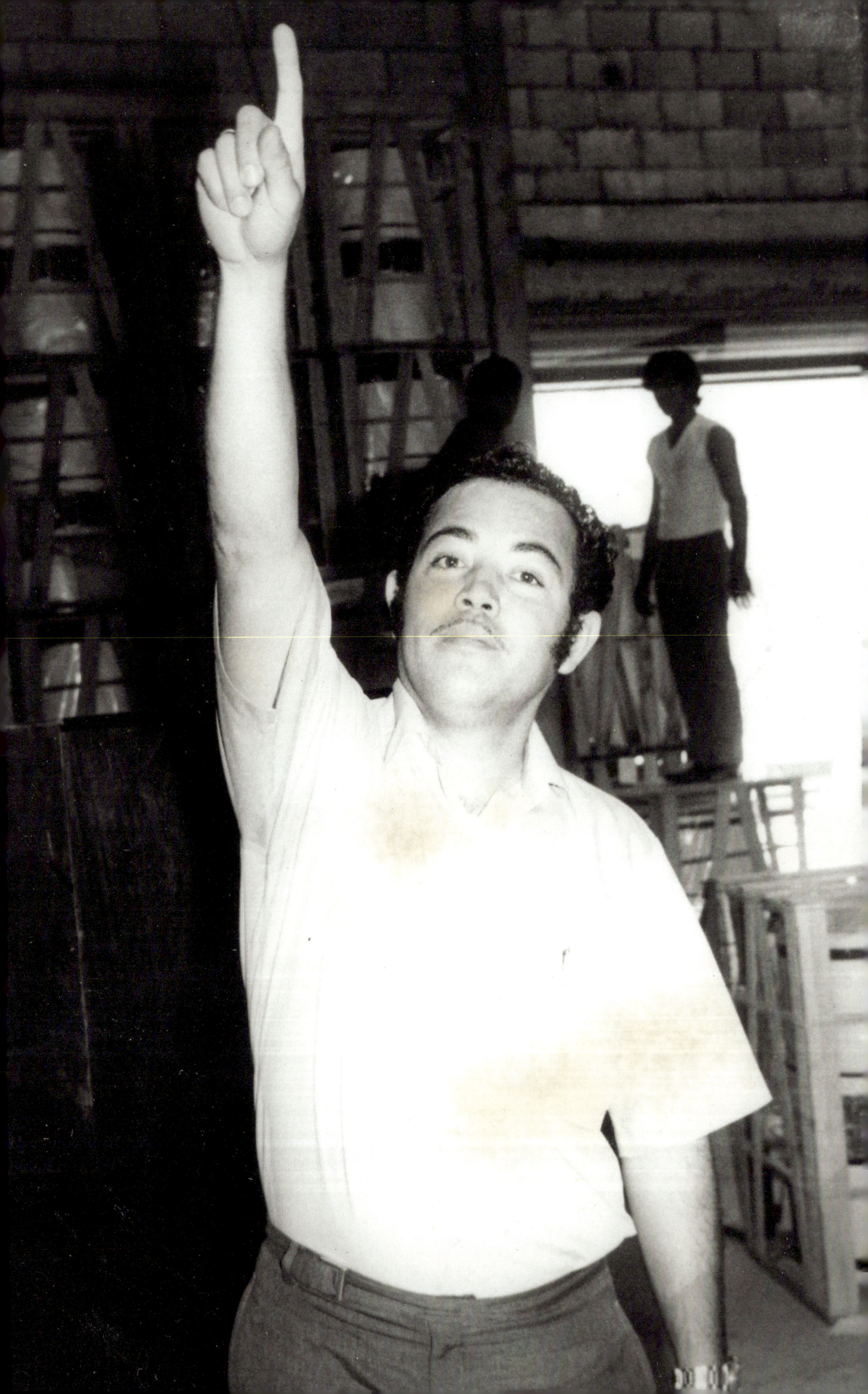

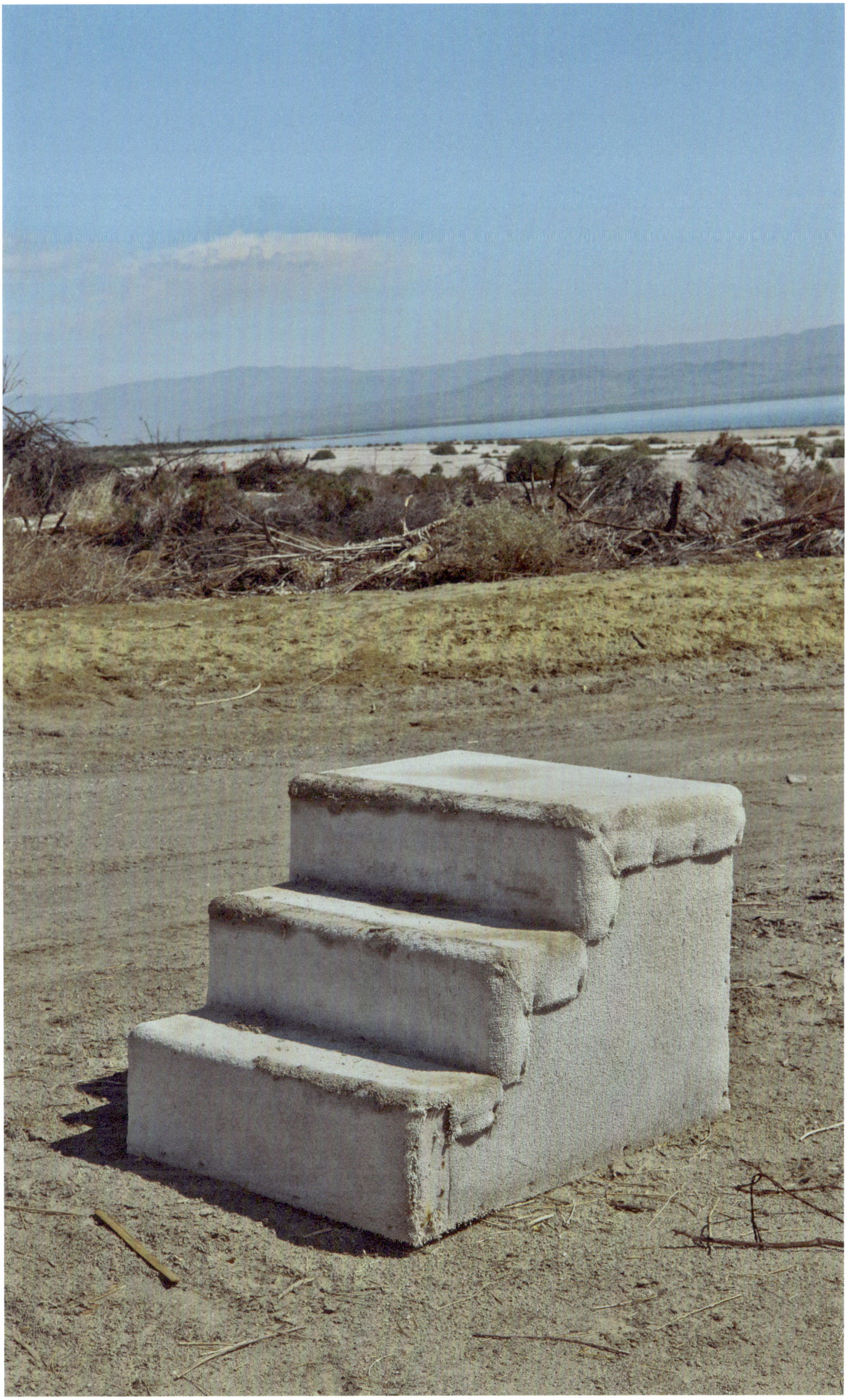

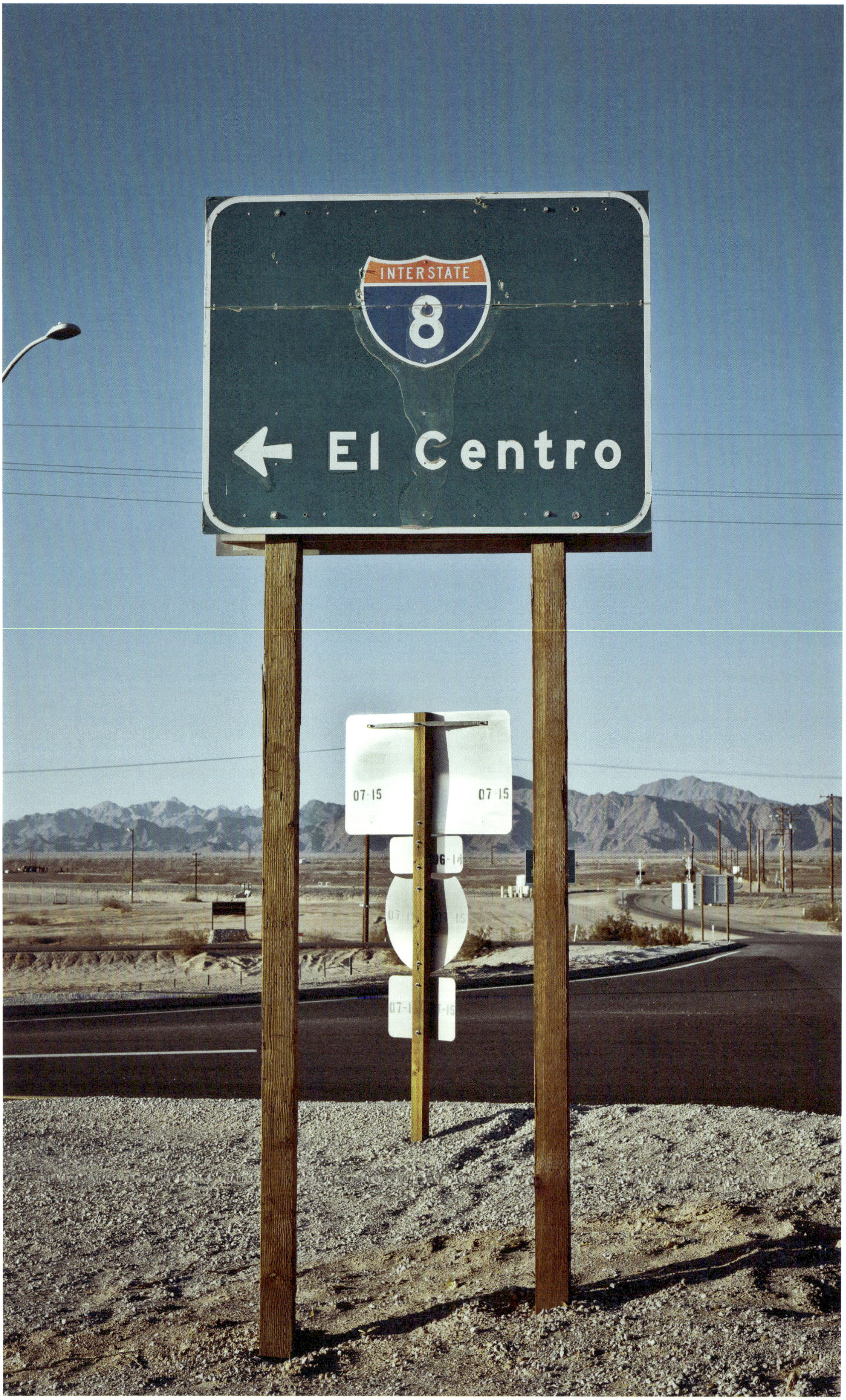
INTERSTATE
8
El Centro
07-15
07-15

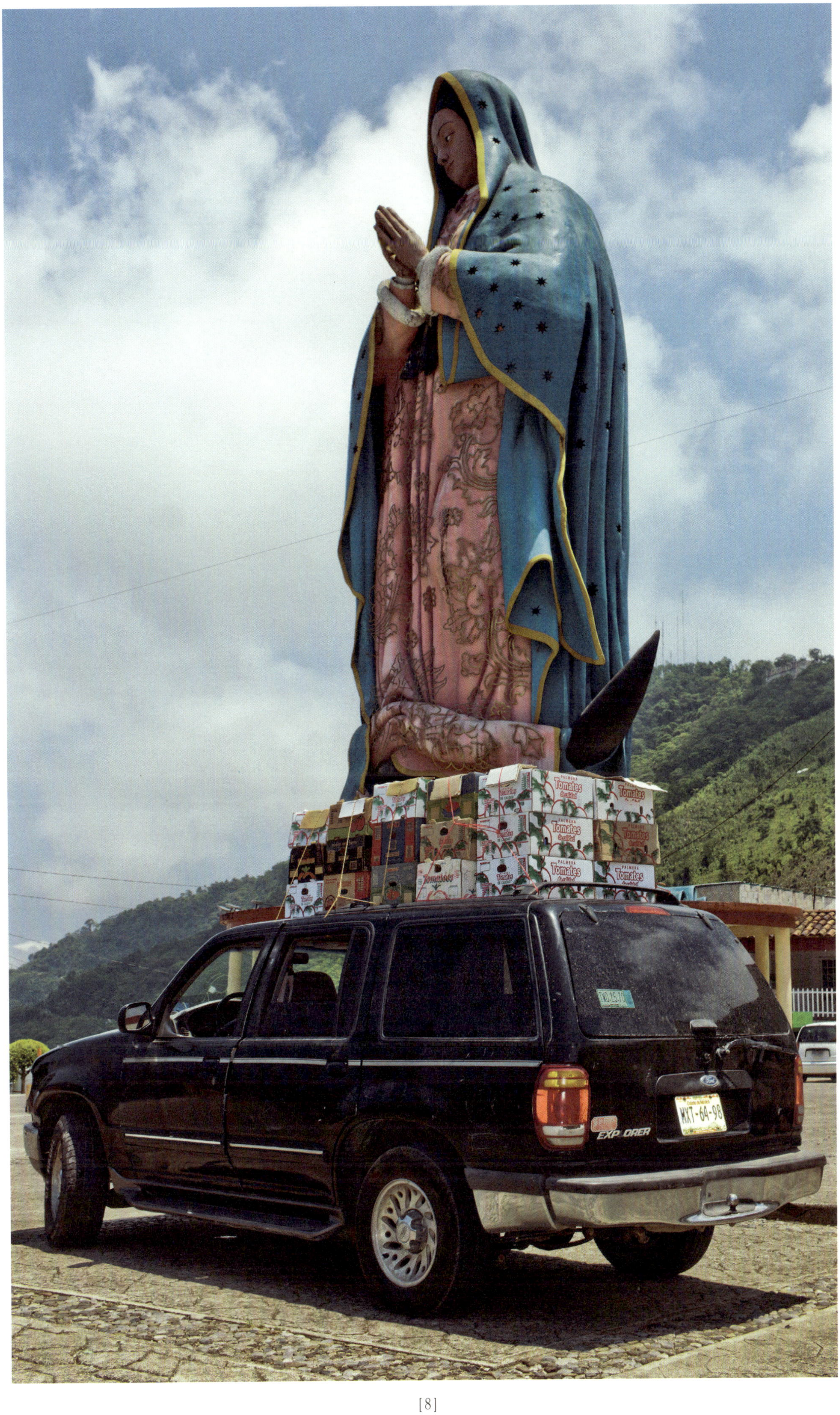
Tomates
EXPLORER
MXT-64-98

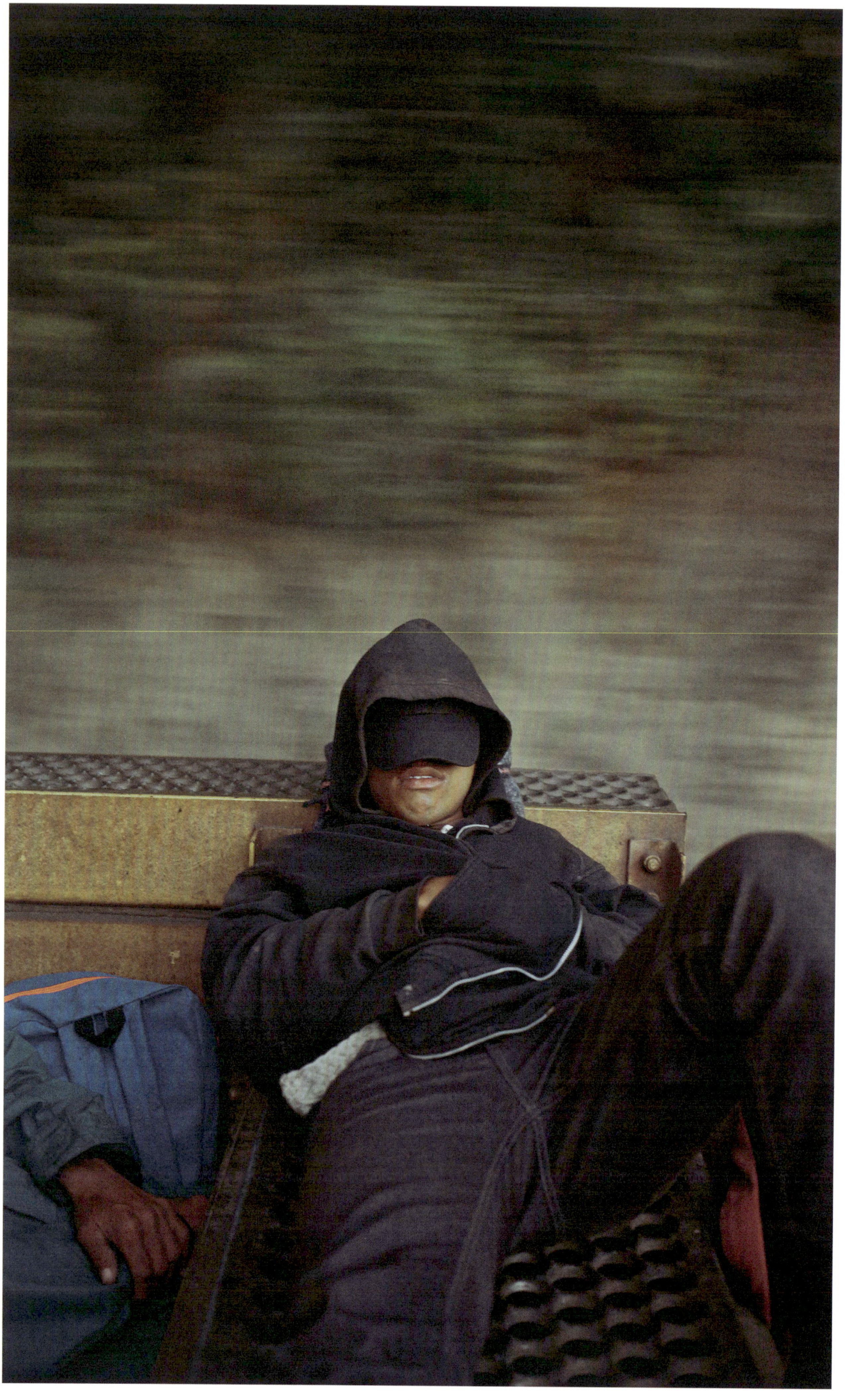

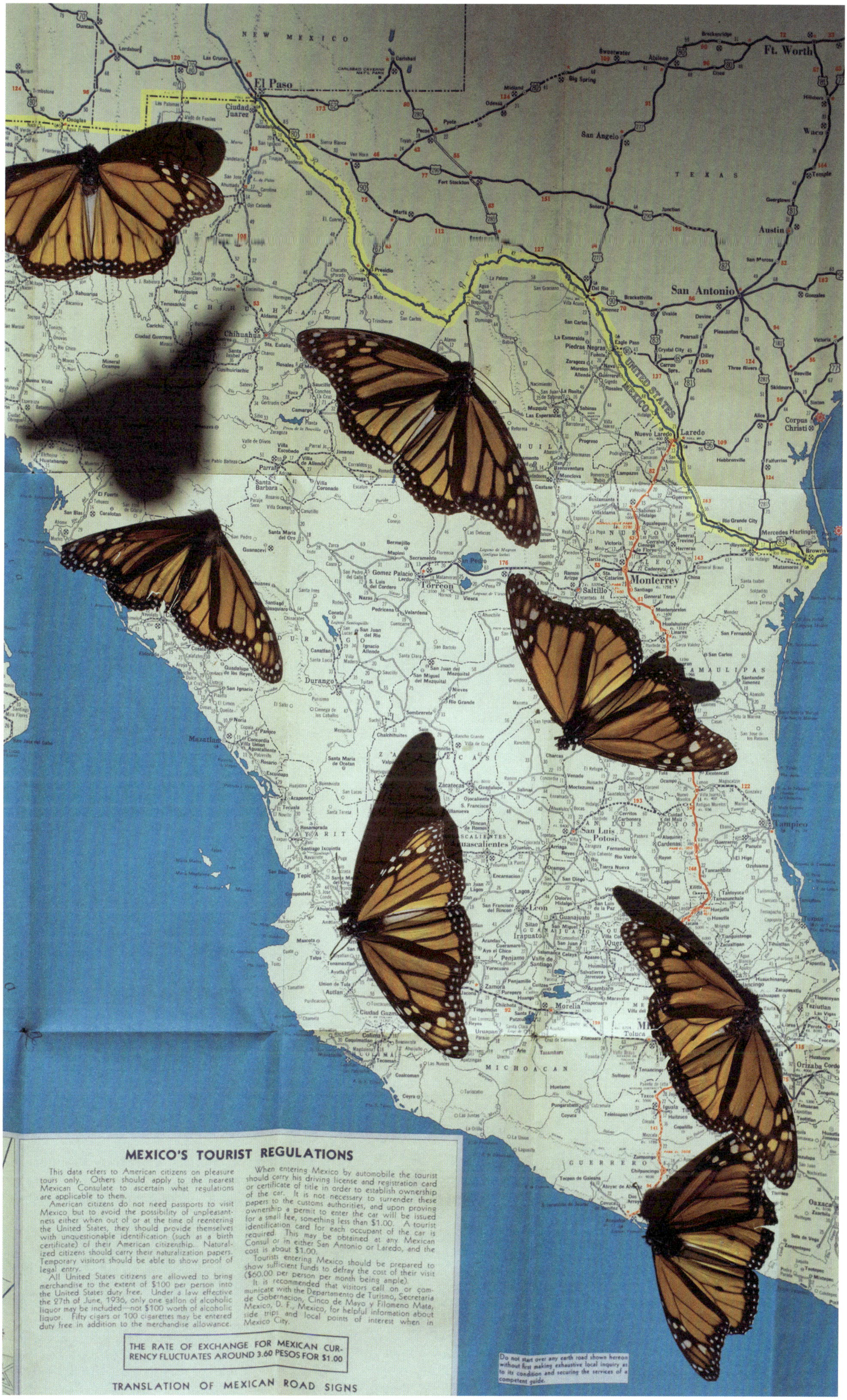
NEW MEXICO
El Paso
TEXAS
Ft. Worth
San Angelo
Austin
San Antonio
Laredo
Nuevo Laredo
Monterrey
Chihuahua
Torreon
Durango
Tampico
MEXICO'S TOURIST REGULATIONS
This data refers to American citizens on pleasure tours only. Others should apply to the nearest Mexican Consulate to ascertain what regulations are applicable to them.
American citizens do not need passports to visit Mexico but to avoid the possibility of unpleasantness either when out of or at the time of reentering the United States, they should provide themselves with unquestionable identification (such as a birth certificate) of their American citizenship. Naturalized citizens should carry their naturalization papers. Temporary visitors should be able to show proof of legal entry.
All United States citizens are allowed to bring merchandise to the extent of $100 per person into the United States duty free. Under a law effective the 27th of June, 1936, only one gallon of alcoholic liquor may be included—not $100 worth of alcoholic liquor. Fifty cigars or 100 cigarettes may be entered duty free in addition to the merchandise allowance.
When entering Mexico by automobile the tourist should carry his driving license and registration card or certificate of title in order to establish ownership of the car. It is not necessary to surrender these papers to the customs authorities, and upon proving ownership a permit to enter the car will be issued for a small fee, something less than $1.00. A tourist identification card for each occupant of the car is required. This may be obtained at any Mexican Consul or in either San Antonio or Laredo, and the cost is about $1.00.
Tourists entering Mexico should be prepared to show sufficient funds to defray the cost of their visit ($60.00 per person per month being ample).
It is recommended that visitors call on or communicate with the Departamento de Turismo, Secretaria de Gobernacion, Cinco de Mayo y Filomeno Mata, Mexico, D. F., Mexico, for helpful information about side trips and local points of interest when in Mexico City.
THE RATE OF EXCHANGE FOR MEXICAN CURRENCY FLUCTUATES AROUND 3.60 PESOS FOR $1.00
TRANSLATION OF MEXICAN ROAD SIGNS
Do not start over any earth road shown hereon without first making exhaustive local inquiry as to its condition and securing the services of a competent guide.

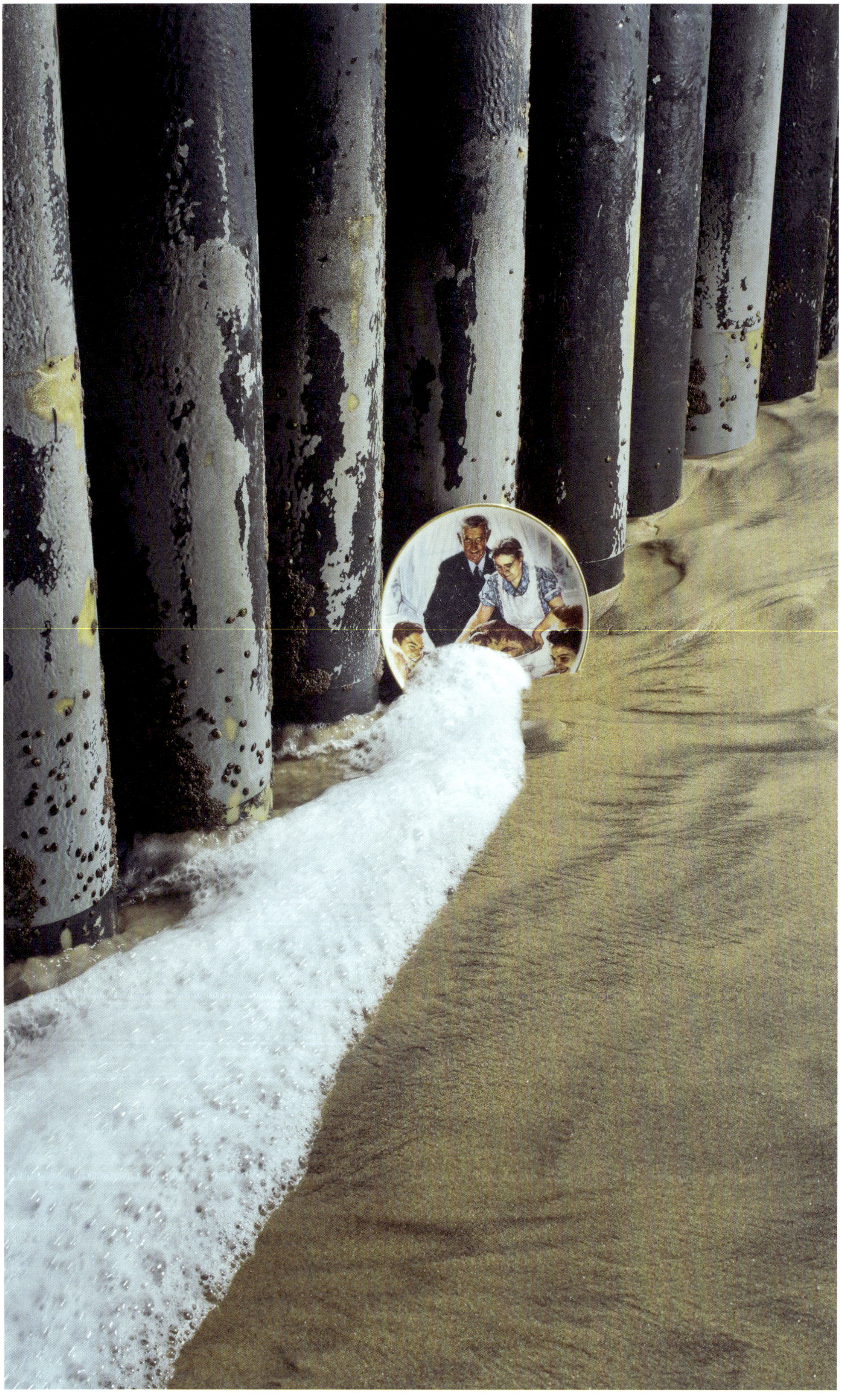

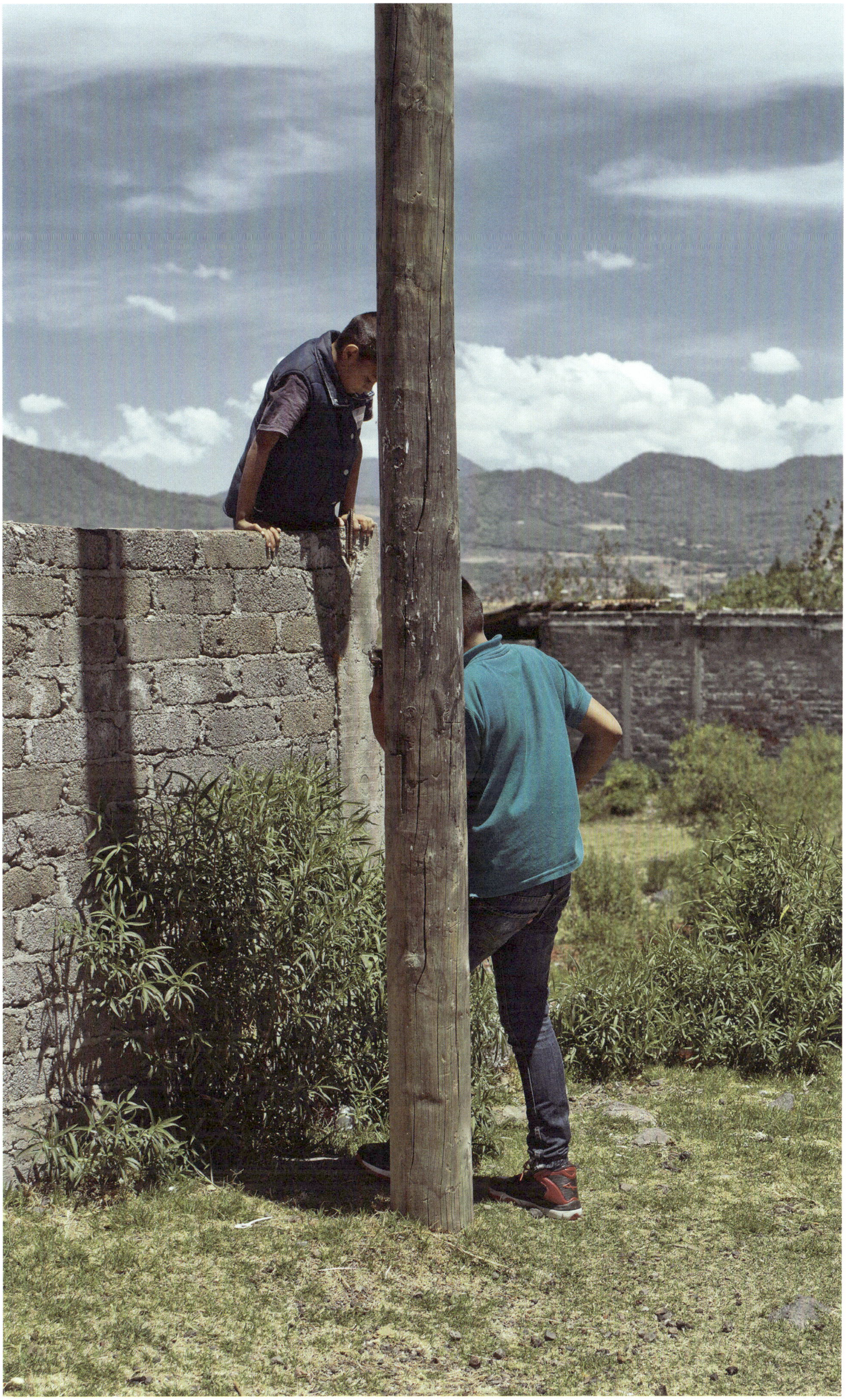

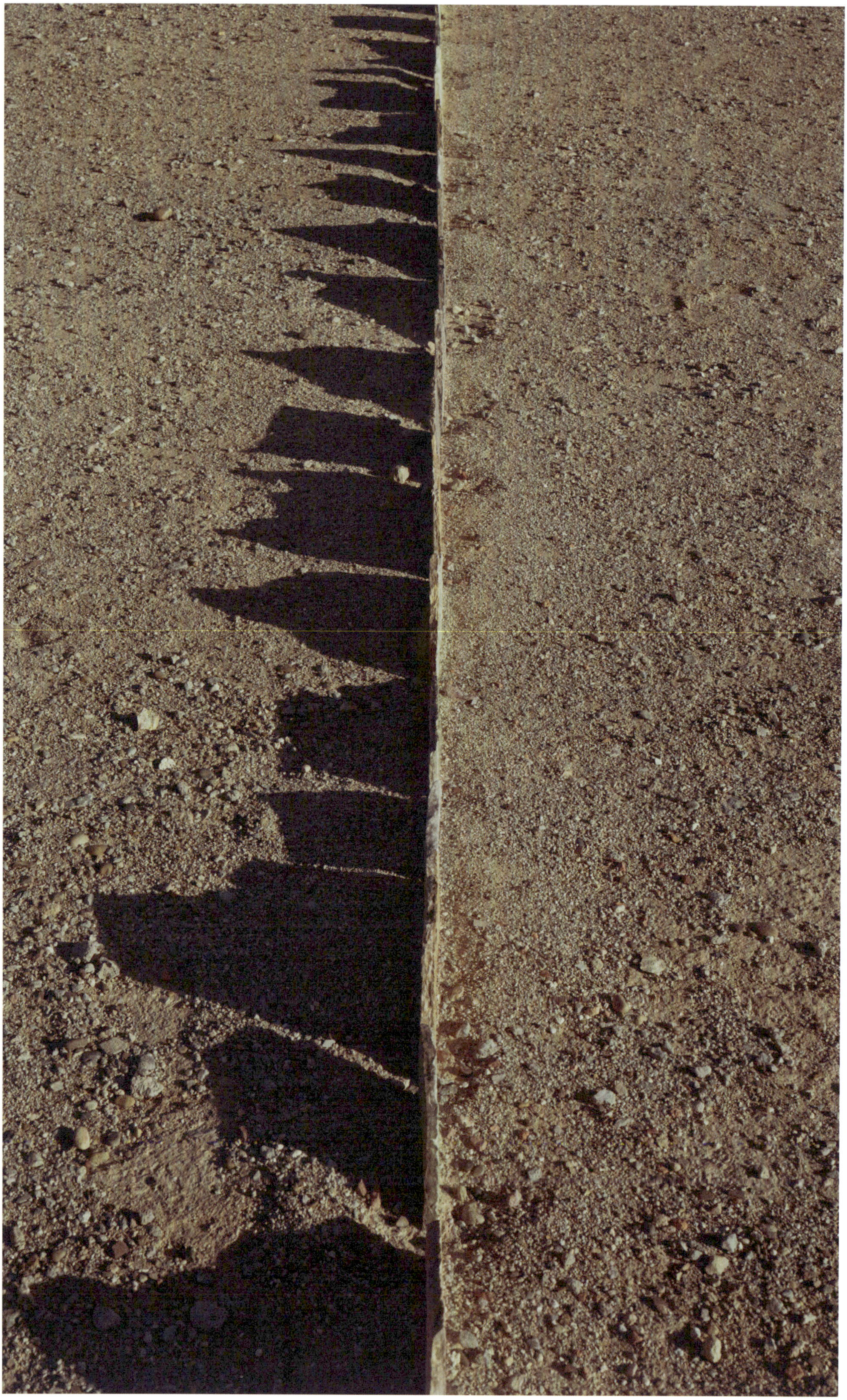

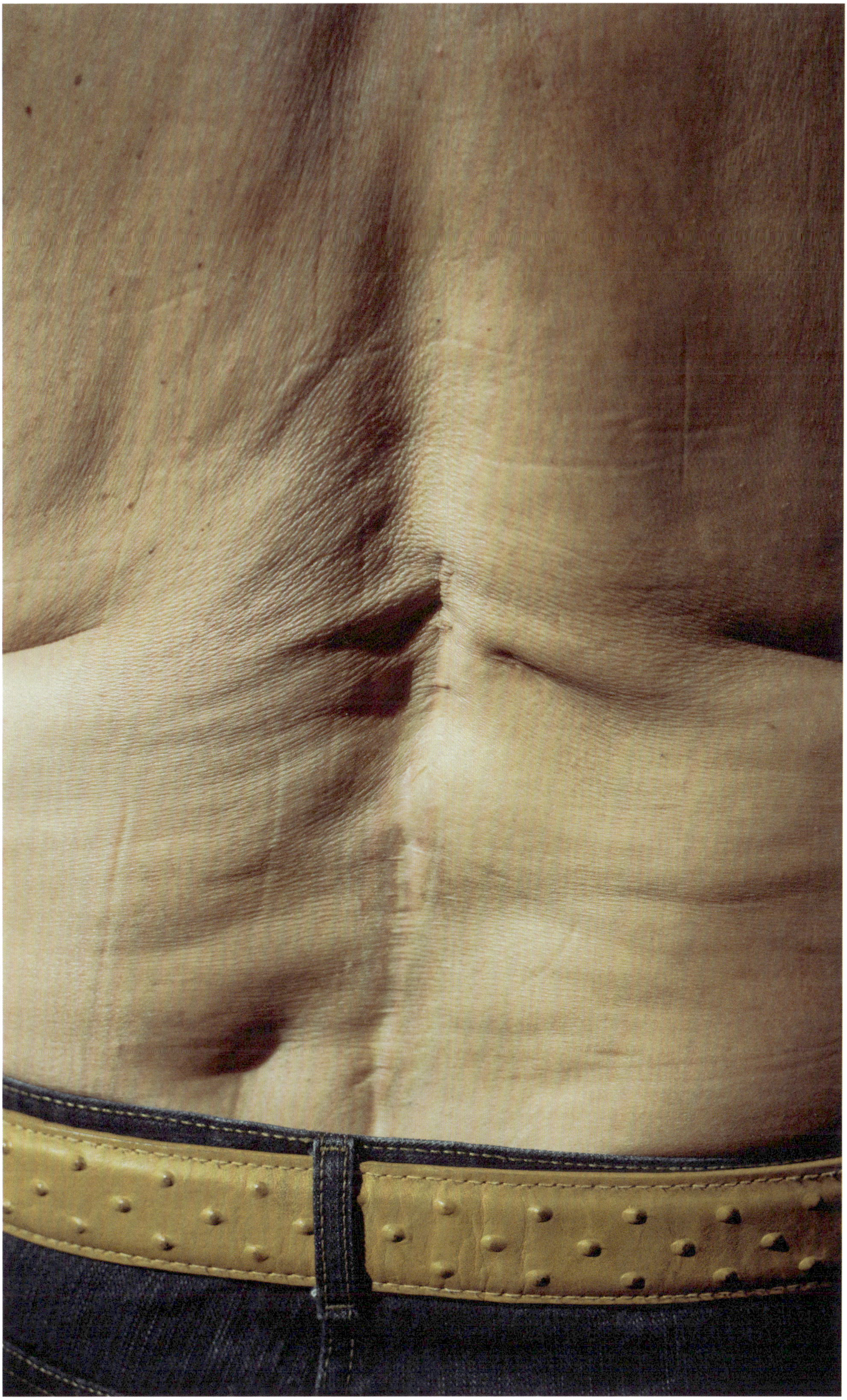

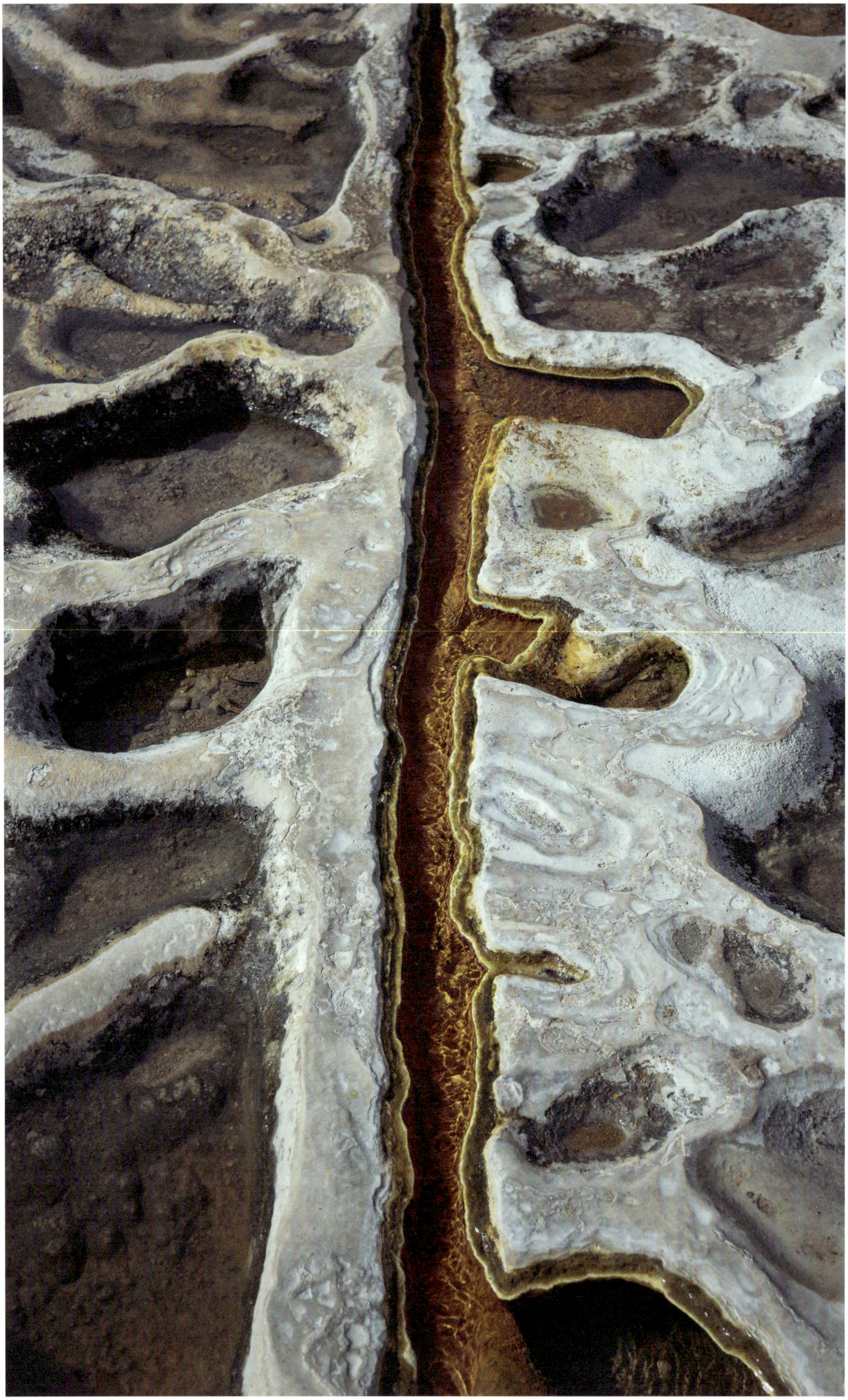

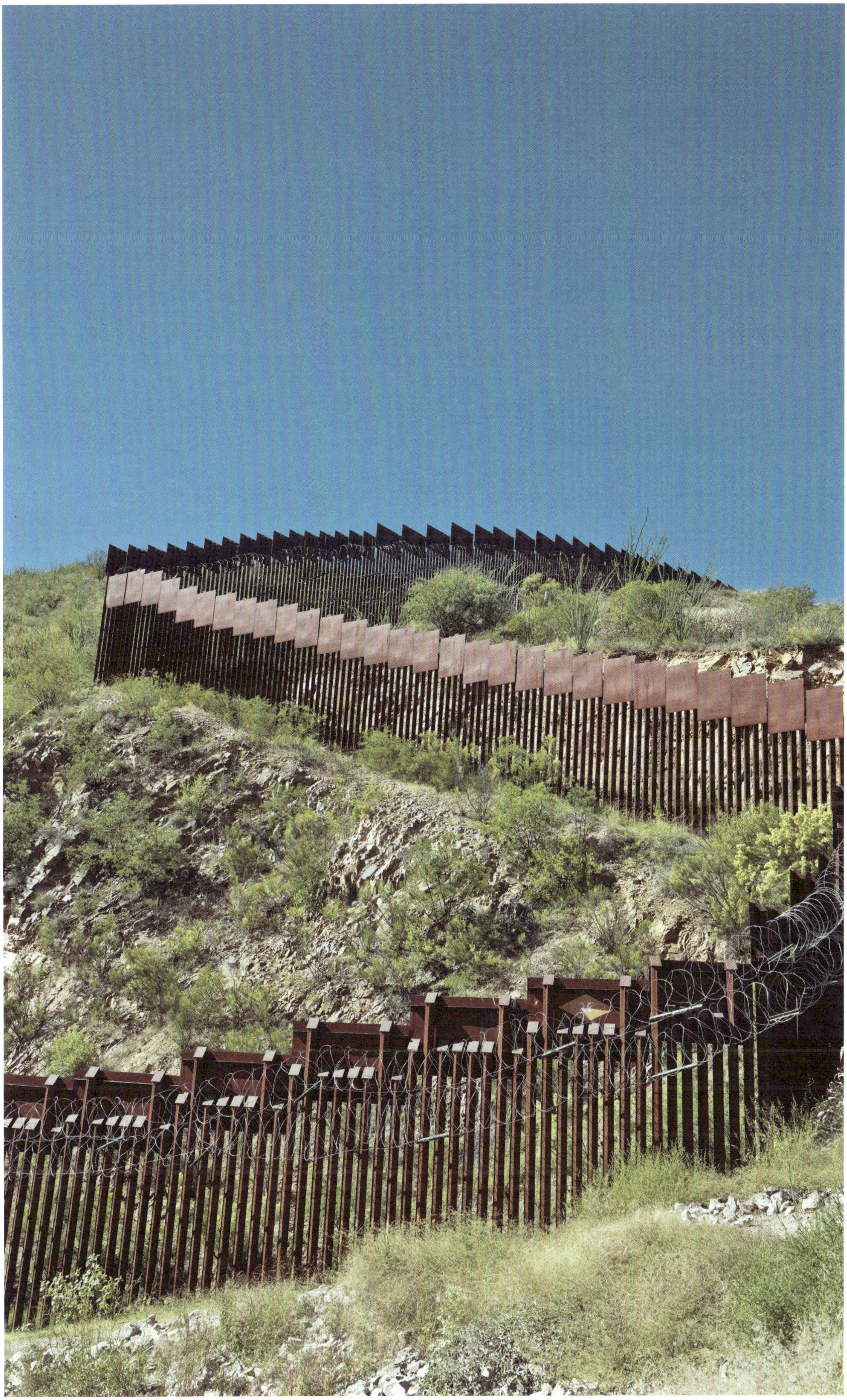

Regarde, me dit-il, et regarde bien ! il faut prendre des leçons d'abîme !

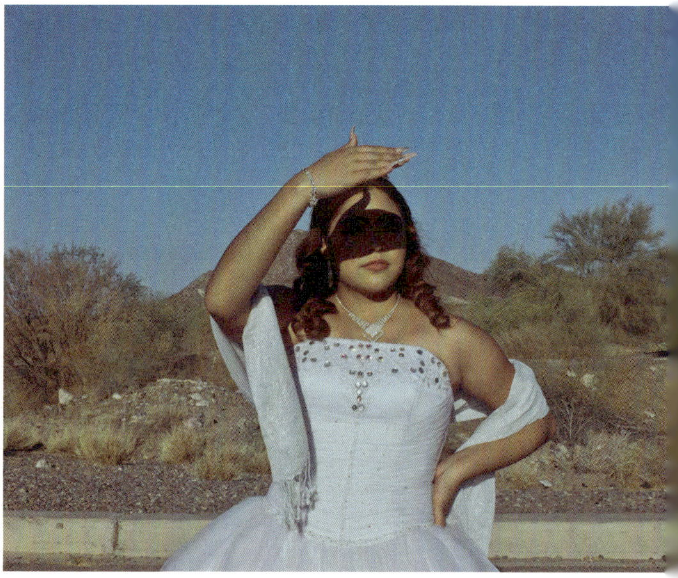

Look down, he cried, and look down well! you must take lessons in abysses.

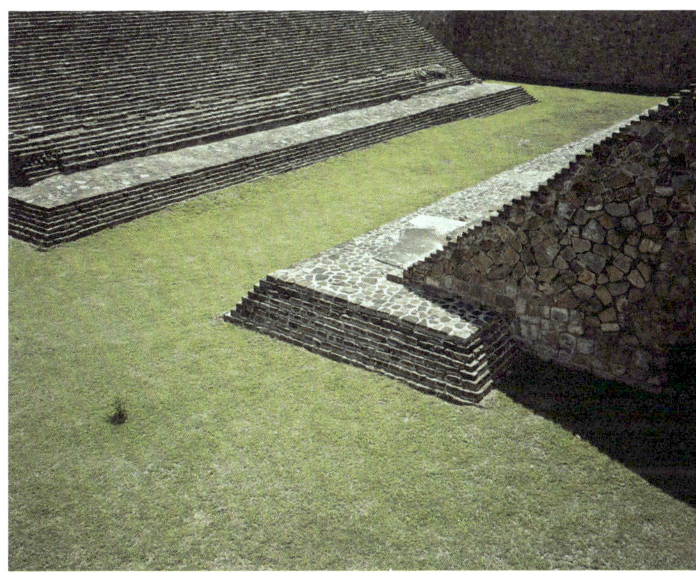
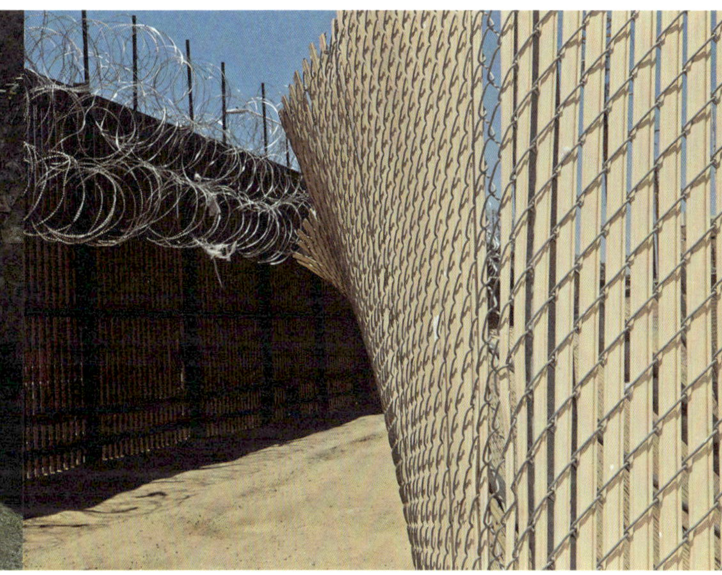
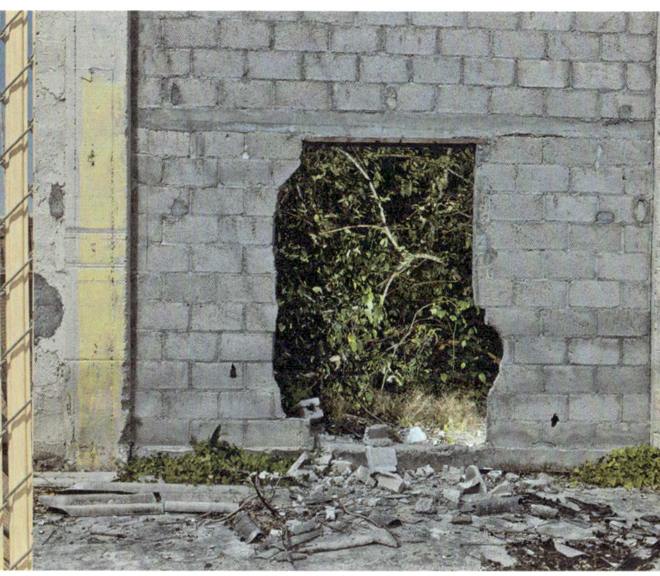

¡Mira!, me dijo, ¡y mira

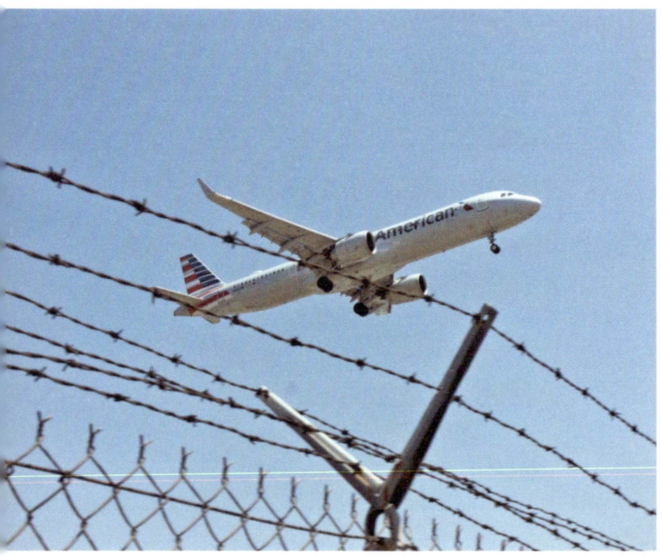

con atención! es preciso que tomes lecciones de abismo.

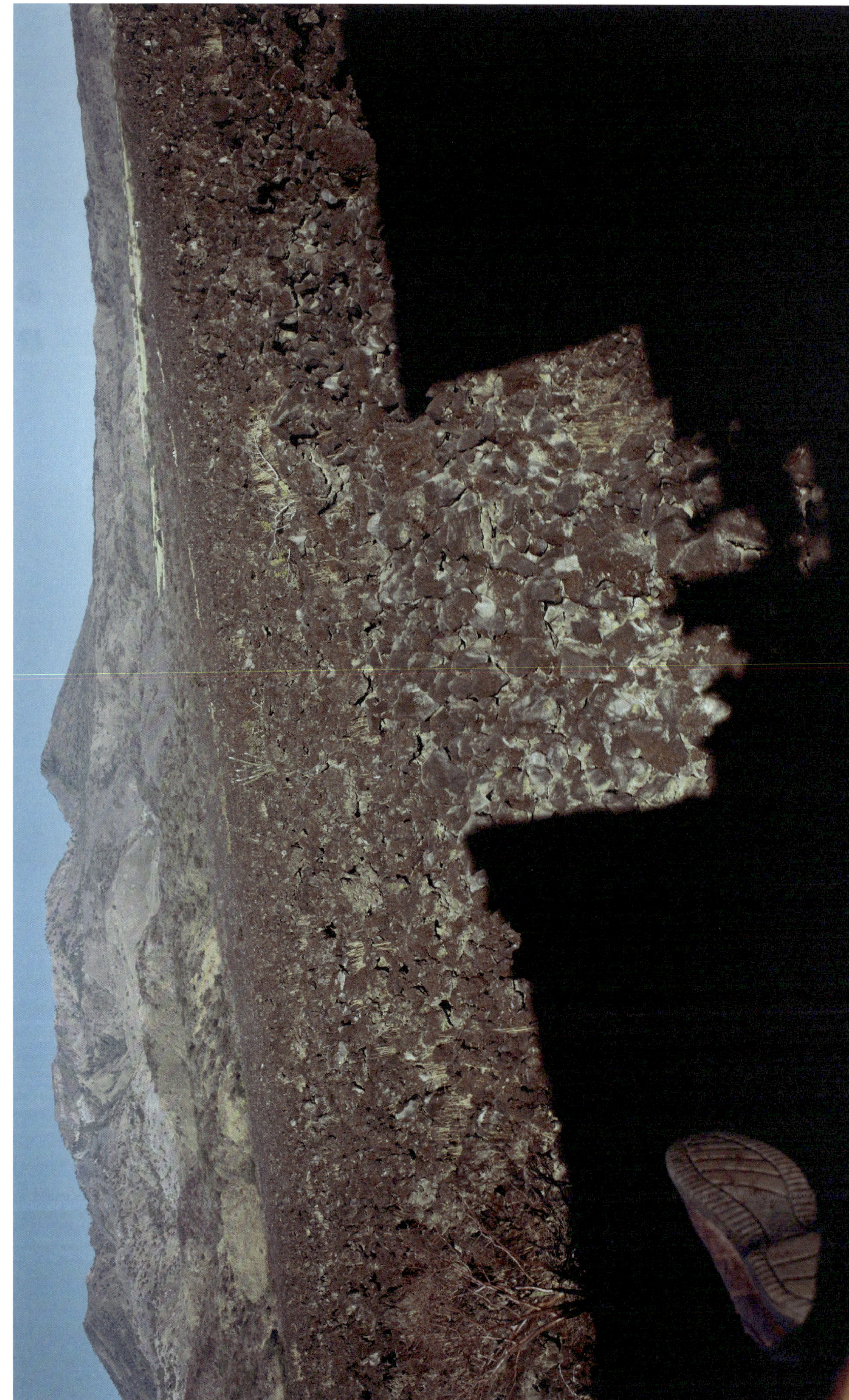

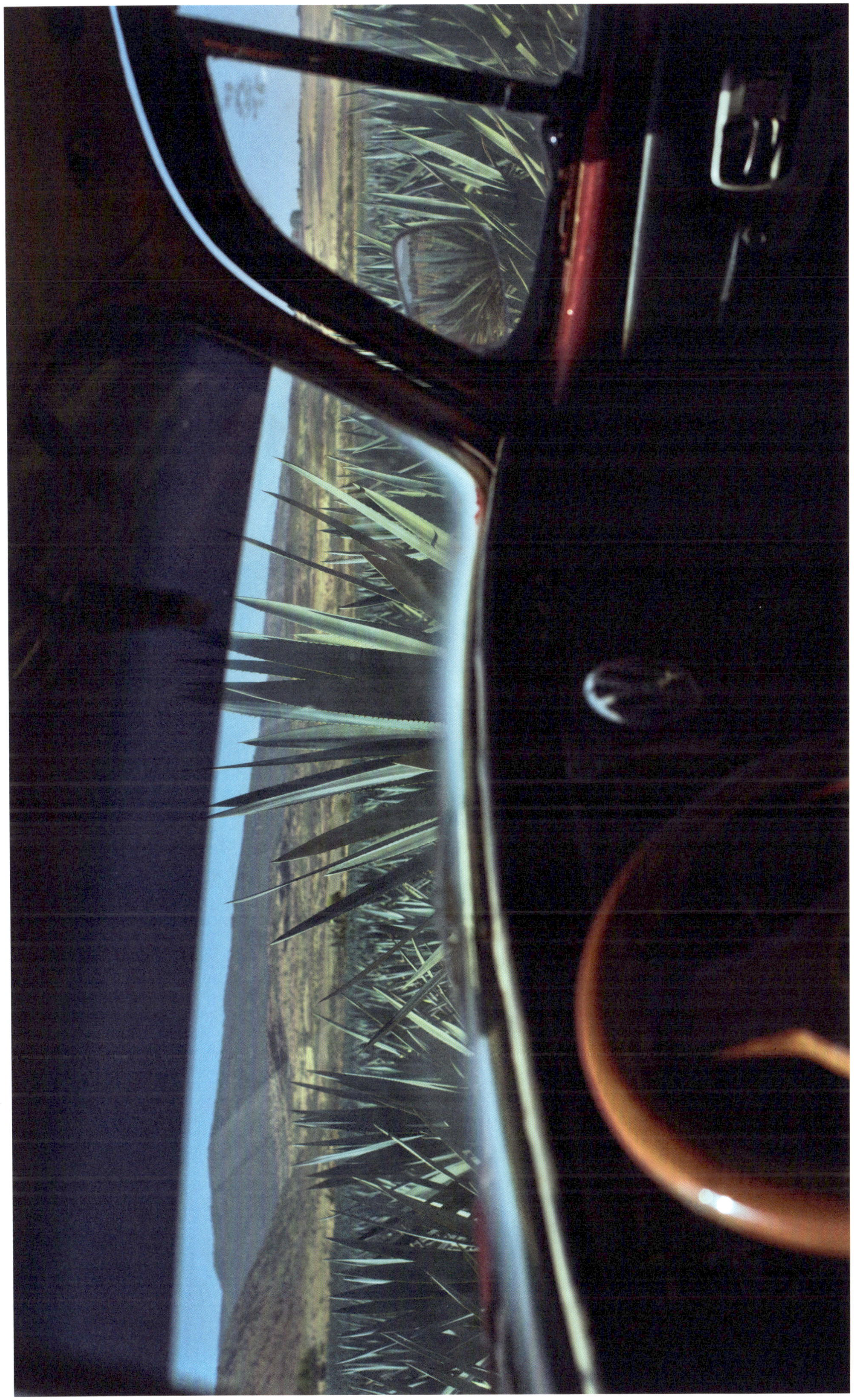

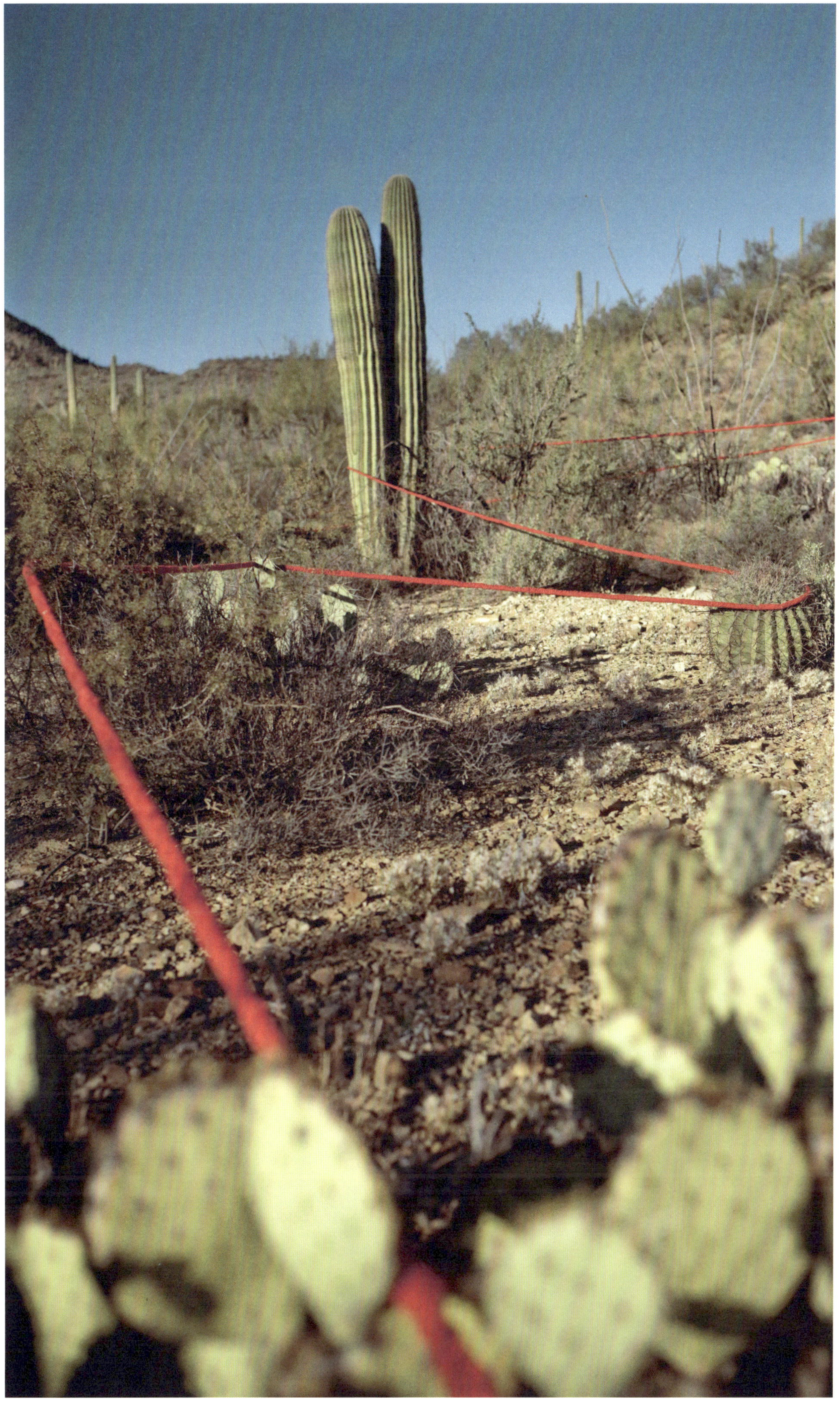

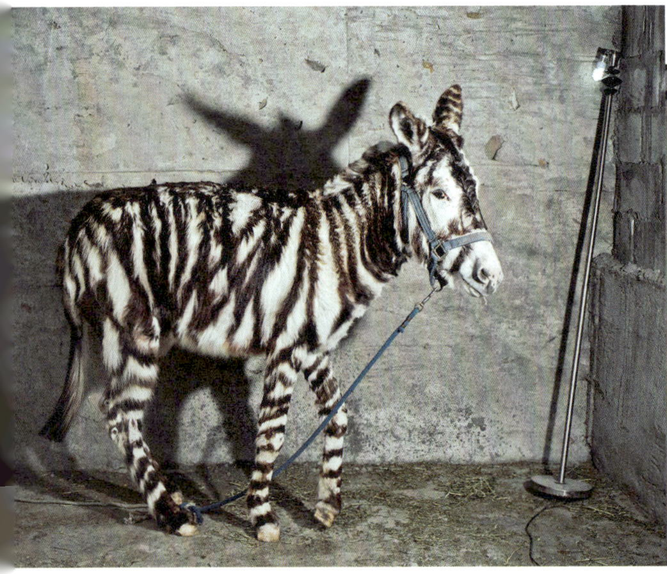

[16]

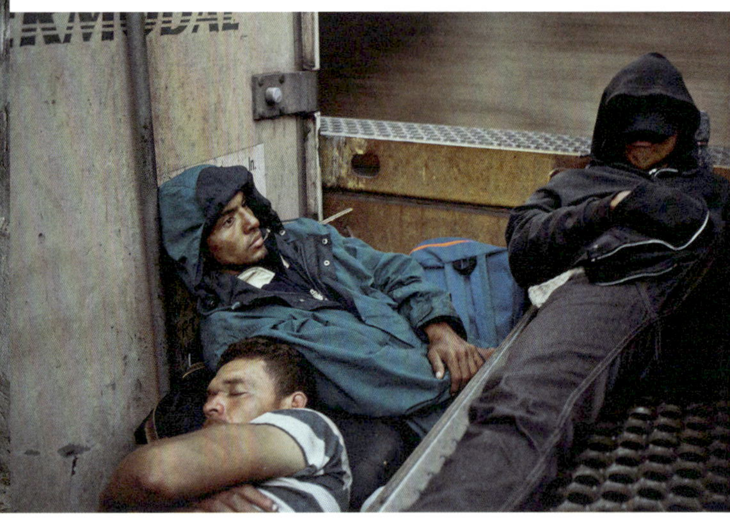

[17]

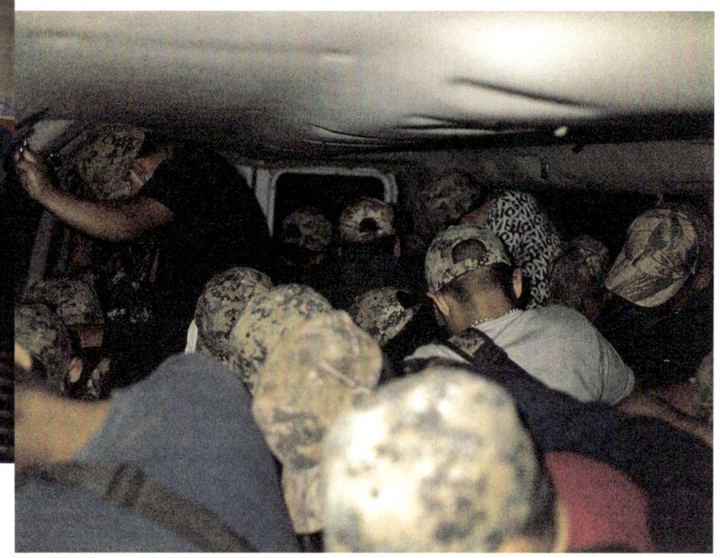

[18]

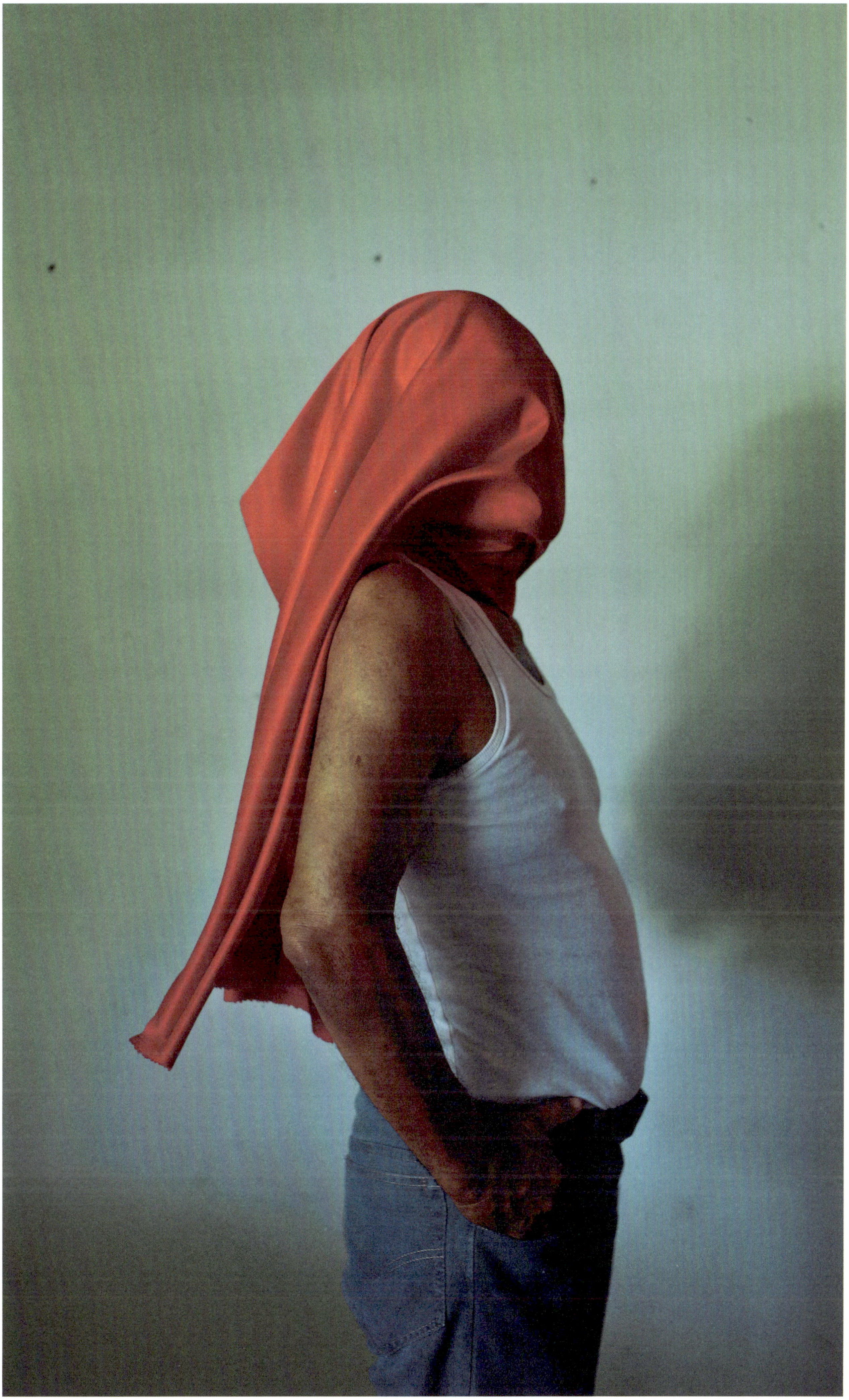

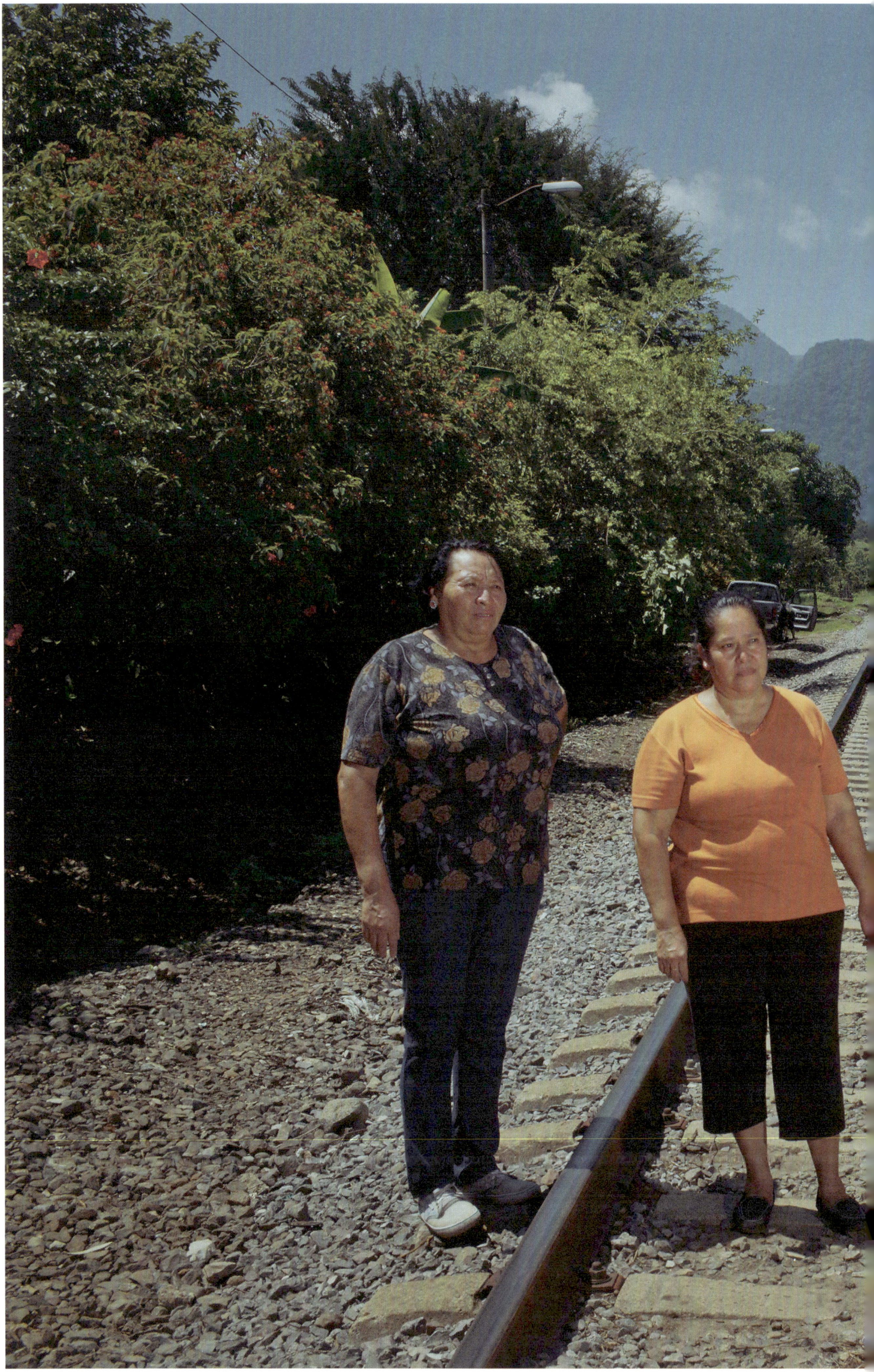

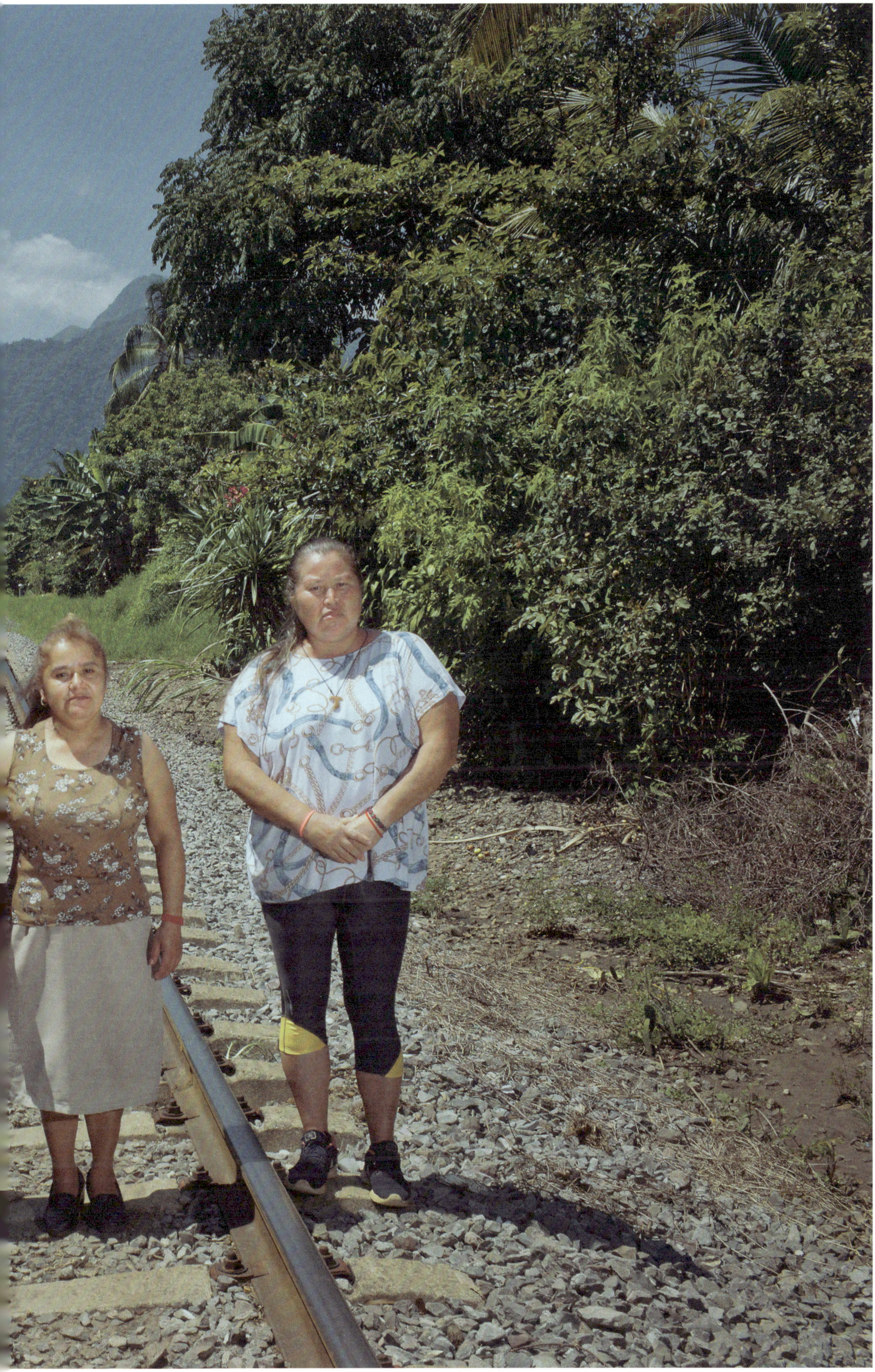

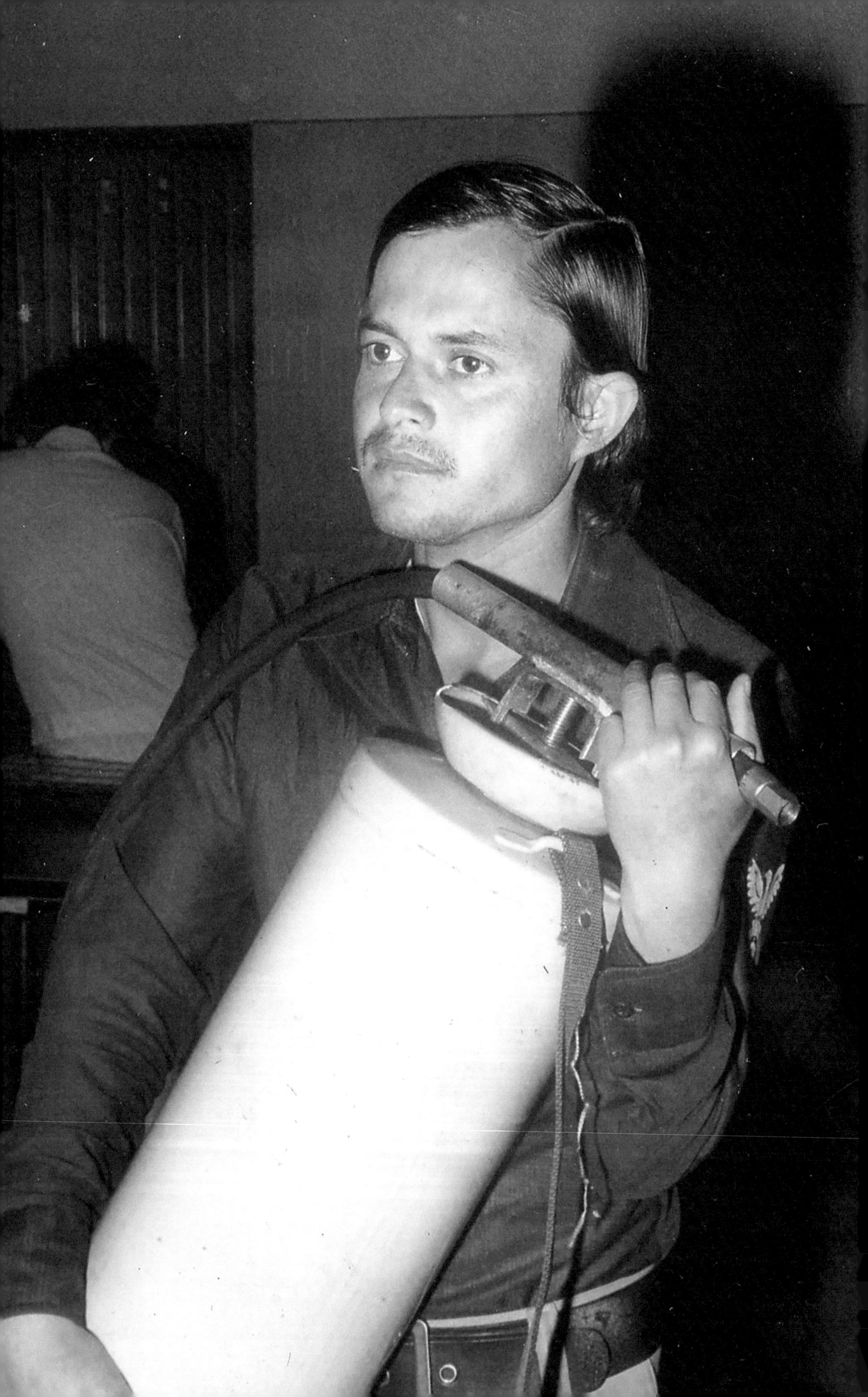

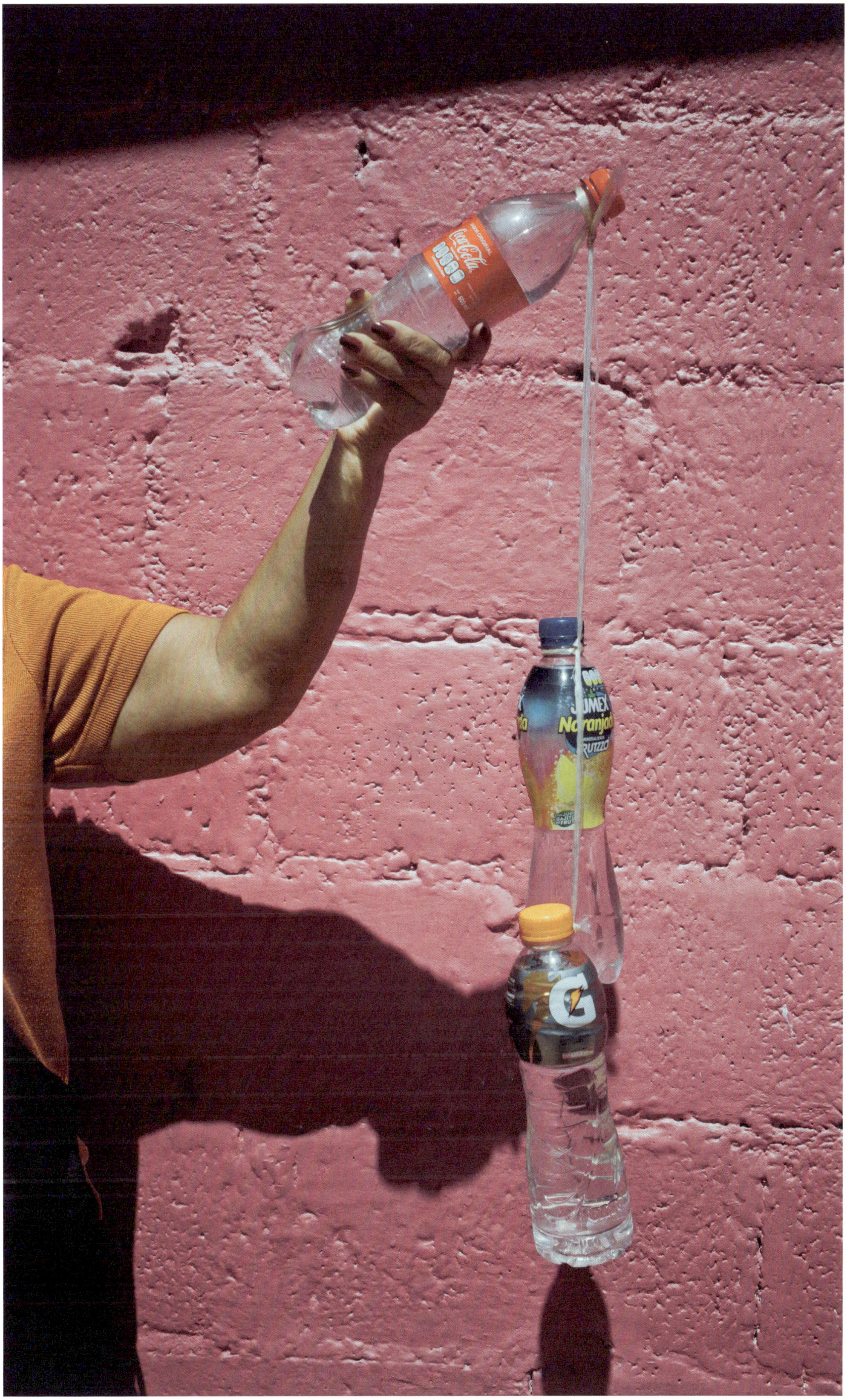
JUMEX

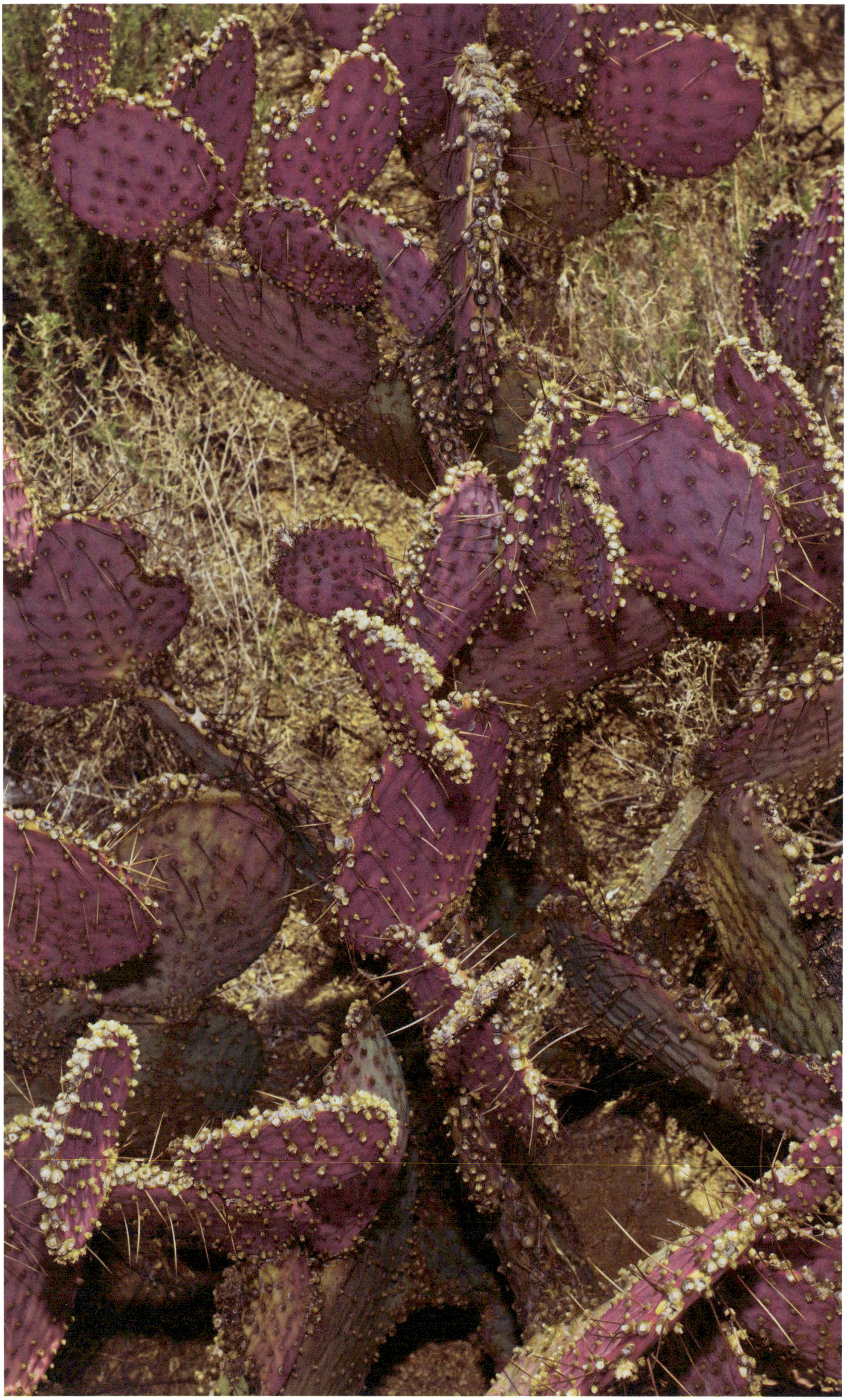

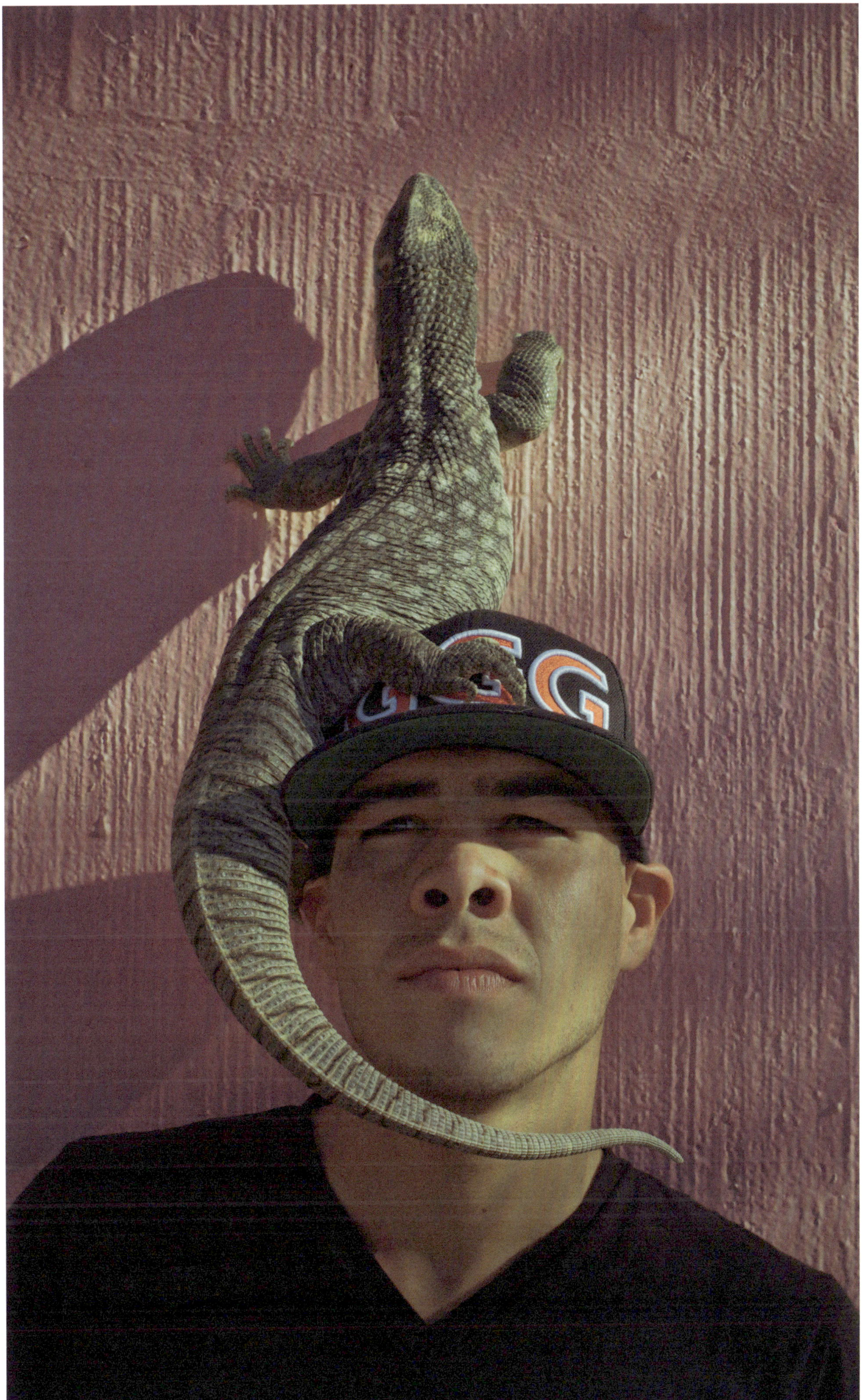

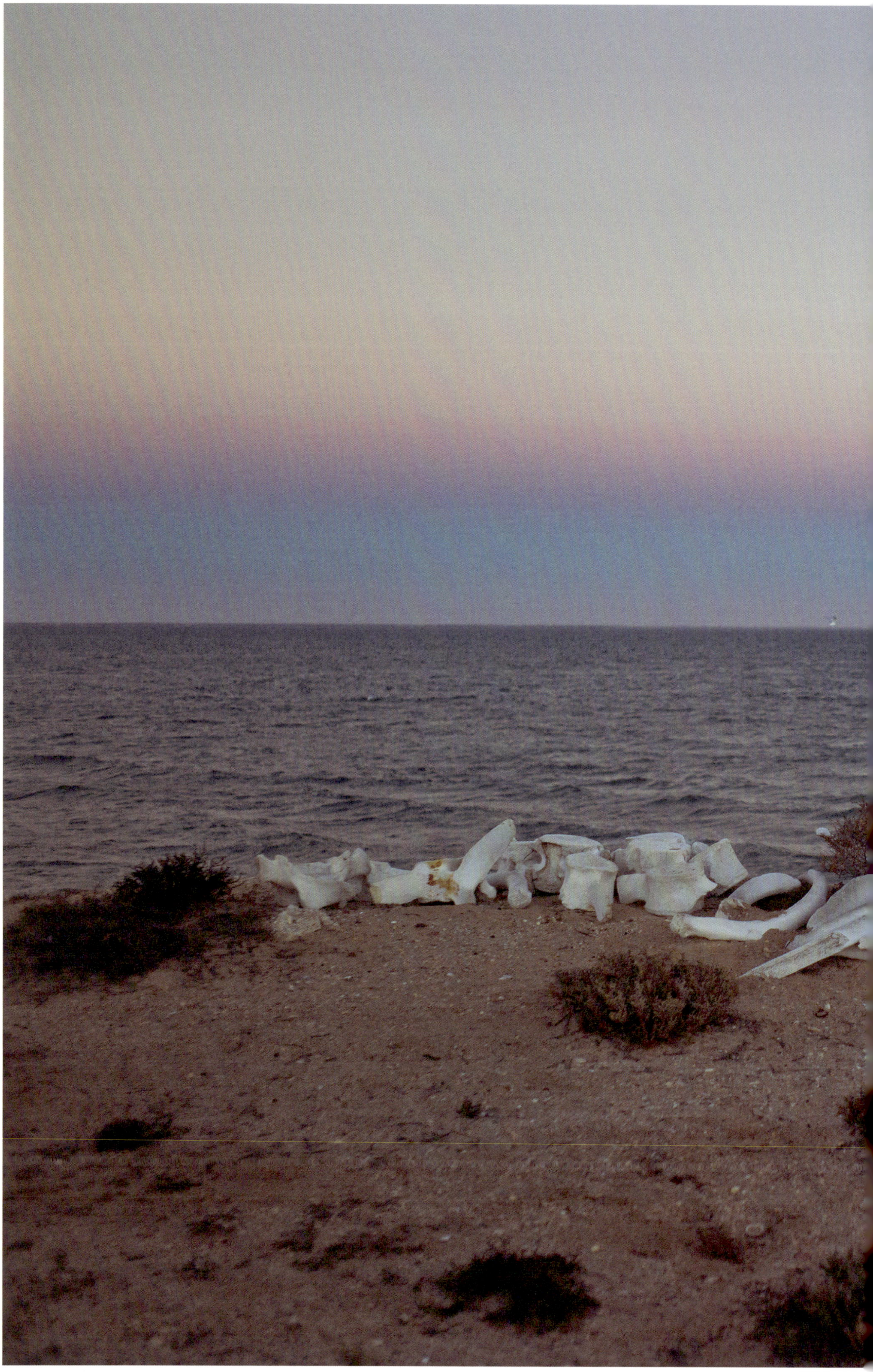

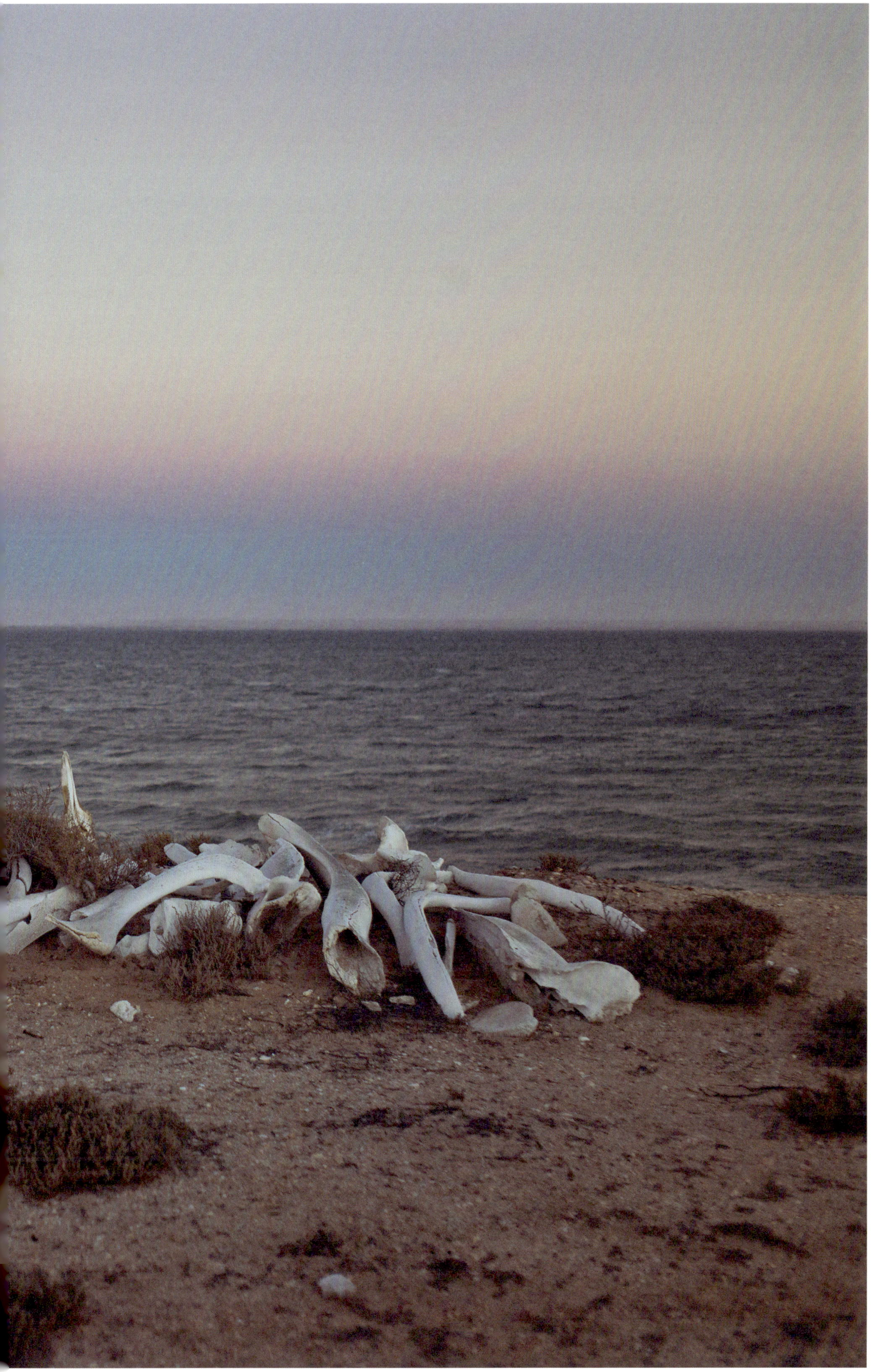

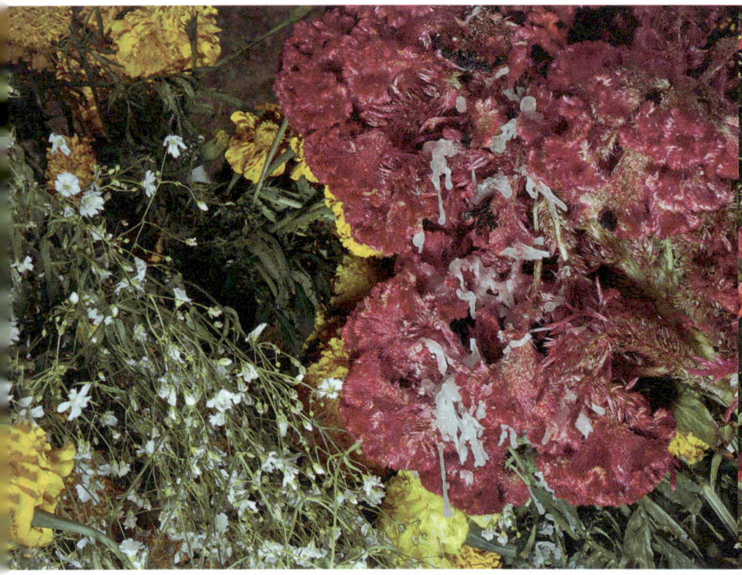

[24]

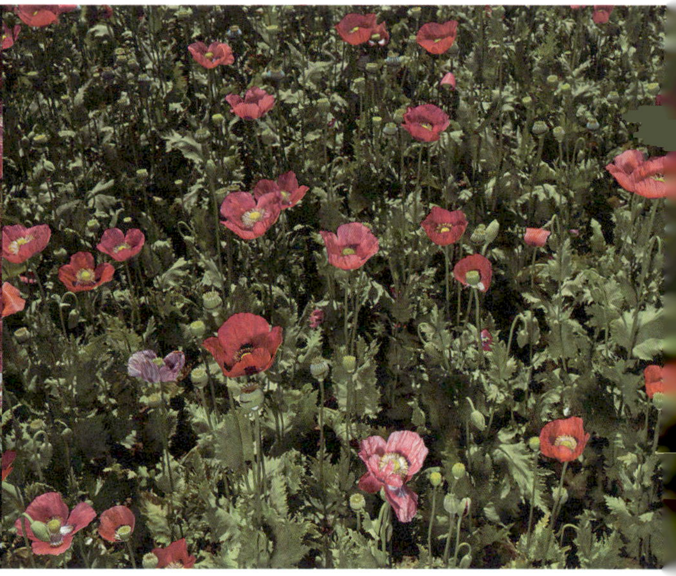

[25]

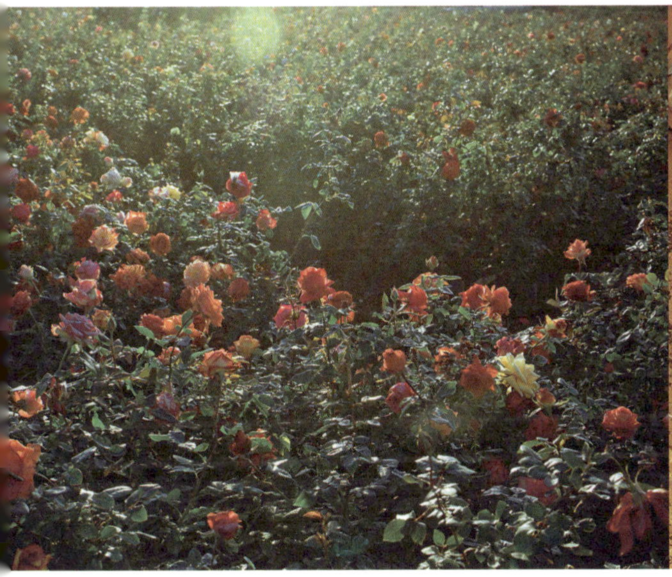

[26]

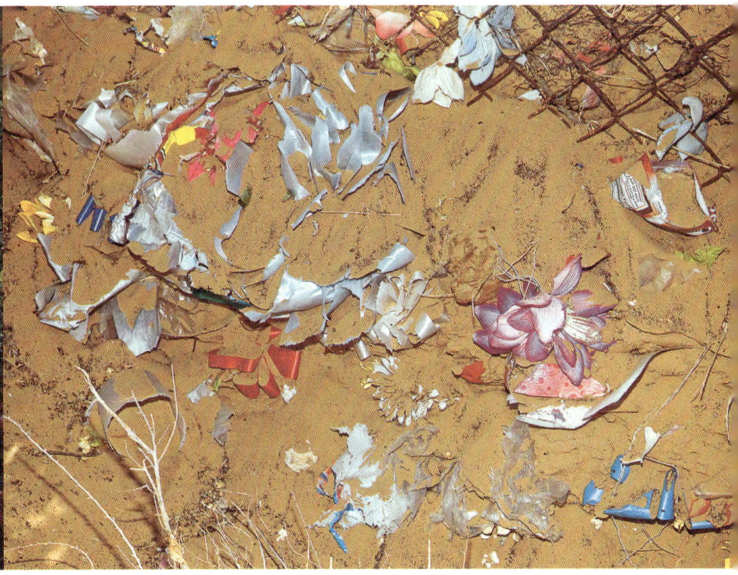

[27]

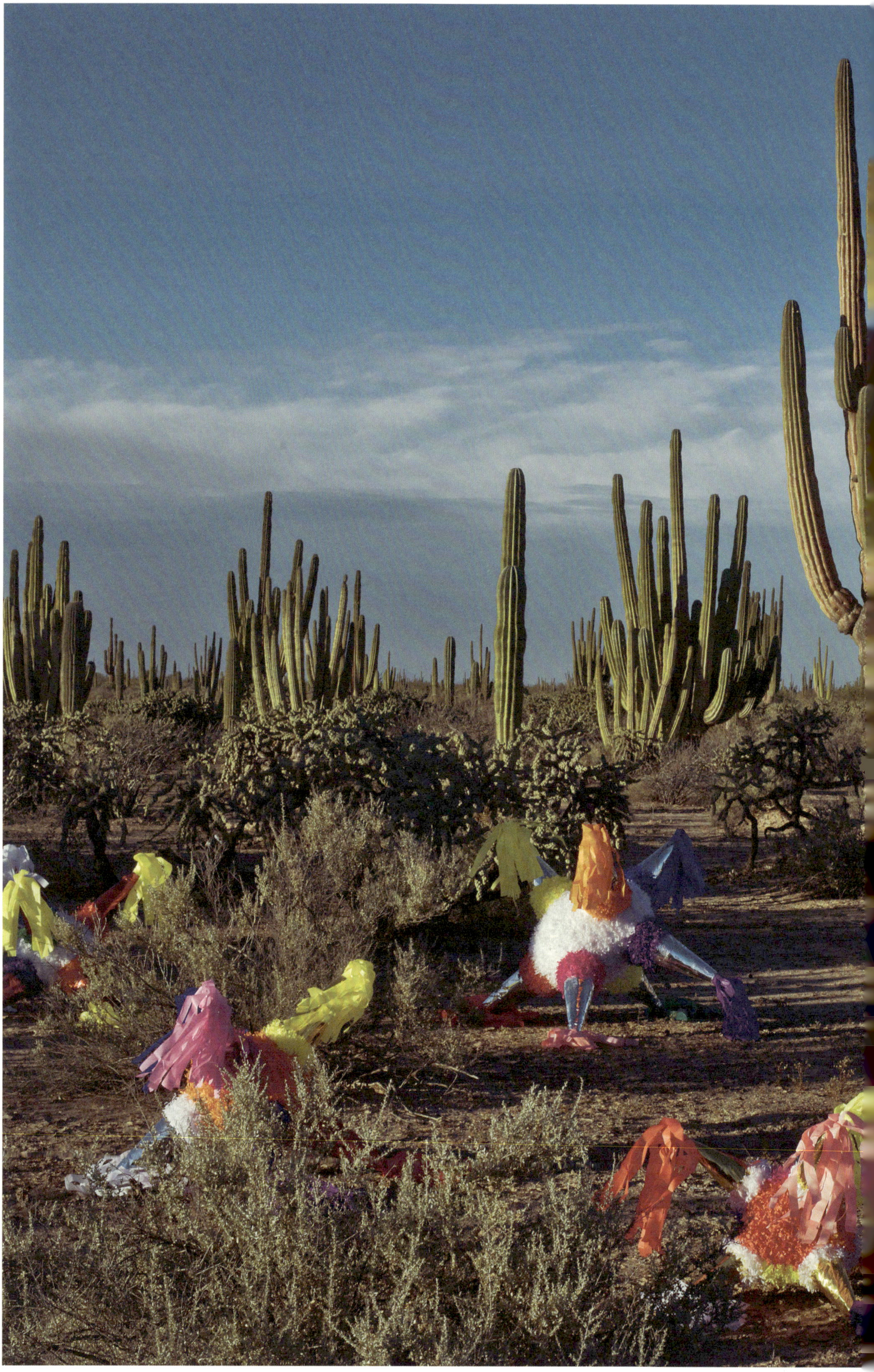

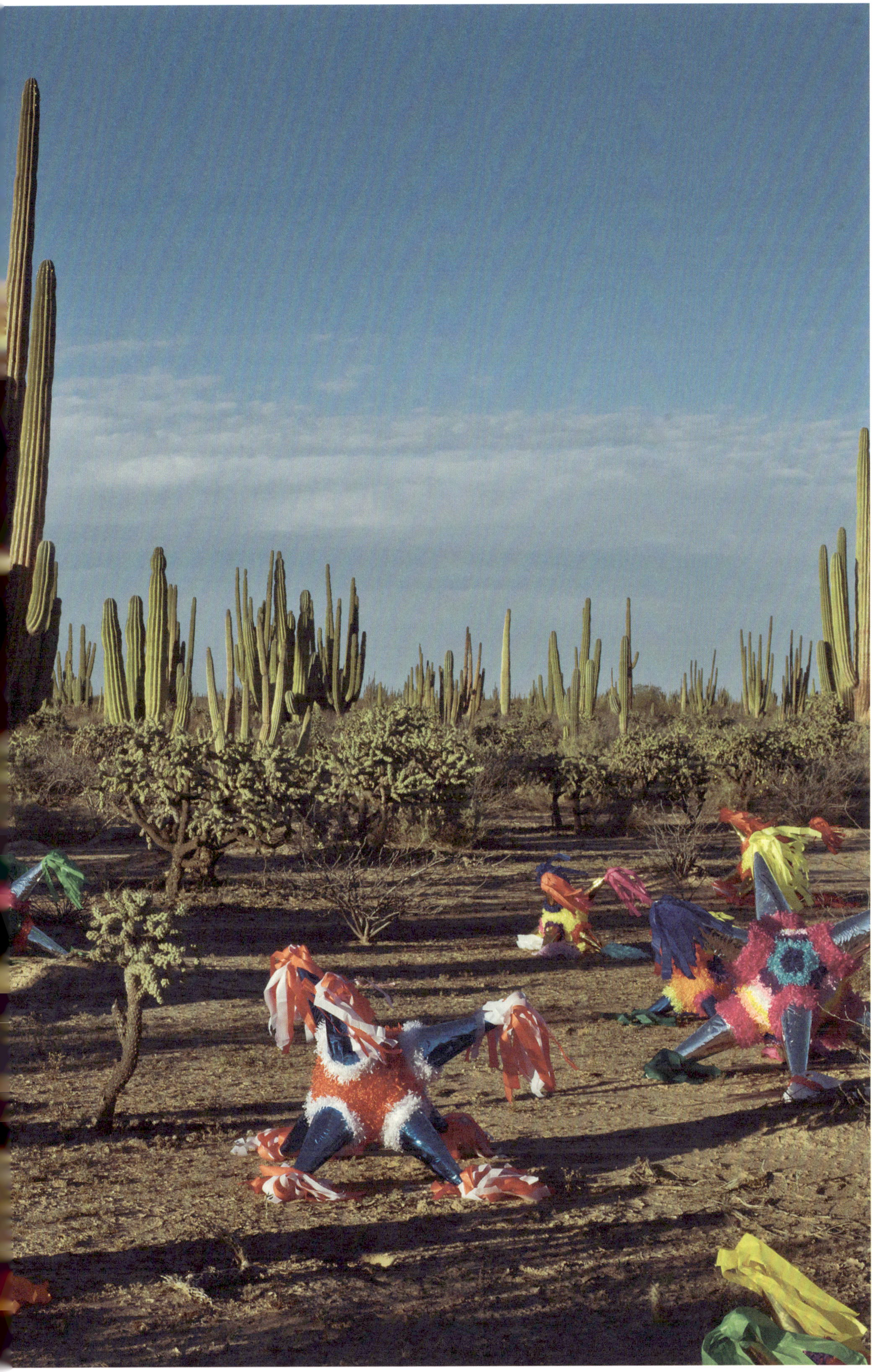

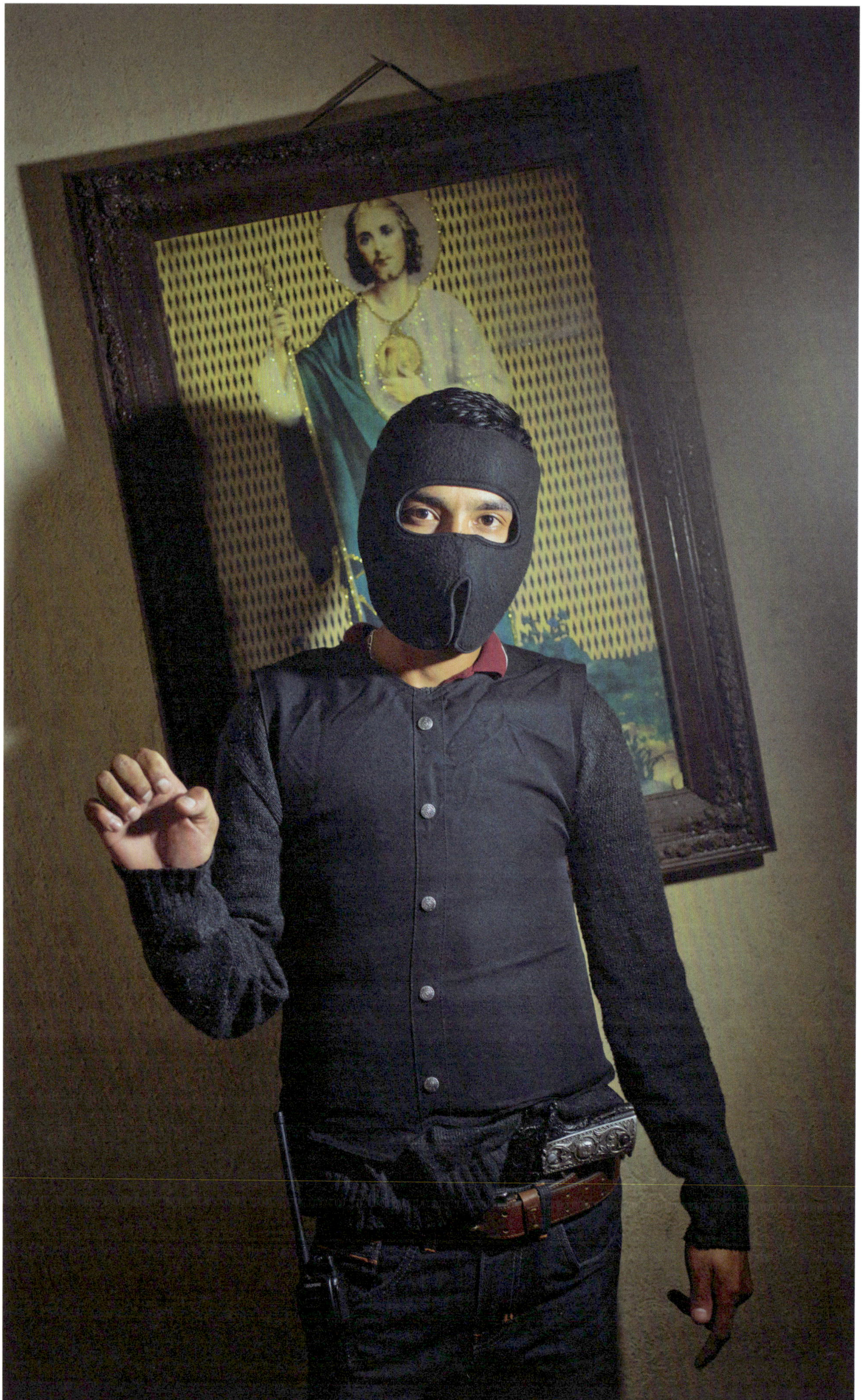

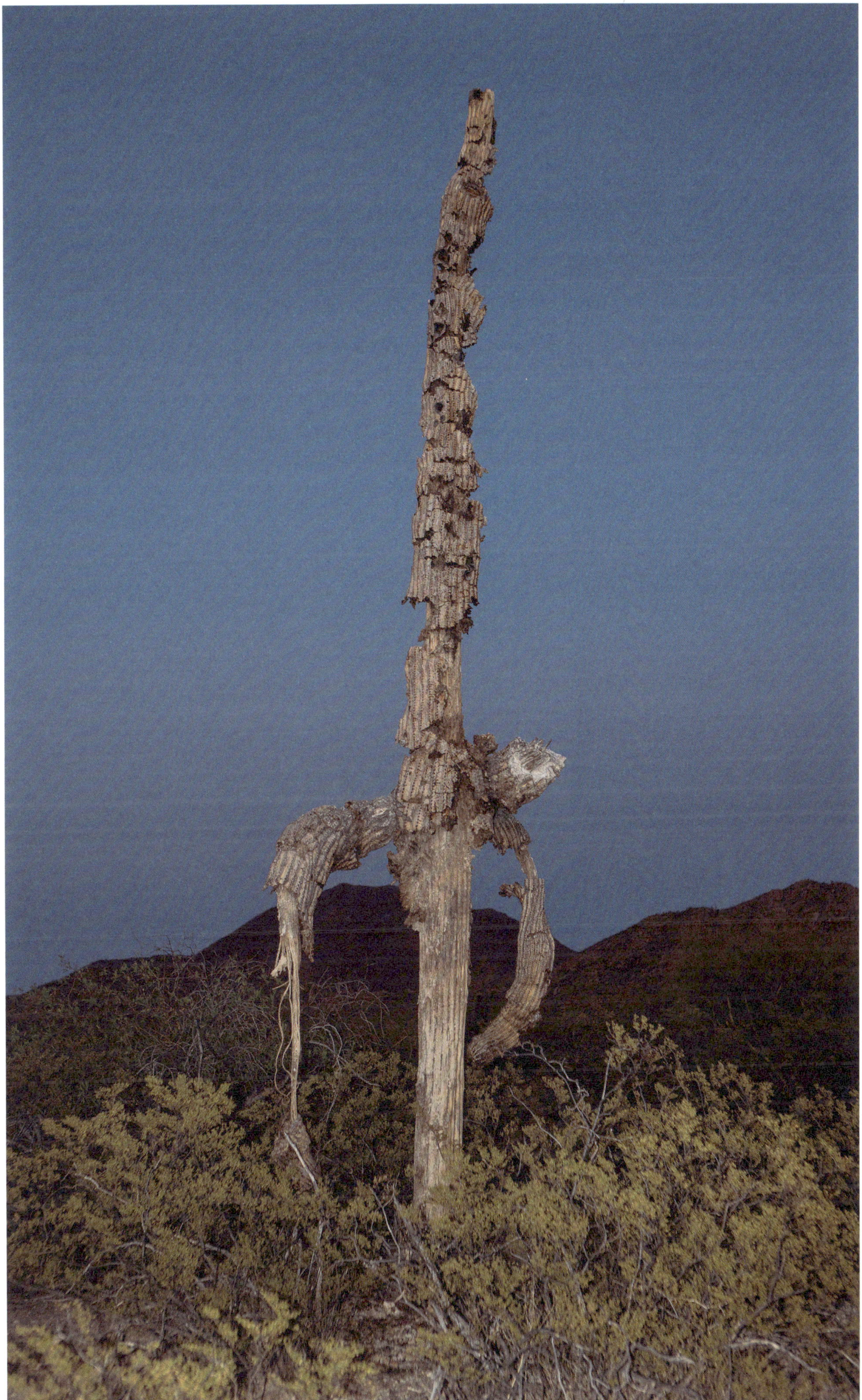

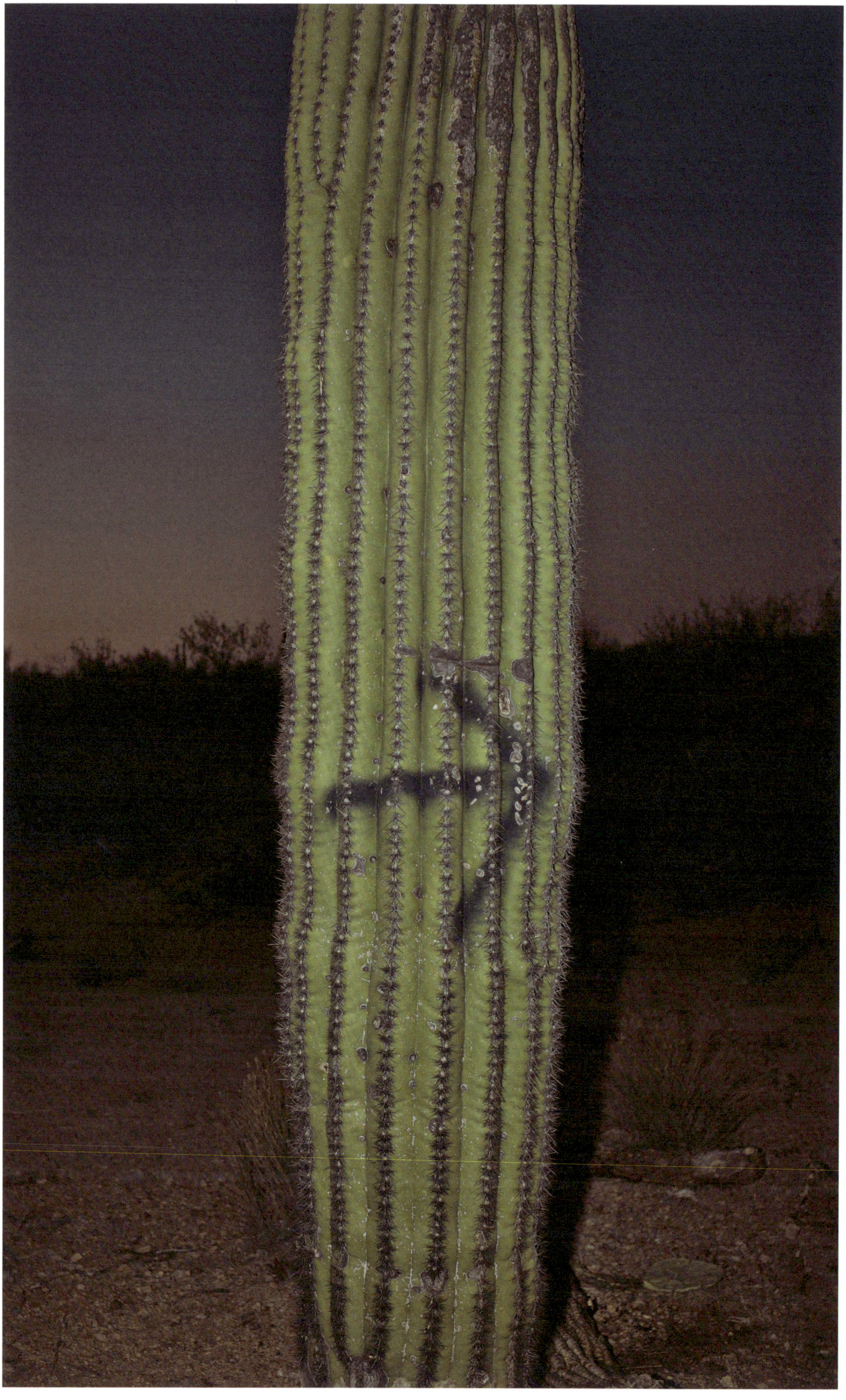

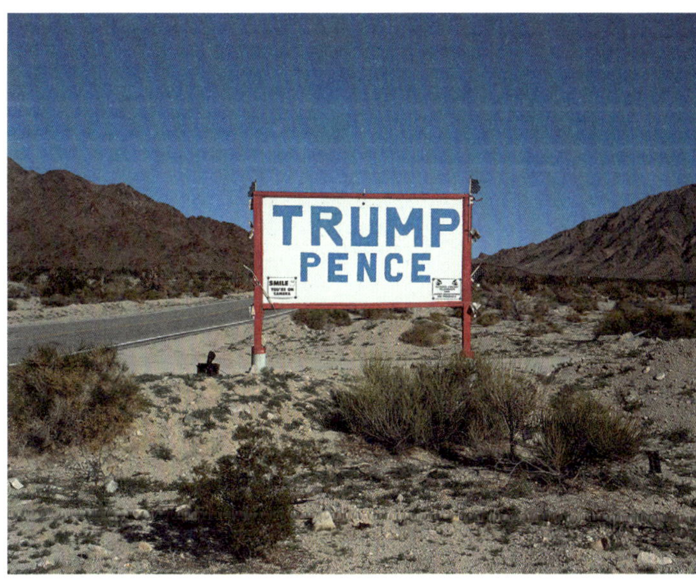
TRUMP
PENCE

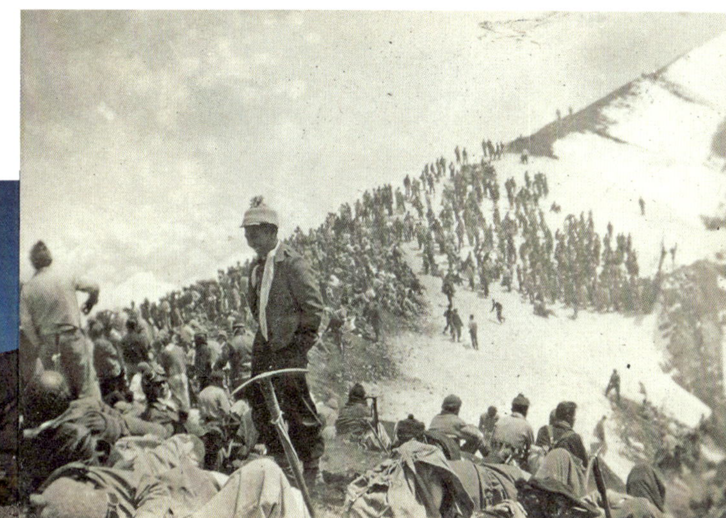

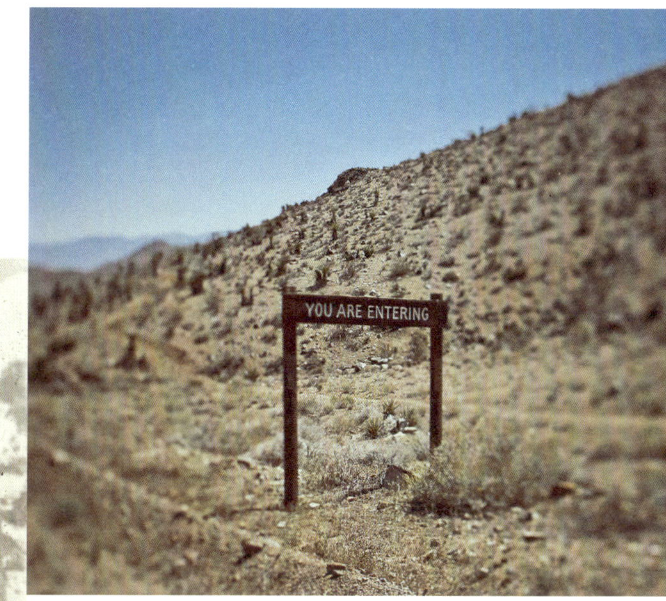
YOU ARE ENTERING

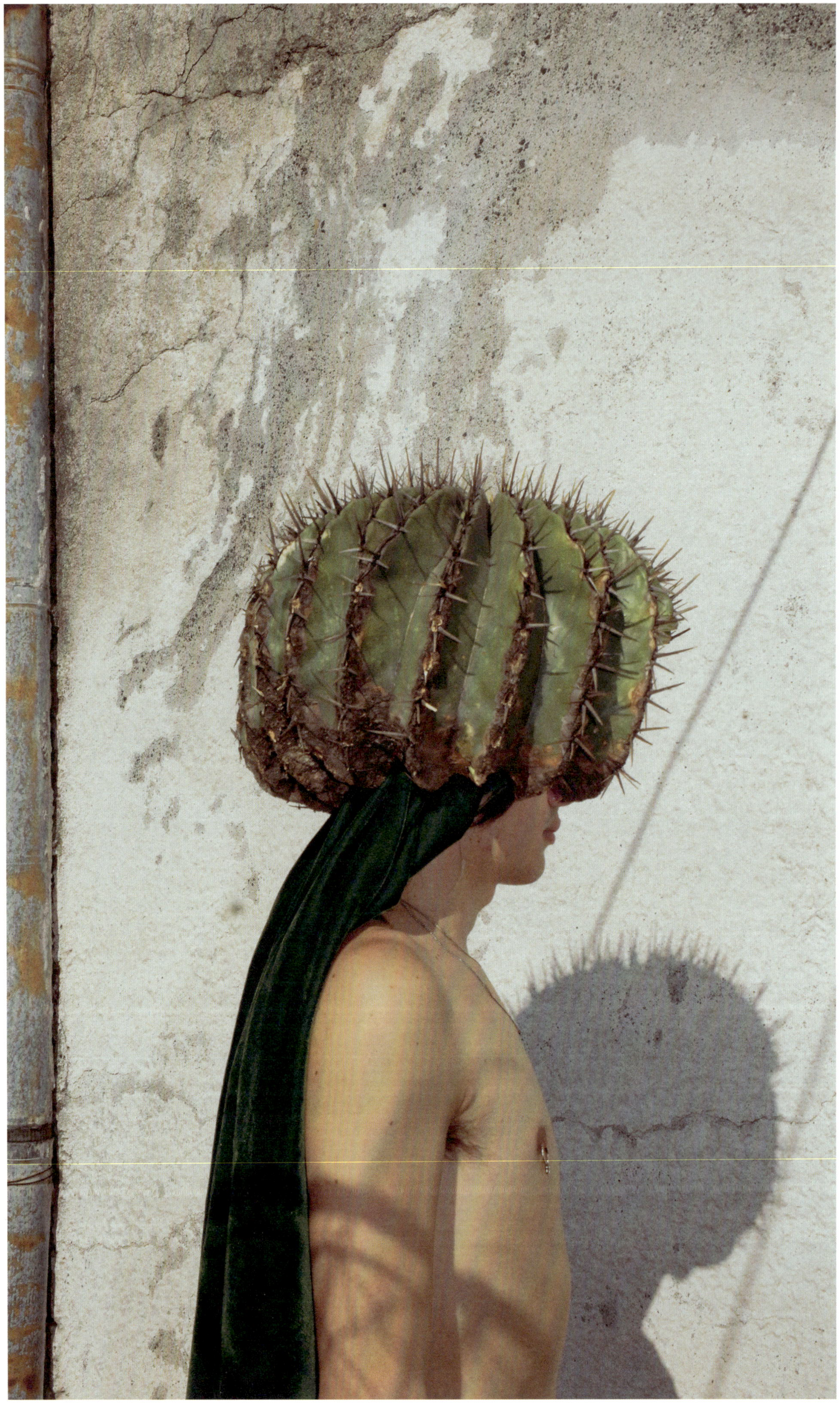

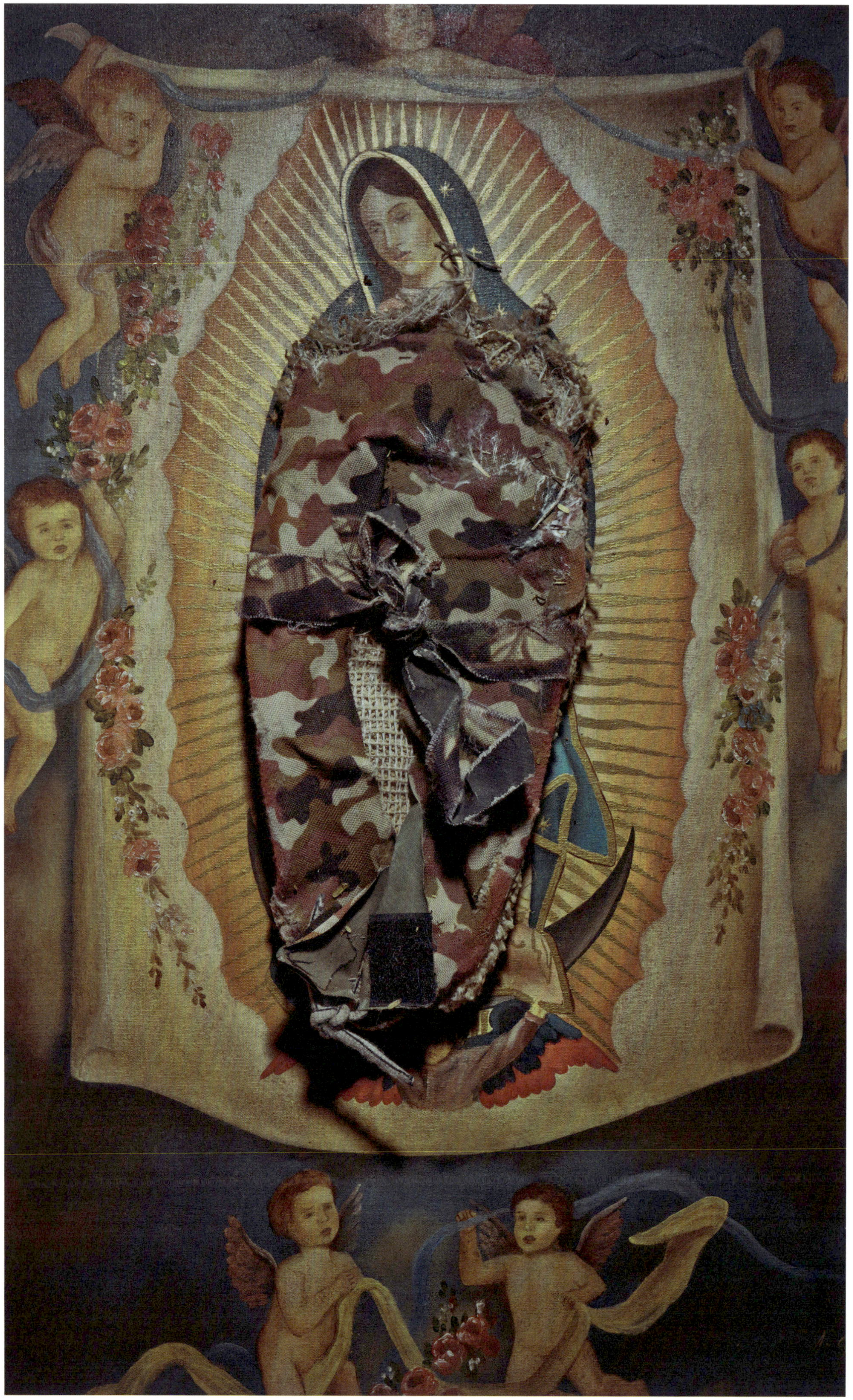

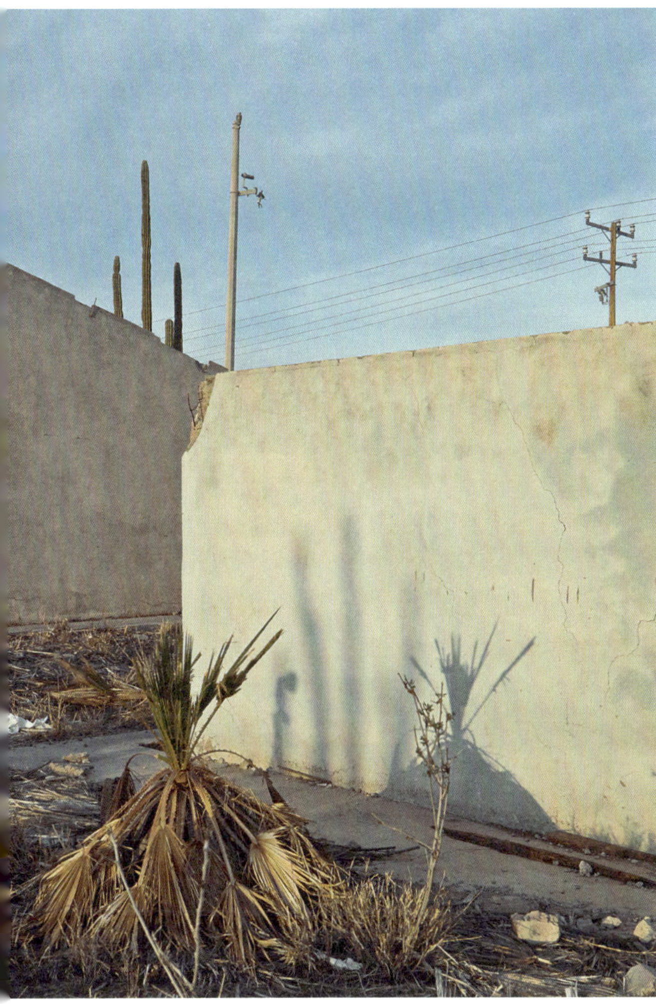

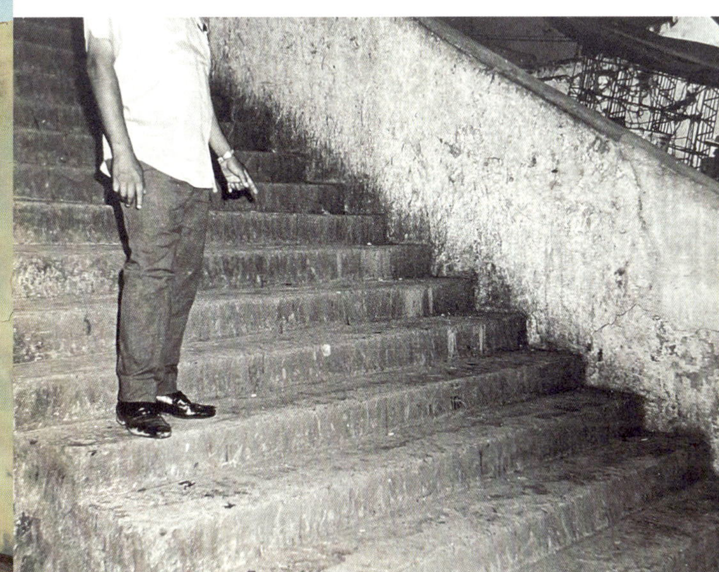

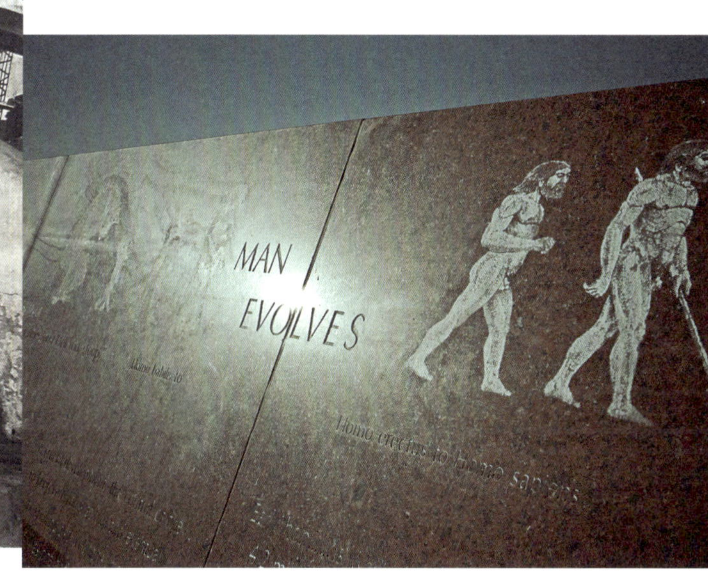

[31]

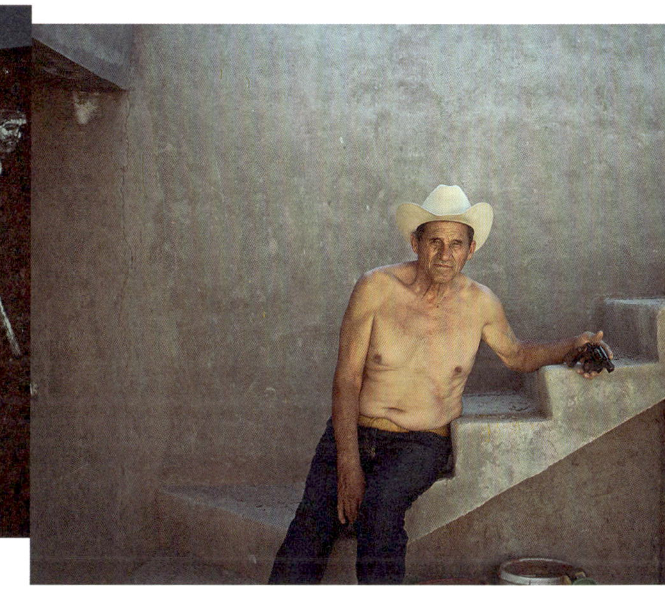

[32]

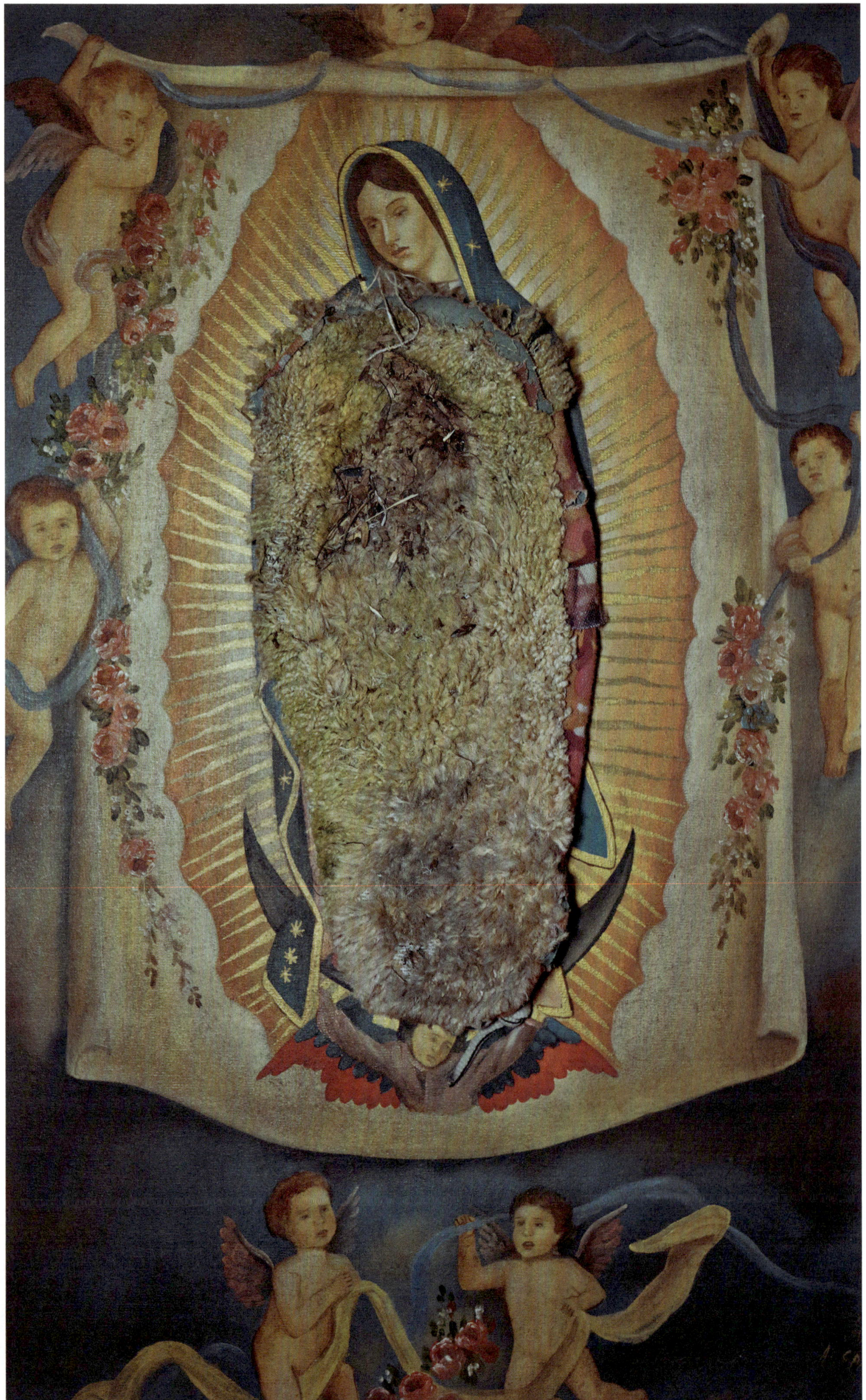

NOÉMIE, HAÏTI

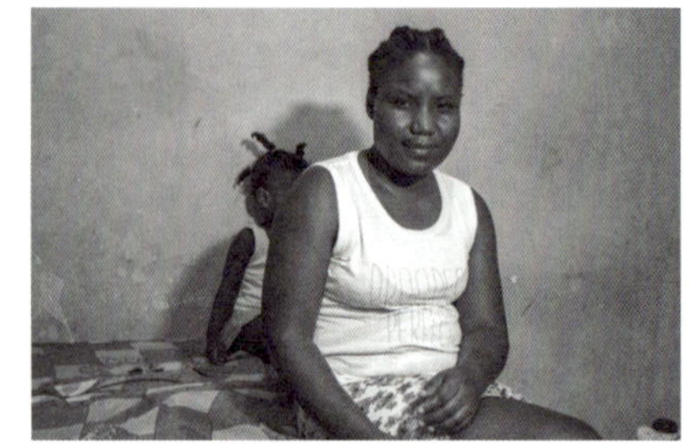

I am Noémie, born on 04/02/90 in Port-au-Prince. I have a sister and a brother. I completed my studies but did not finish university due to a lack of funds. Life in Haiti is not easy because if you are poor, you lack everything to live: food, clean water, hospitals. Moreover, there is rampant insecurity and violence. I decided to leave Haiti and go to Chile because I had no other options due to injustice, violence, and insecurity.

On August 17, 2016, I left Haiti to go to the Dominican Republic before taking a flight to Chile, but the journey was not easy because I was not familiar with the Dominican Republic. I had to find a hotel to wait for the day of the trip. On August 20, 2016, I arrived in Chile, and it was so cold that I couldn't bear it. However, my husband, who had been there for a year, came to pick me up. Since that day, my confidence began.

When I arrived home, he left for work, but life was not easy for me due to the temperature. As I did not speak Spanish, I could not go out for anything, and I spent 6 months doing nothing but learning Spanish on my phone. After 6 months, I went out on the street with a friend to look for work. At that time, all Haitians could enter Chile without a visa, and upon arrival, you were given a visa for 3 months if you found a job with a work contract that you had to submit to immigration for a 1-year visa. But for me, it was different because I spent 6 months at home. When I had to go out to the street to look for work, I couldn't find any because they said there were none for women, but I did not give up. I continued to search until I became pregnant and couldn't go out. I spent 2 years at home without work, and my family in Haiti needs my help because life is not easy for them, and my husband doesn't earn much to send every month. I had to suffer a lot because of this.

When my baby could go to daycare, I went out again to look for work to help my husband and my family in Haiti who need my assistance. There, I was not given a job due to racism, discrimination, and the color of my skin. Every time I went out on the street, I was treated very badly, and they told me, "go to your country, cursed," and when I asked for work, I was told that there was no work for Haitians. I spent 3 years and 4 months without working, and my husband's salary cannot support our needs. That's why my husband discussed with me to leave the country and seek a stable life elsewhere to be able to help our family in Haiti and provide a better life for our child. That's how we decided to go to the United States, a path that is not easy because we don't have a visa, and we have to take a bus journey to reach the saddest part of my story.

On December 29, 2019, I left Chile for the United States. I took a bus from the capital to the last point called Arica. When we arrived, we walked on foot to the border. The police didn't want anyone to pass, but we watched and ran across. Crossing the Chilean border, we reached the border with Peru, and we were asked for $50 USD per person to pass, but it's not legal because the police have what is called a "salvoconducto" to continue the journey. Then we took a bus to go to Colombia, and when we arrived, exhausted after several days of bus travel with a child, there was no hotel to rest, and we had to sleep on the ground near the sea for two days. We bought a ticket for a 2-hour boat ride, and during the boat journey, I faced death with tears and waves that almost capsized the boat. Fortunately, by the grace of God, we came out unharmed. The "salvoconducto" that immigration gave us when we descended from the boat warned us that if it wasn't properly stamped, we would be sent back to the other side of the sea, which is very dangerous.

At 6 pm, we started climbing mountains because we had to cross forests to reach Panama. There were many wild animals. I spent 7 days in the forests and saw a lot of deaths, children, girls, and boys who died in the mountains. On the road, there were injured people who couldn't continue and were waiting for death. We could do nothing for them, even though there were guides to show them the way, but it wasn't easy. There was a man in my group who was sick on the 6th day. It was difficult to get out of the forest with him, but with God's help, we made it. On the 6th day, we encountered armed thieves with guns, machetes, and knives. They took all our luggage, even my baby's milk, and we lost all hope of getting through. We were hungry, cold, and there were wild animals making noise at night. We were scared, and the children asked for food, and we didn't know what to give them. I cried so much that day. I called everyone I knew to save us, but nothing worked. However, God, in His love, heard our cries and protected us from everything.

After the thieves took everything, a woman from my group ran away and fell into the river because in the forests, there are many rivers to cross. People tried to save her, but it was impossible, and sadly, she died, leaving her son and husband on the path. The next morning at 6 am, we resumed the journey, desolate, with much sadness and no hope of reaching, the children almost dead in our arms. But we reached a place with many bananas, and we stopped to cook for ourselves and the children because everyone was almost dying of hunger. At this place, there was also a man, and we asked him how much time we had to reach the Panama refugee camp. He told us three hours if we walked fast, but it was much more than 4 hours of walking, and we arrived at the first Panama refugee camp very tired. The first night, I had a fever, but we were not treated well, and we slept on the ground in a room without doors and with dogs everywhere.

After 5 days there, we left for the second refugee camp, where we were vaccinated and given clothes and food. For sleeping, it was still on the ground. After 4 days, we left for the third camp, which was better and had beds. To leave the first camp, we paid $25 USD per person, the second was $40 USD per person, and for the third, we didn't pay anything, so we stayed for 9 days.

Immigration put us all on a bus to Costa Rica. It's a good country that welcomes people with joy. From the border with Panama, we went to Costa Rica's immigration to take photos. If you have a child, they detain you for a day in a shelter, but if you don't, you can continue your journey the same day with a paper they give you. I spent a month in Costa Rica due to a lack of money because the thieves took everything from me, but everything was fine in the center. We were given food three times a day, soap, milk for the children, but my daughter was hospitalized with fever and diarrhea.

My family sent me $1,300, and I left for Nicaragua, a very difficult country where they made us pay $150 USD per person, even for children. Then we paid for the bus to go to Honduras, but no one can pass through there, and we had to cross a small forest for 4 hours where there were many police and thieves. We had to pay a guide $60 USD per person, and in Honduras, another $187 USD each for the "salvo-conducto." Then we paid for a bus to Guatemala, which had to stop three times on the way for immigration checks and to see if people hadn't brought fraudulent things. When we were almost at the Guatemala border, some people got on the bus. They were the guides because we couldn't pass through the border, and we had to cross a small forest for 2 hours. But that day, there was a lot of rain and cold, and it was impossible to walk. To pass, we had to pay the police $30 USD per person, and they put us in a hotel. After a few minutes, the guides arrived to ask us for $155 USD to reach the Mexican border.

That day was one of the worst days of our lives. They moved us at 8 pm from the hotel to the Mexican border, and we couldn't go by bus; it was a private car to avoid attracting the attention of the police. We arrived at 5 am at a place where a man was waiting for us, and he said he would cross the Mexican border with us. He brought a freight truck to transport us to the border like animals. It was very hot, and inside, we couldn't see anything because they locked us with a padlock. But thanks to God, we arrived at 8 am near the border, where we waited until 2 am and crossed a very short river. Then they put us in a house to check if there were any police. After 30 minutes, the agents came with 2 buses to transport the people to Tapachula. We got on the buses with fear because we didn't want to go to prison after all the miseries we endured.

Before reaching Tapachula, there was a bridge where there are always immigration police, and if they find you on the bus entering Mexico illegally, you go straight to prison. But if you pass, you can get a residence for 5 years. For us, that was the case because we didn't see the police, and we arrived in Tapachula at 3 am. We took a taxi to the place where they give you the temporary visa, and afterward, we looked for a place to rest. We had no money or anything to eat, but we went to a place that helps migrants and is called ACNUR. After the interview, they gave us money to pay for a room for 3 months.

I have been in Tapachula for 5 months now, and the situation is not very good. I no longer receive help to eat and buy things for the house and my daughter. We live day by day, difficultly, and my husband has not found work for 4 months. I filed the papers in immigration for a visa, but so far, I am not yet recognized as a refugee, and immigration works very slowly.

This story is not yet finished because I have not yet reached my destination, but I think that one day, in the future, I will have the chance to tell you how it ends.

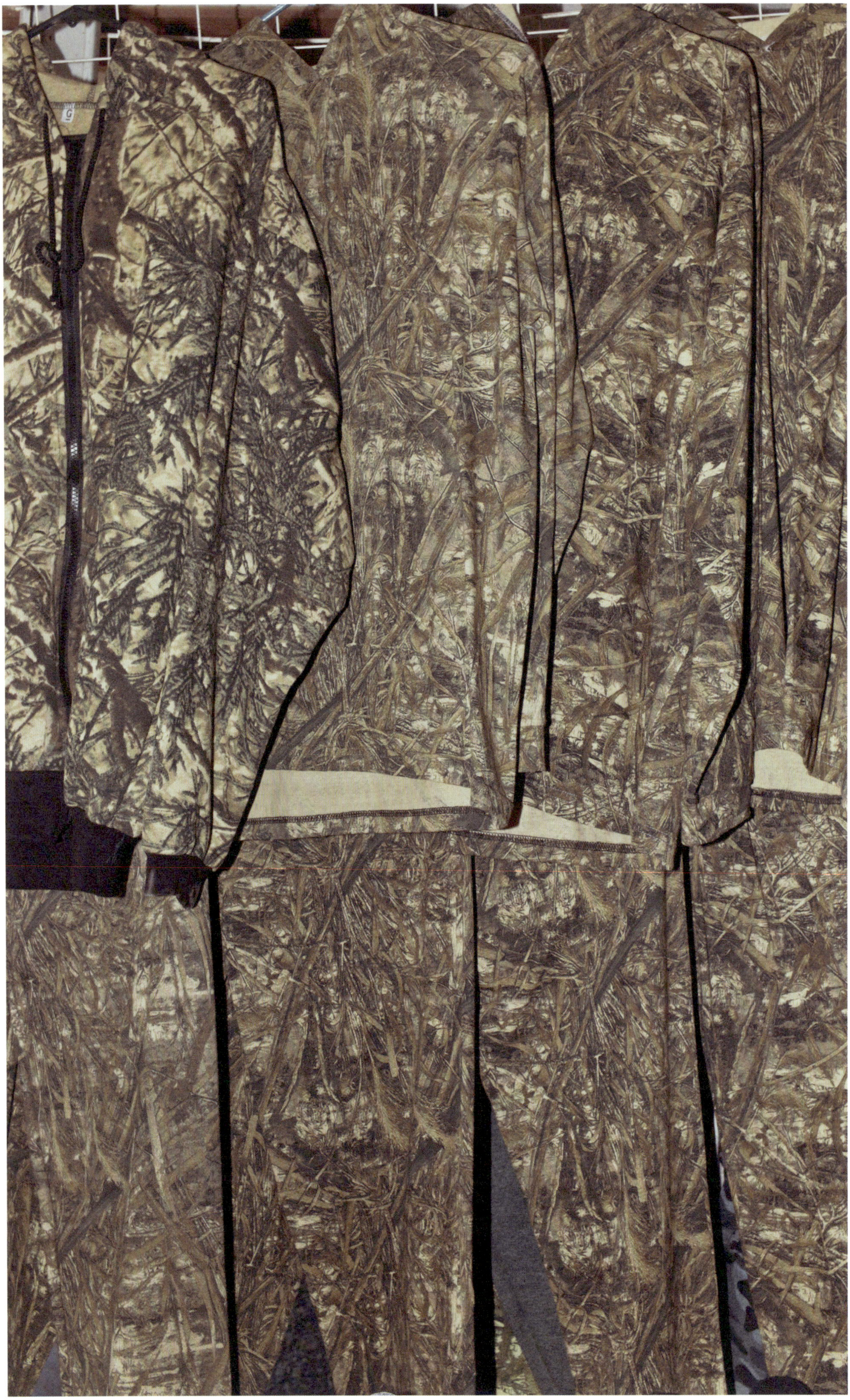

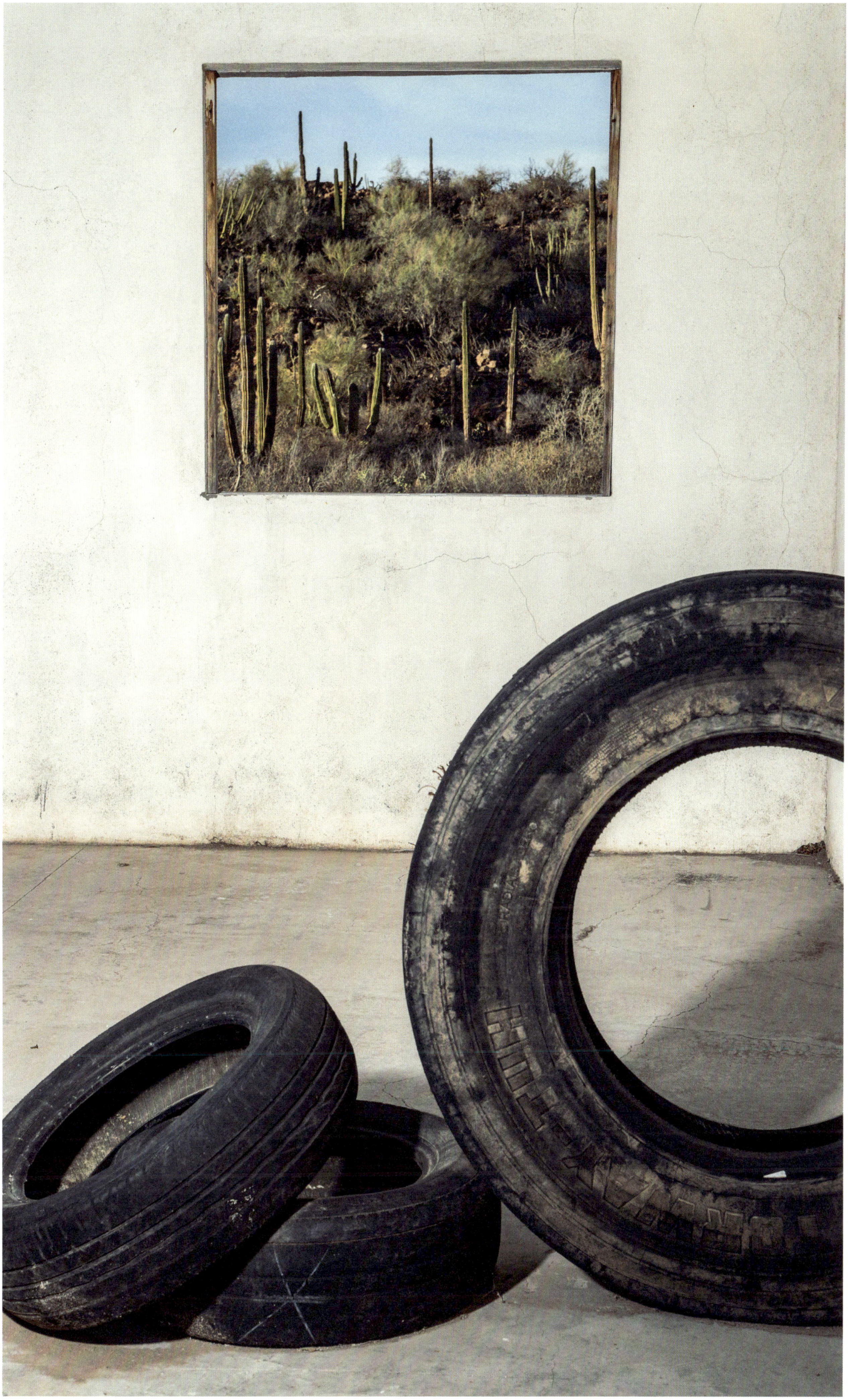

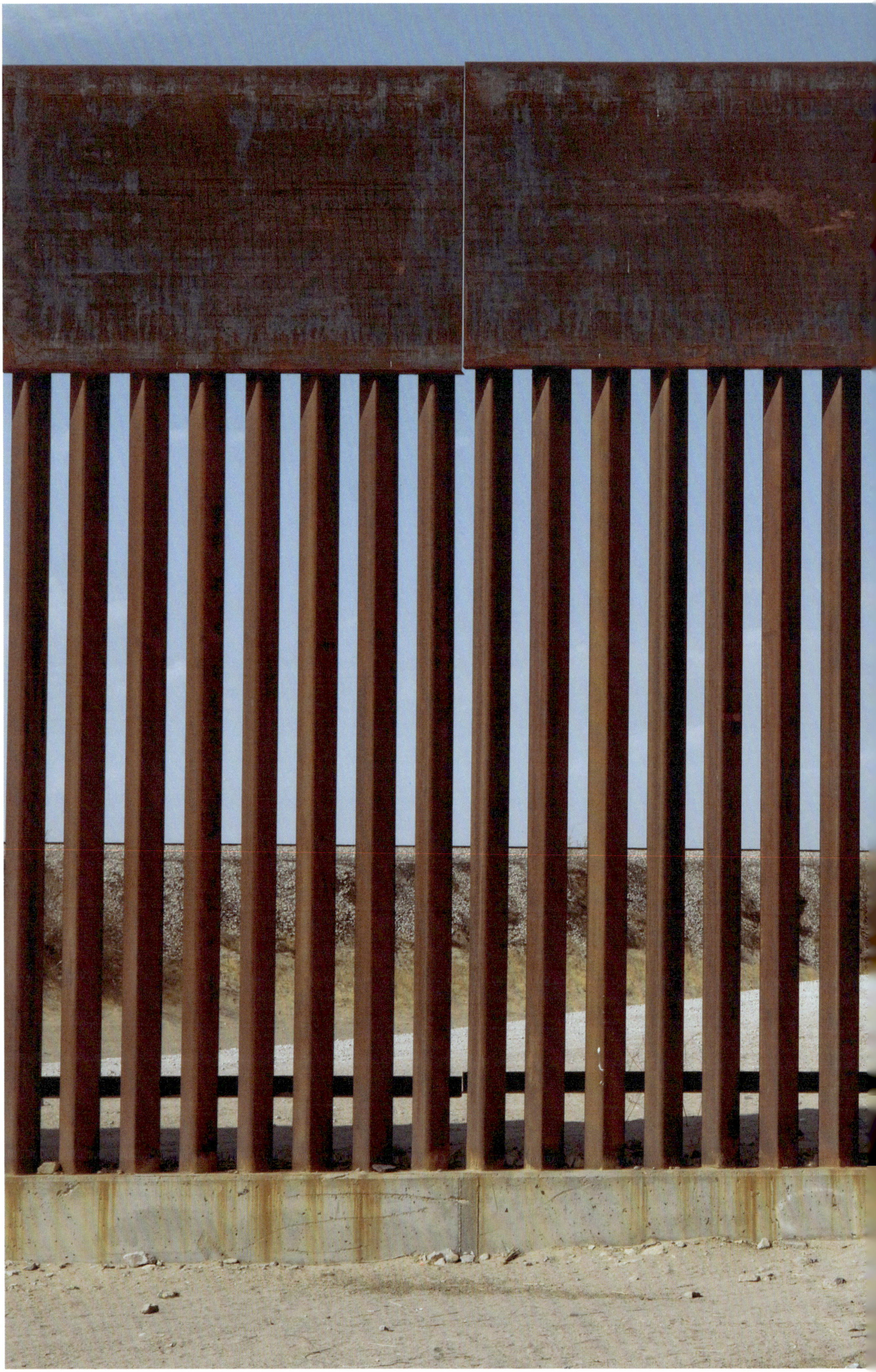

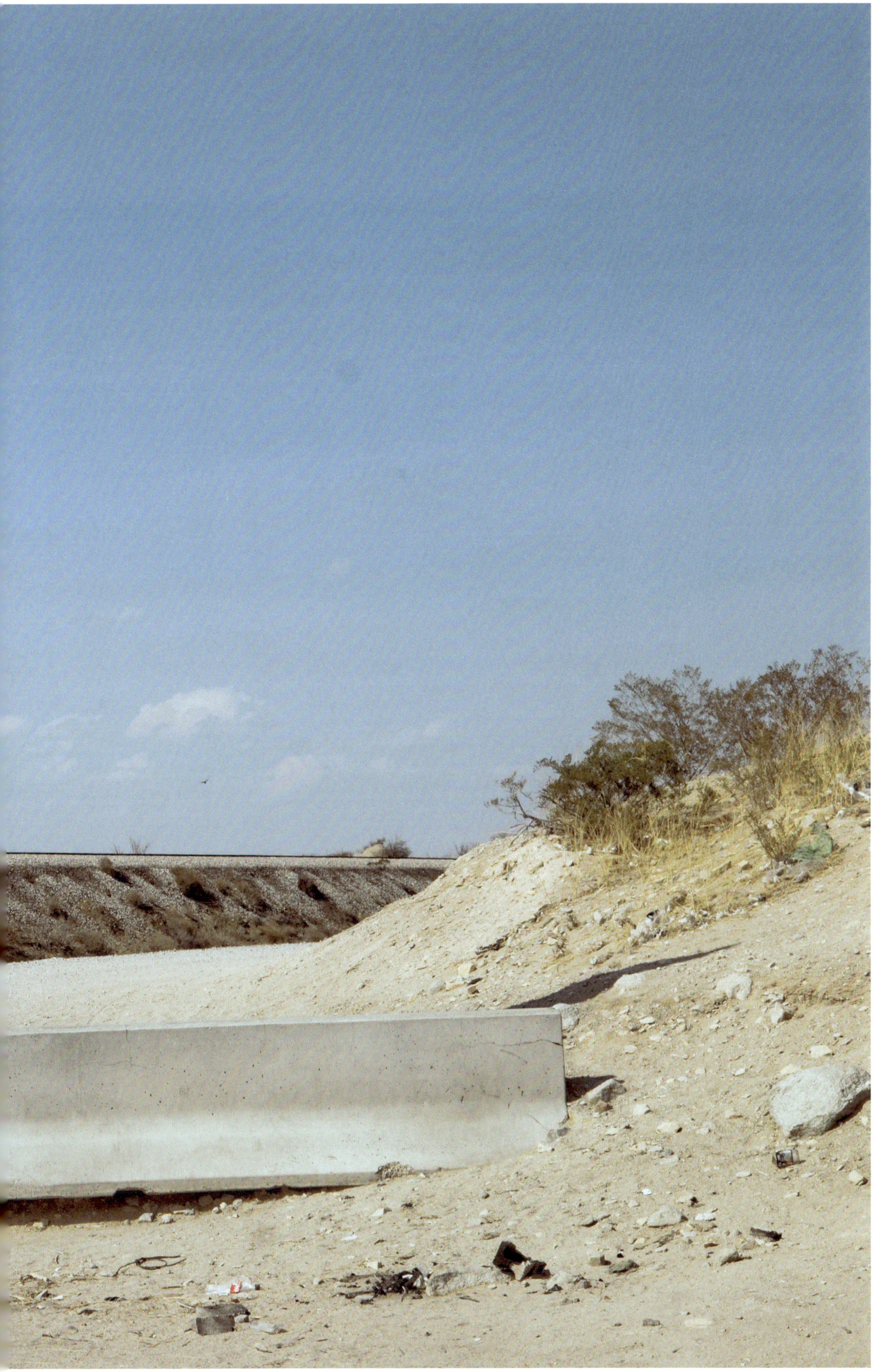

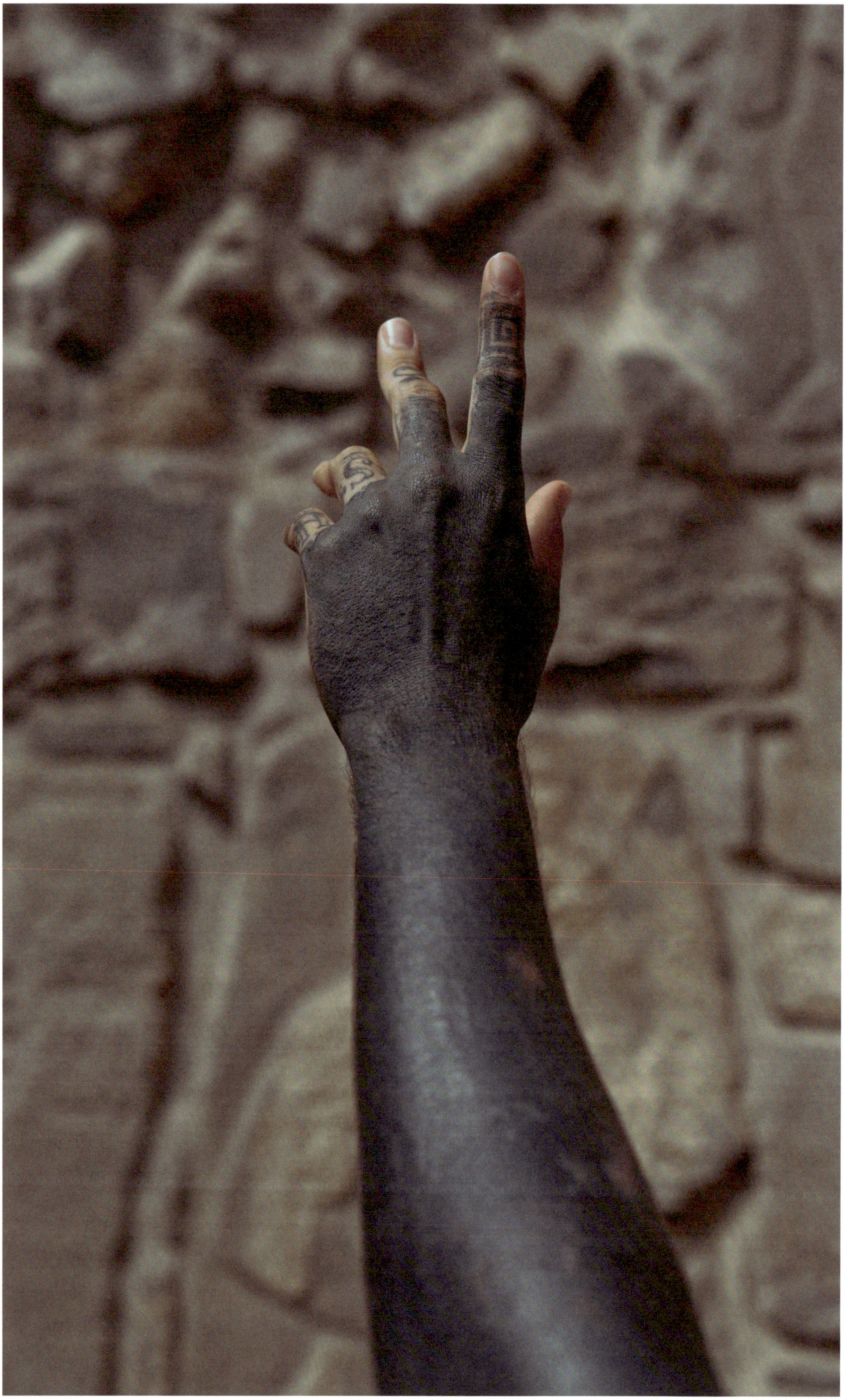

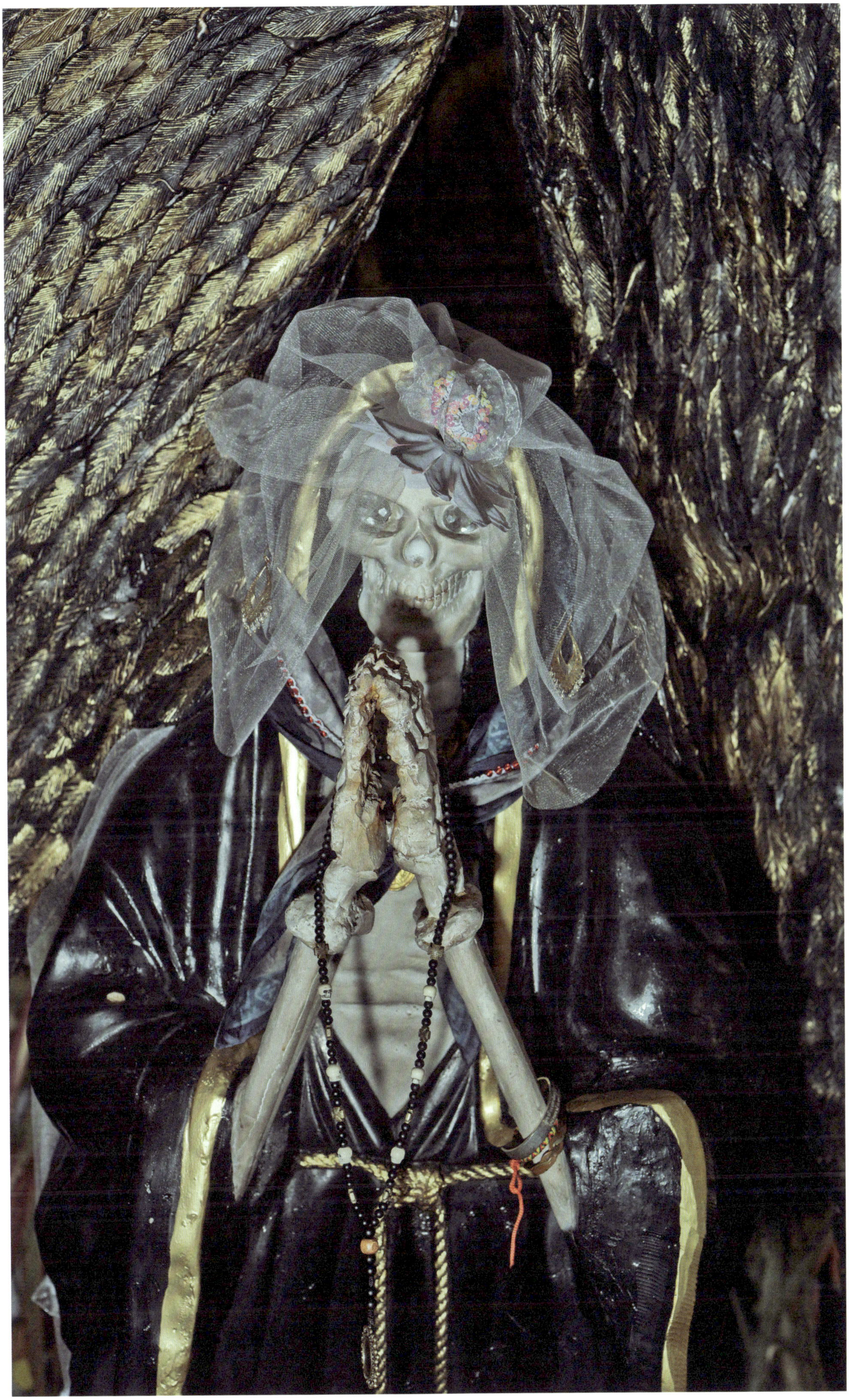

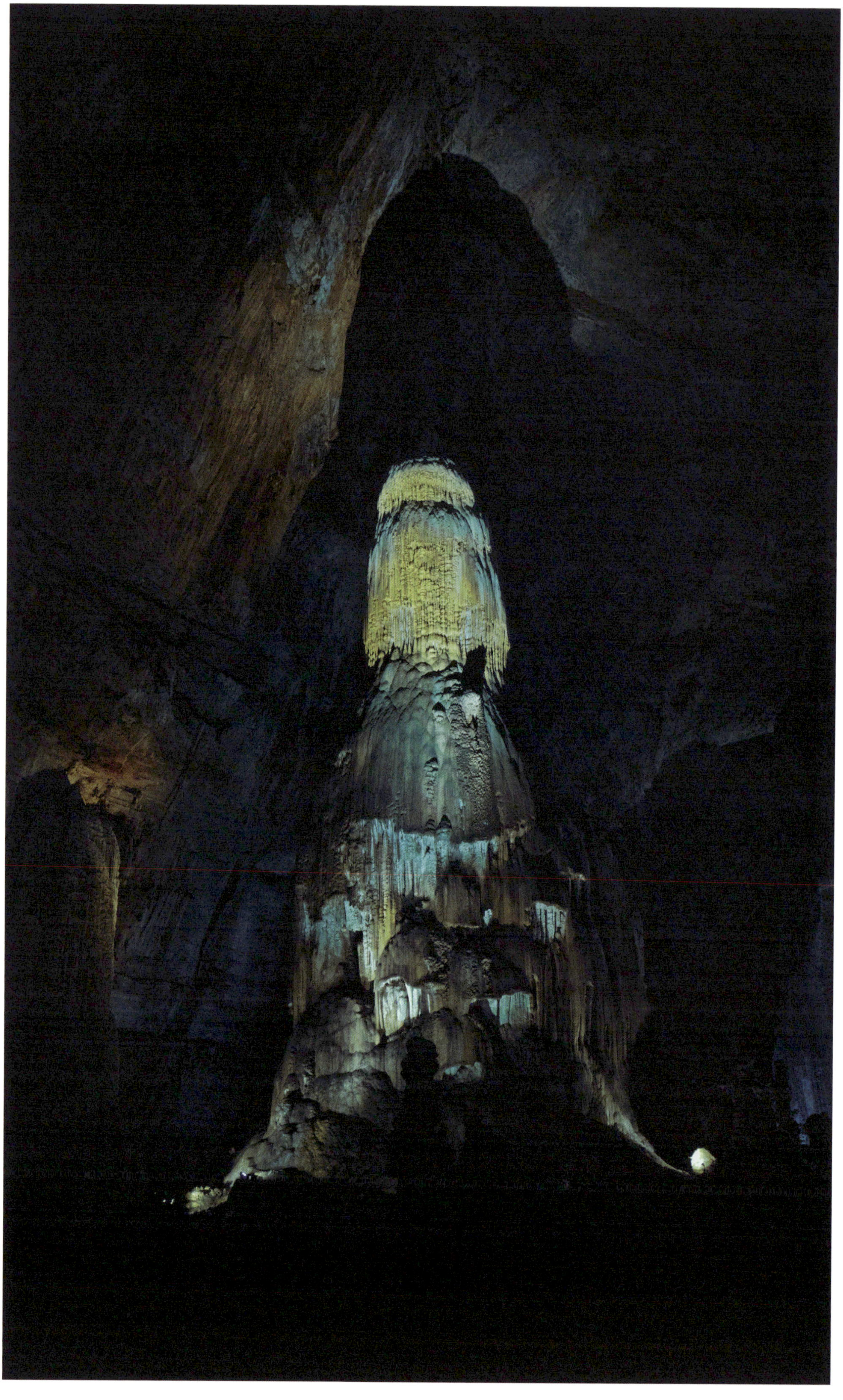

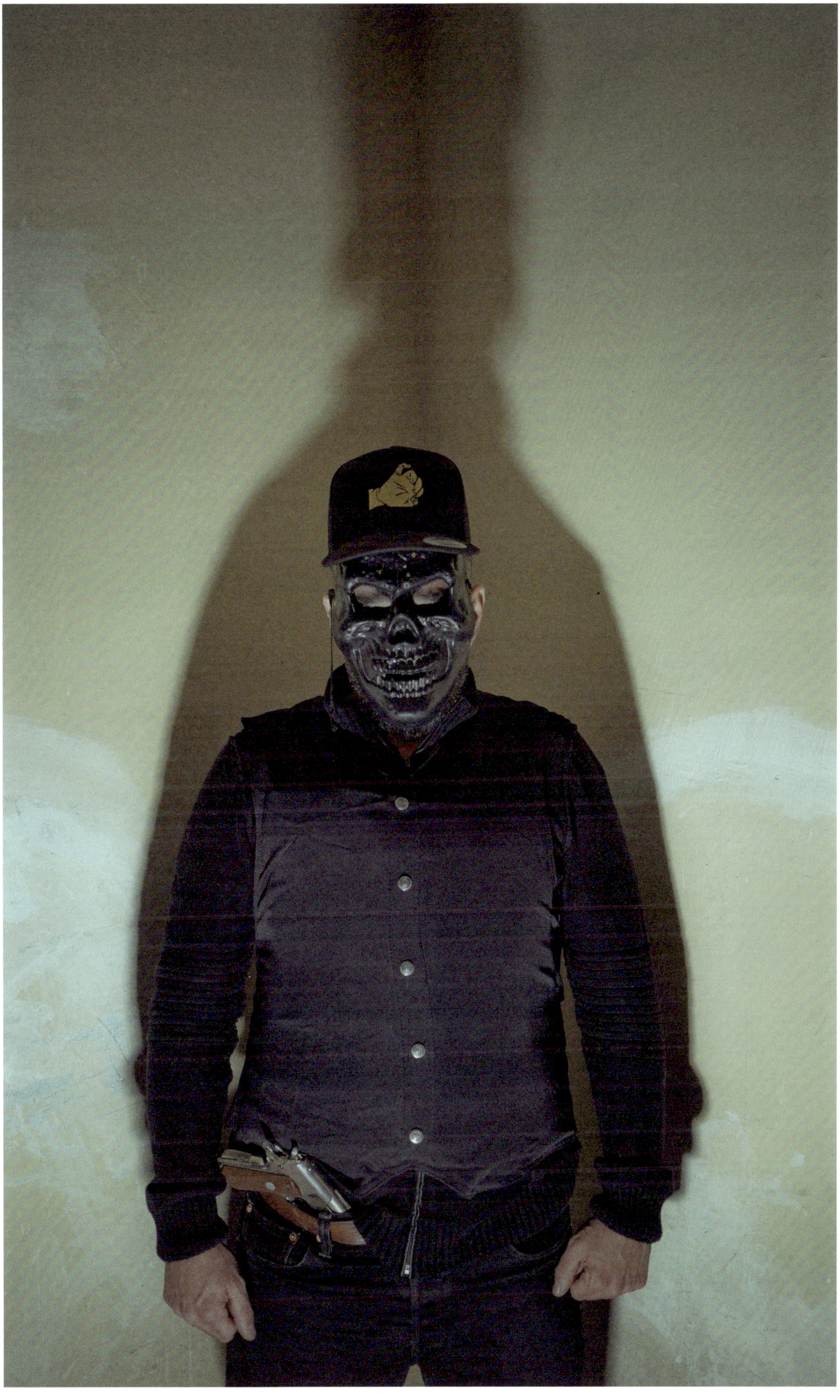

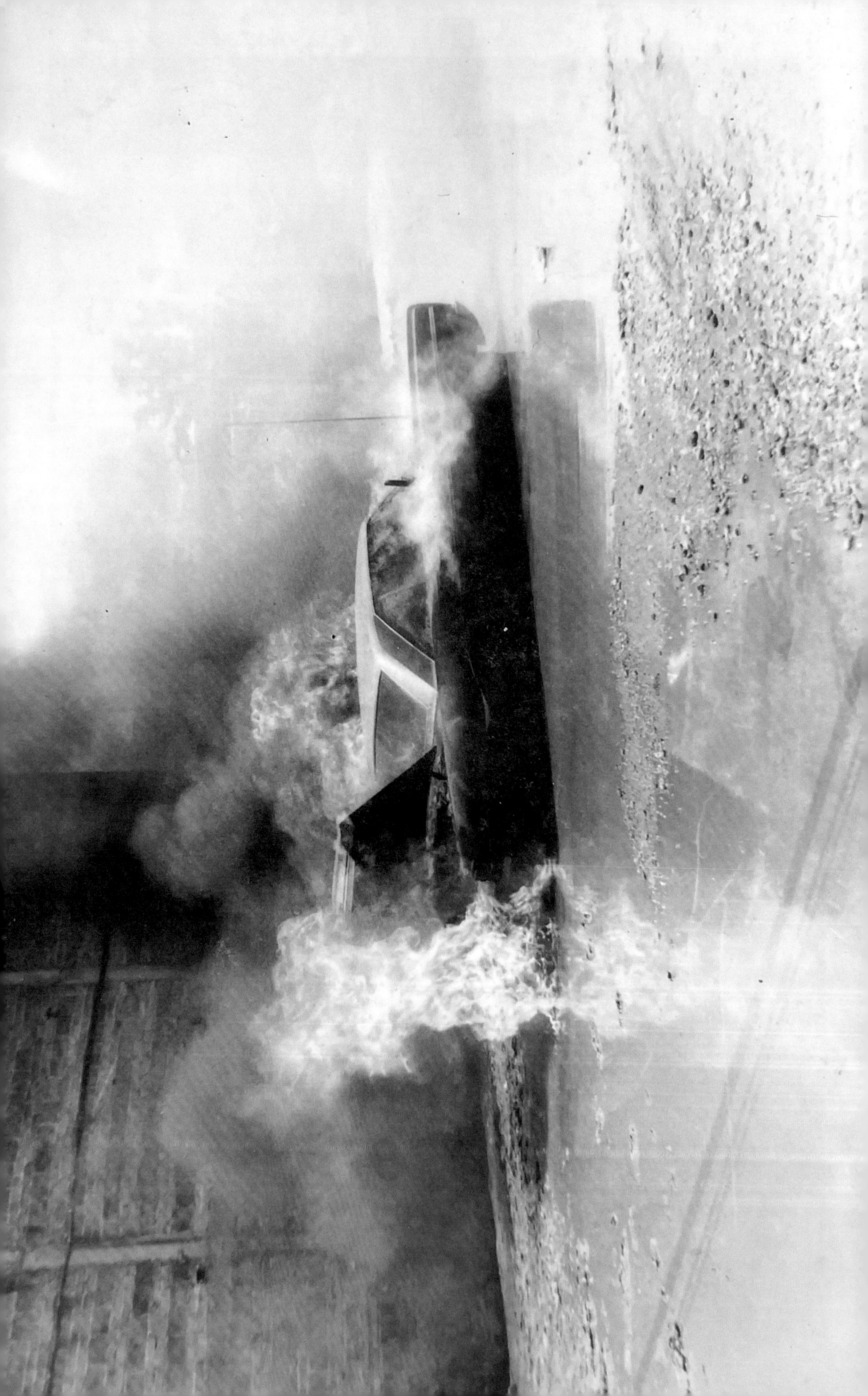

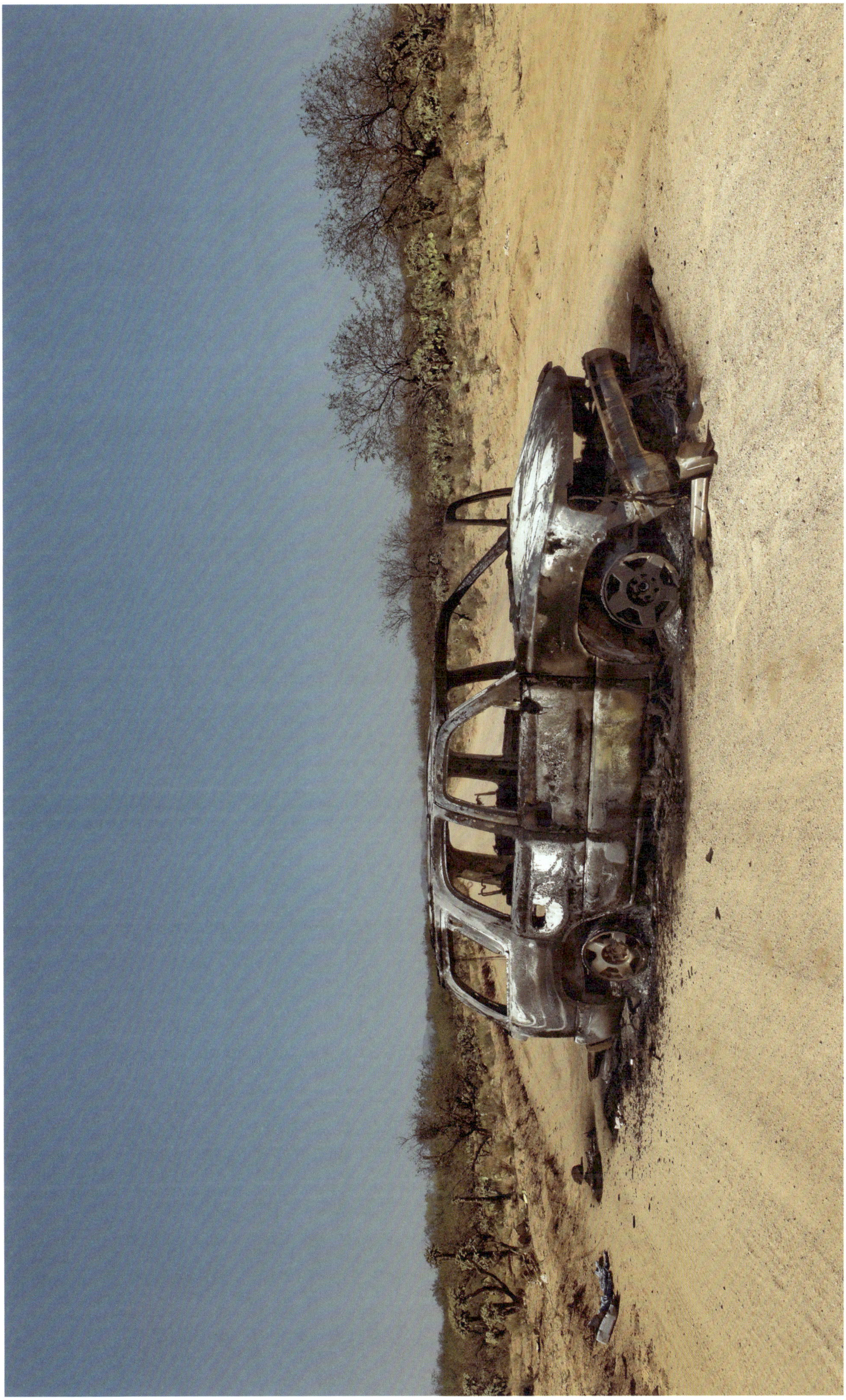

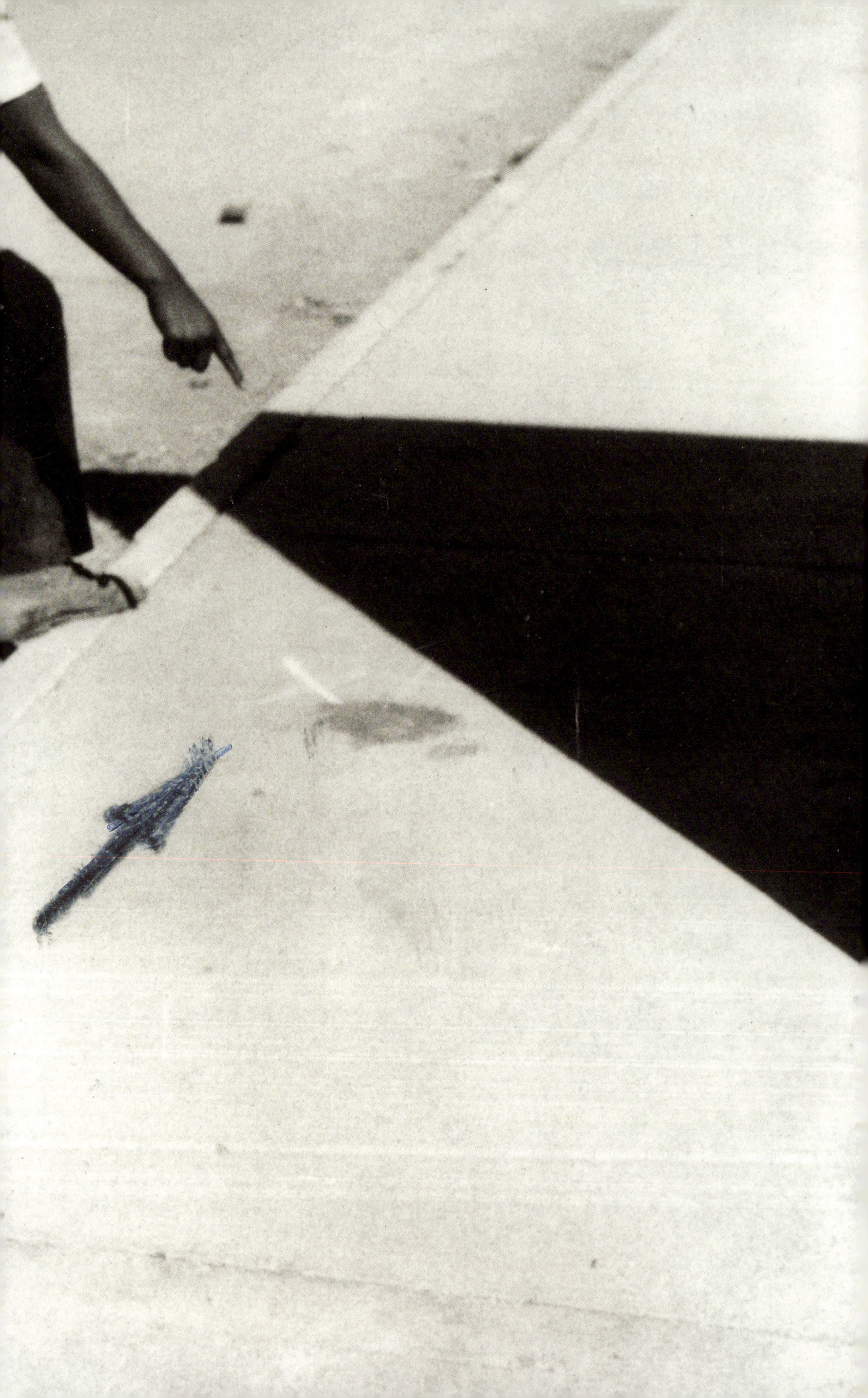

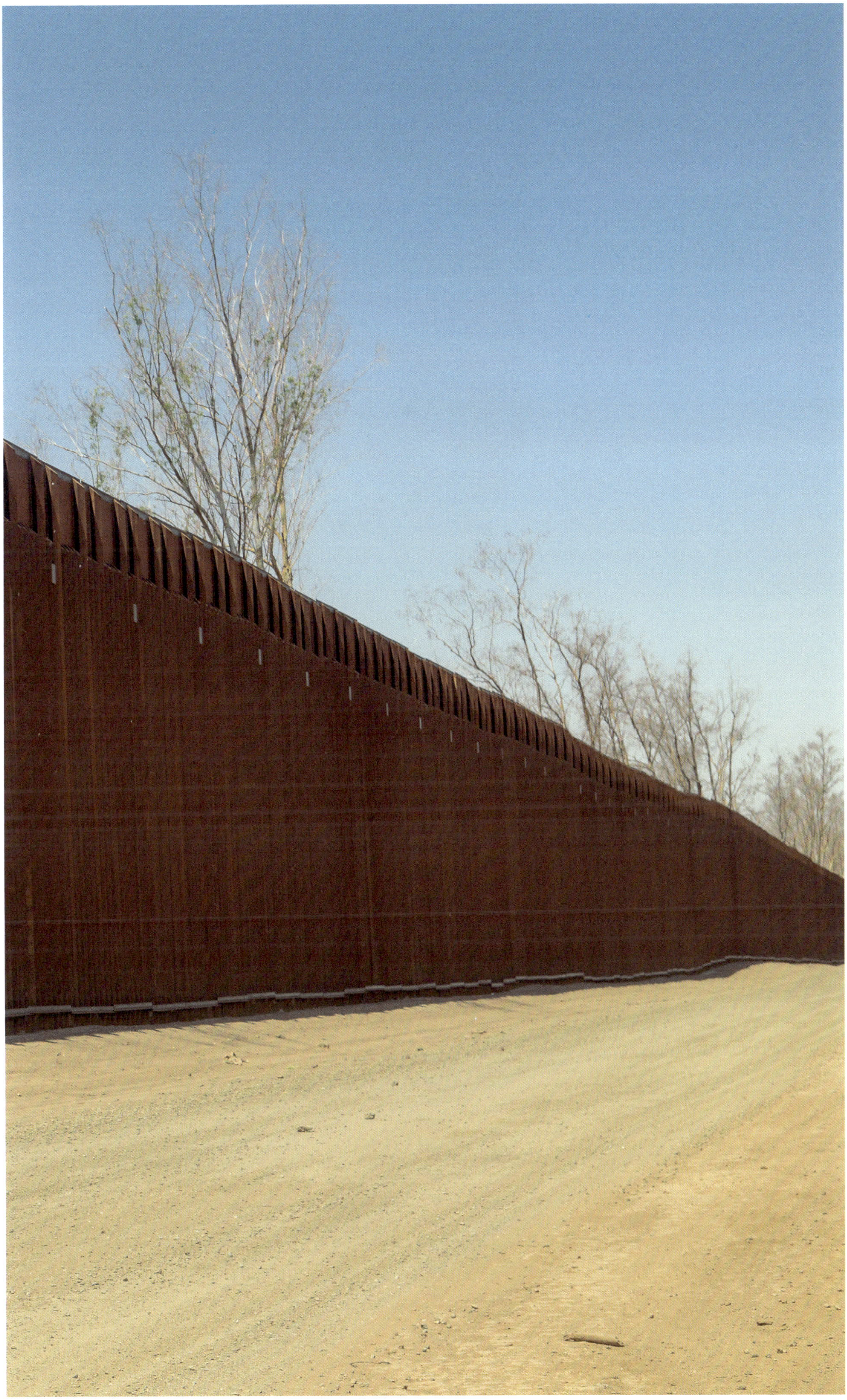

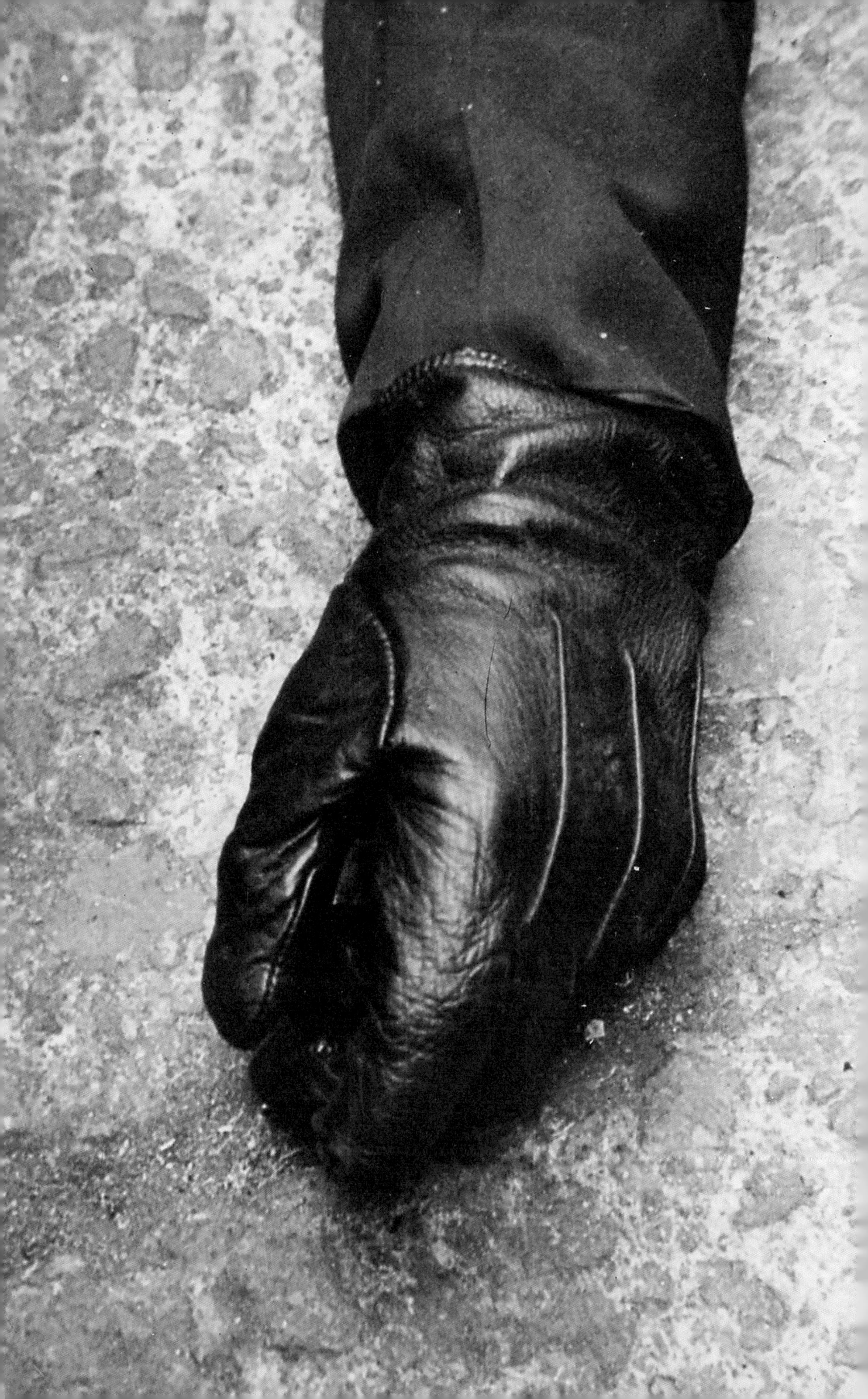

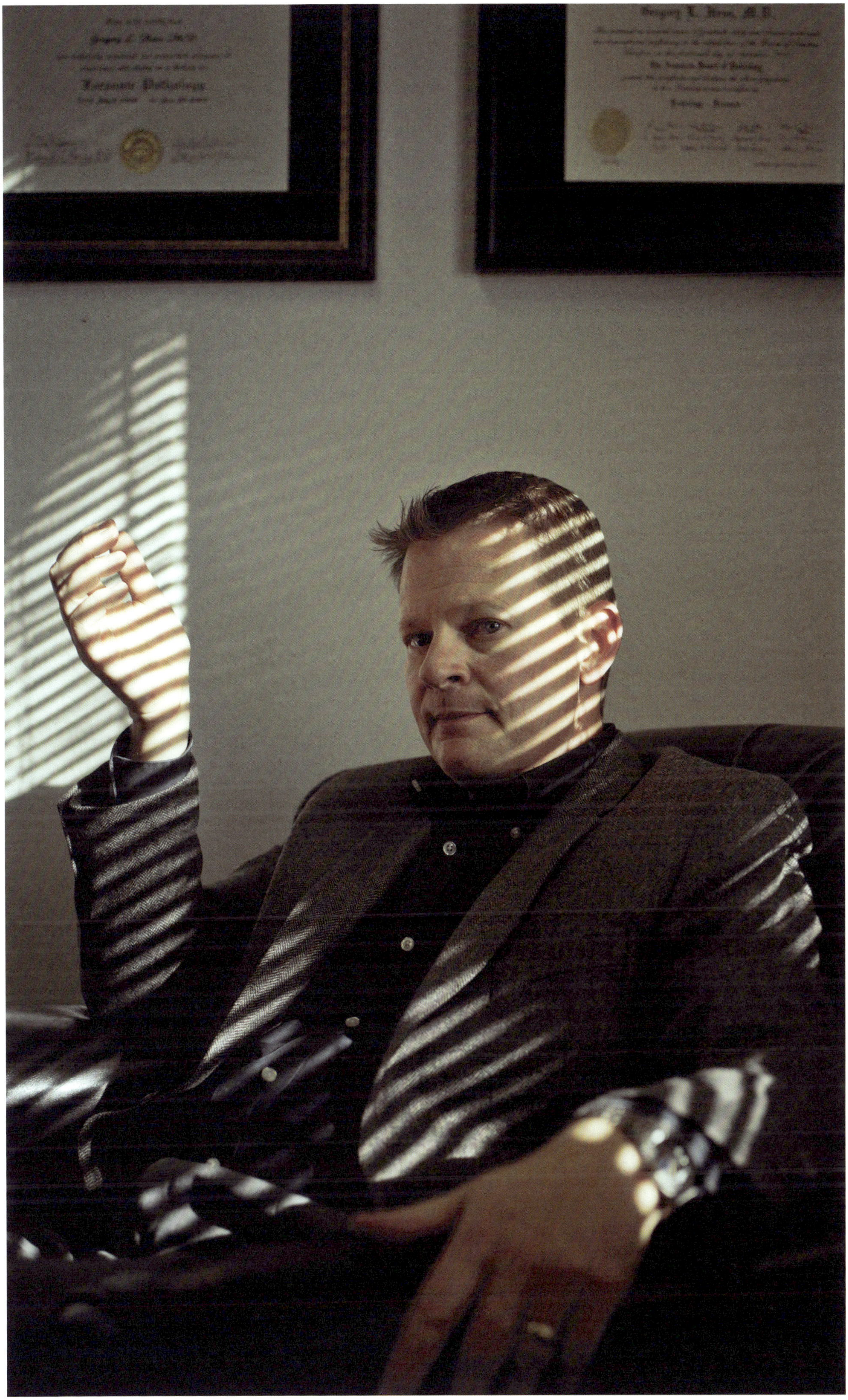

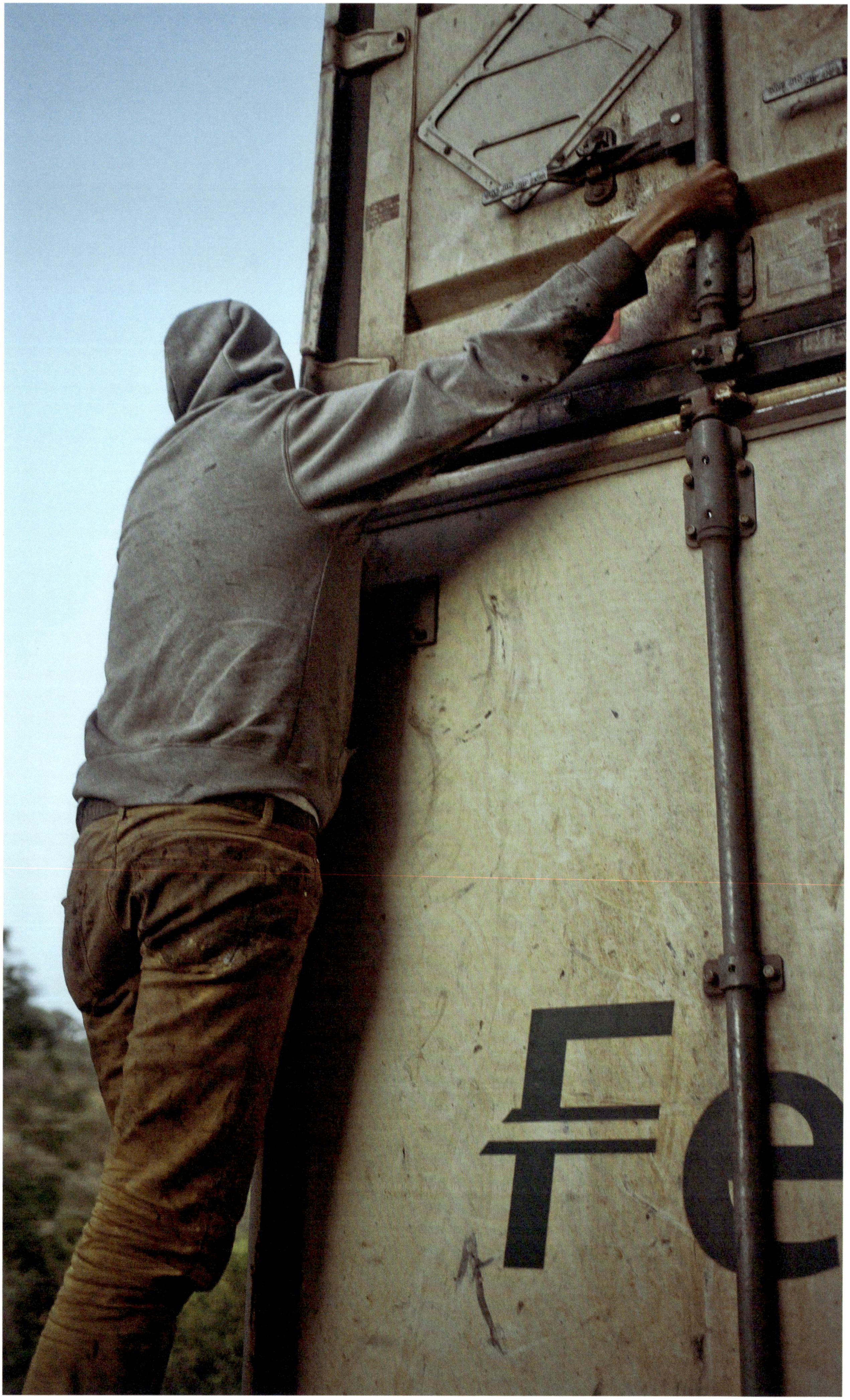

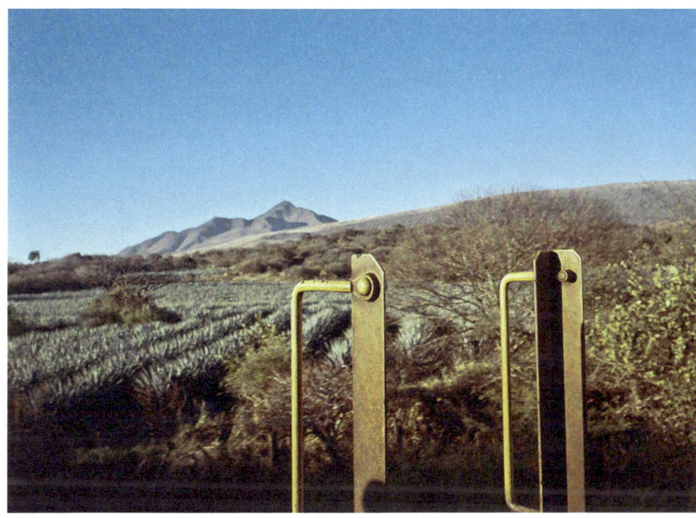

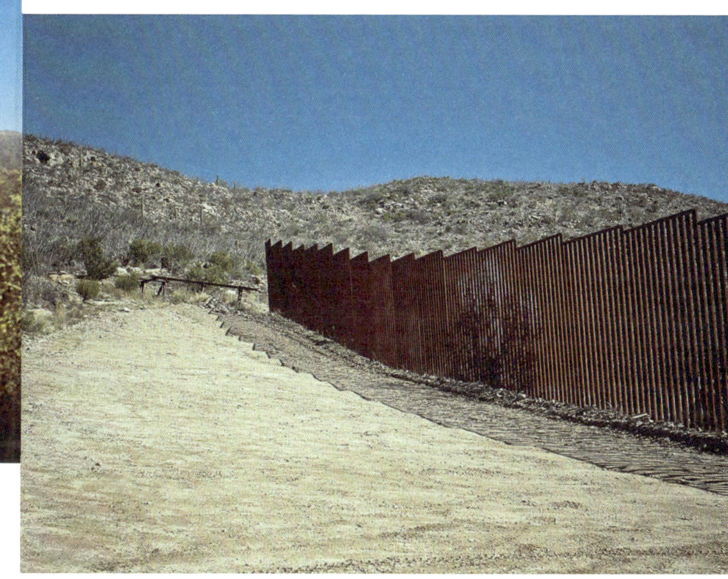

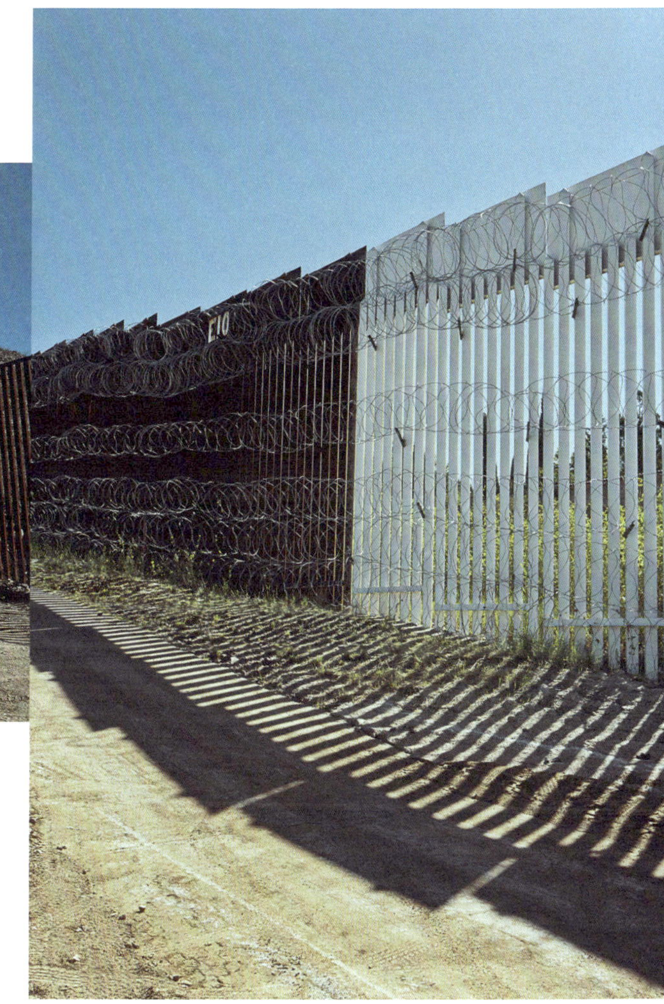

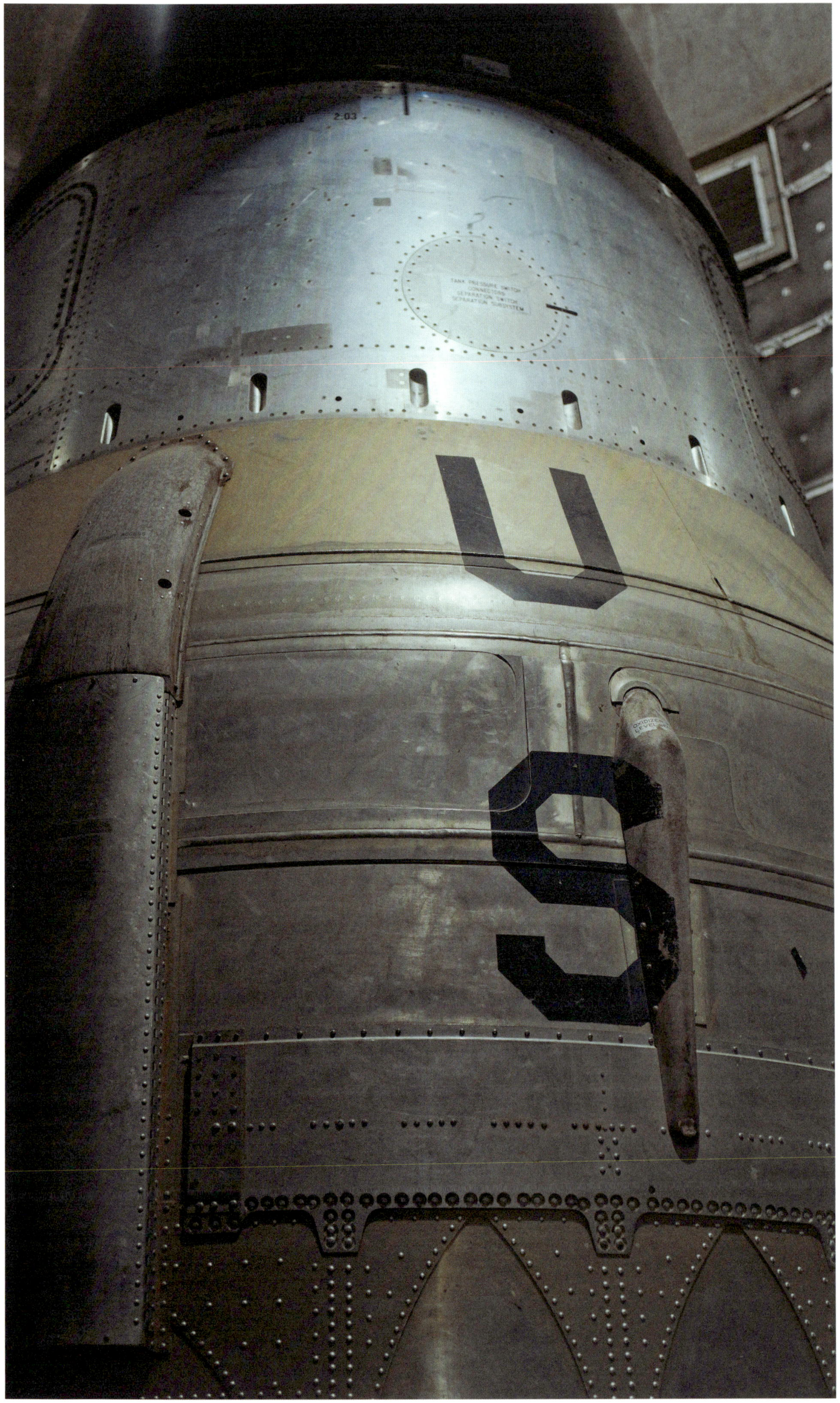
U
S

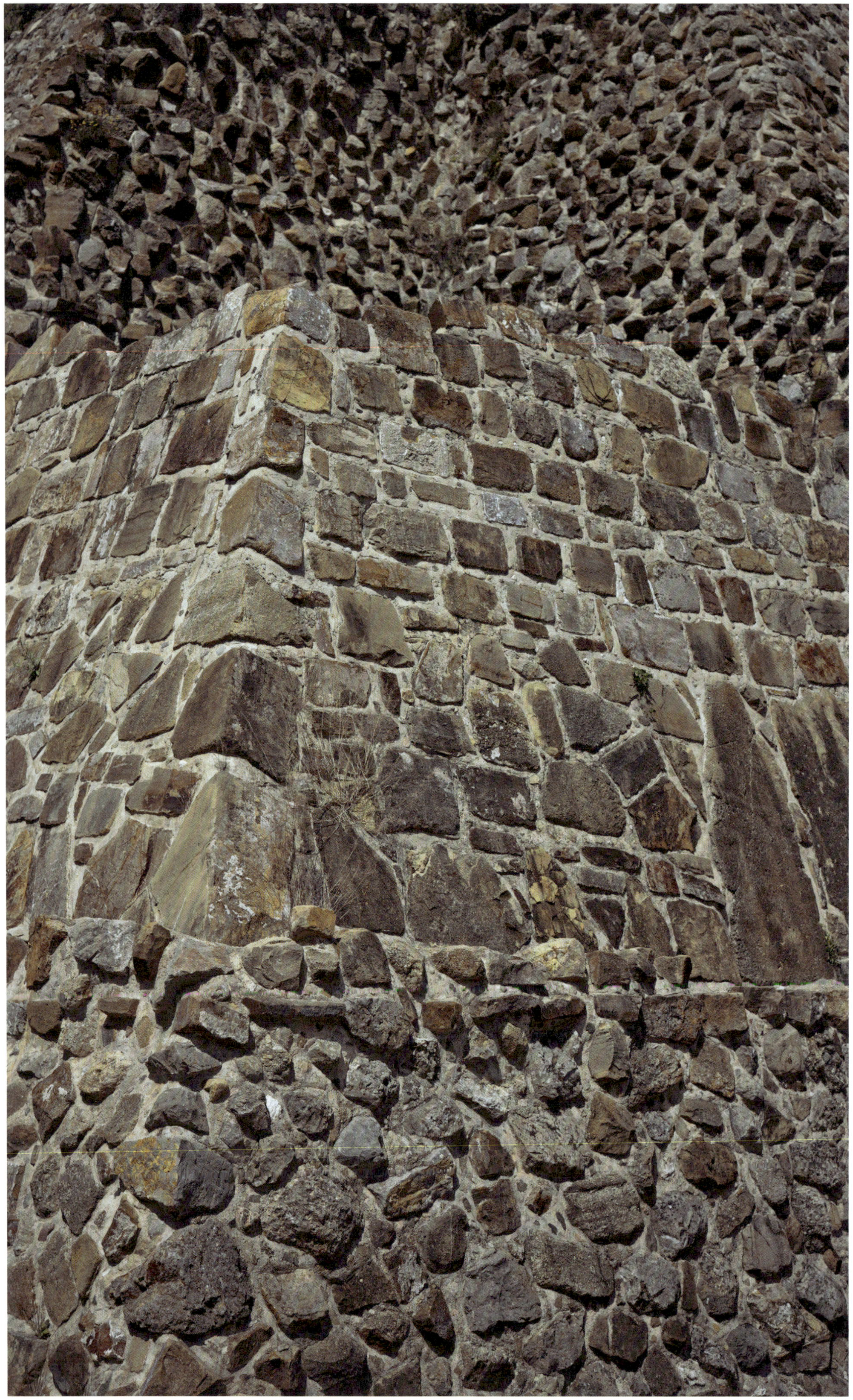

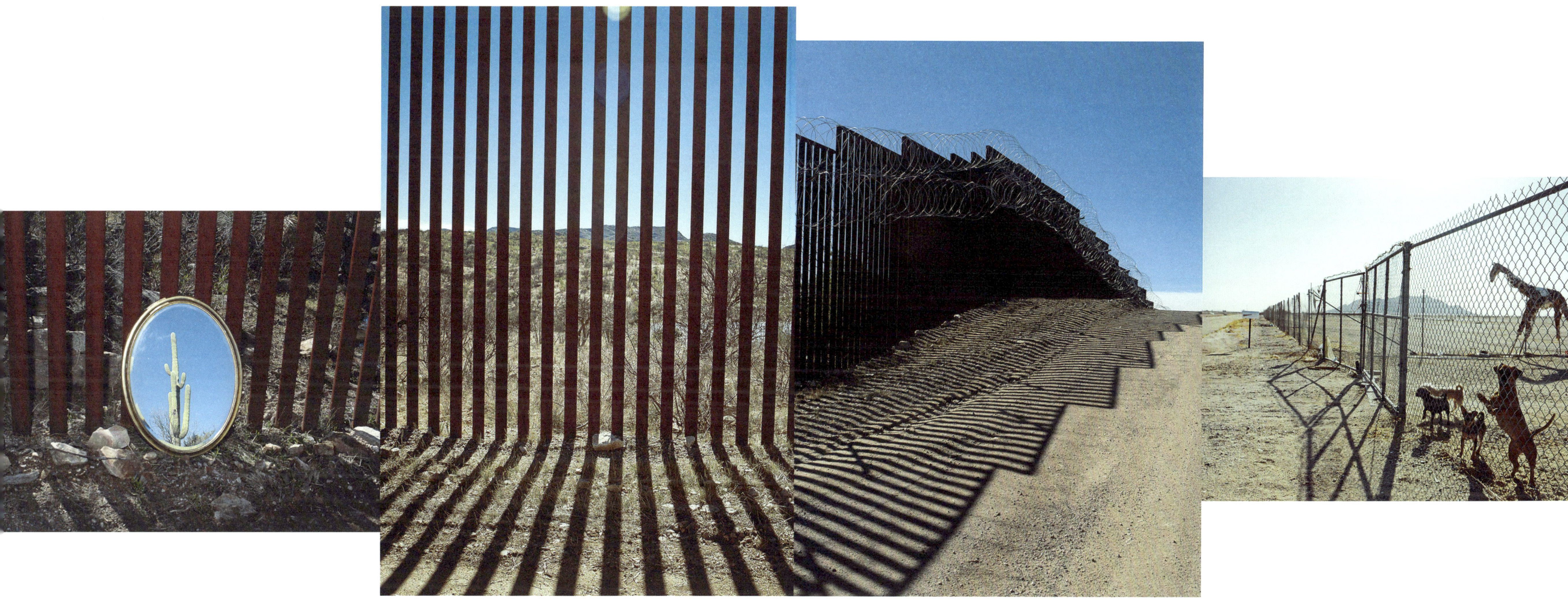

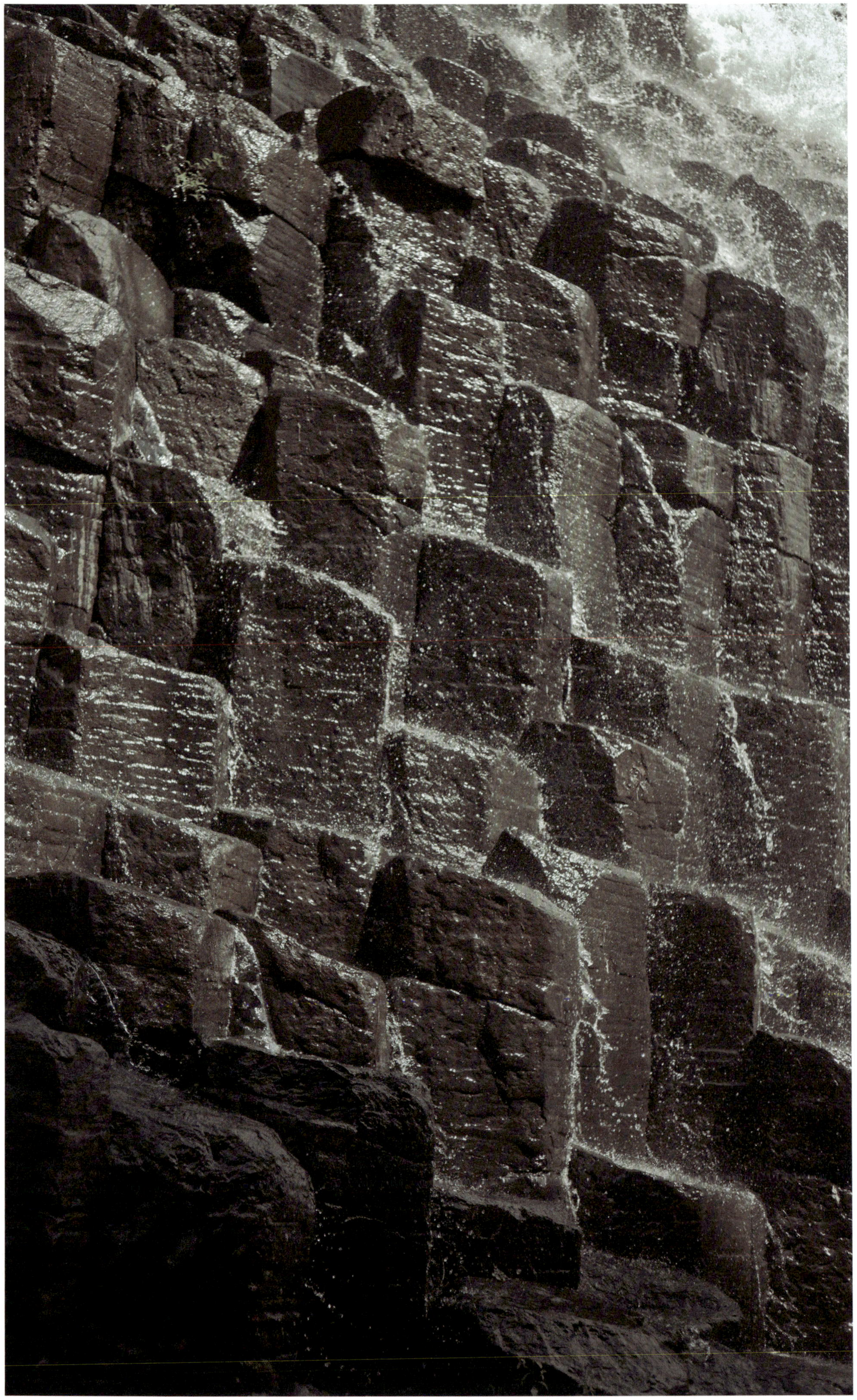

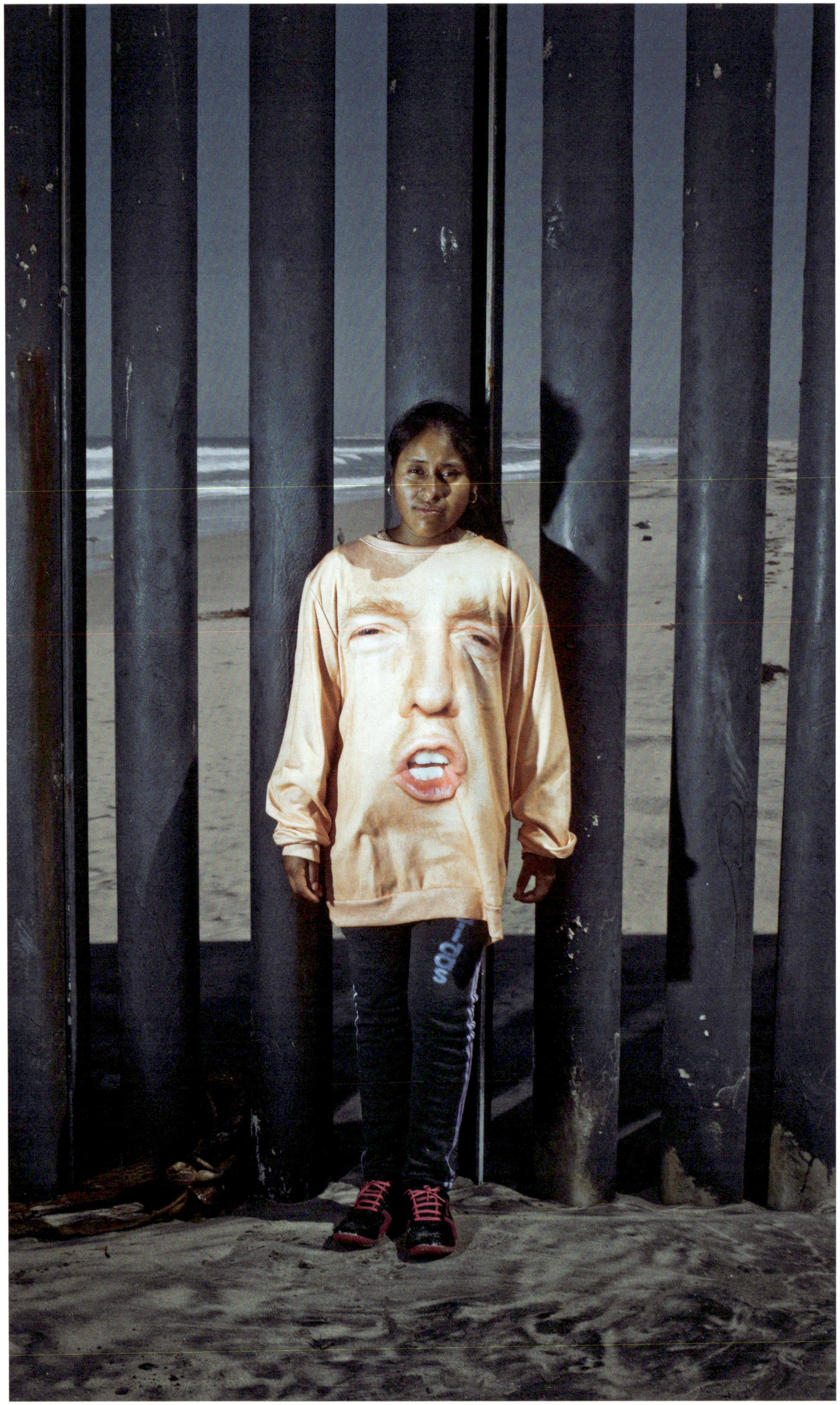

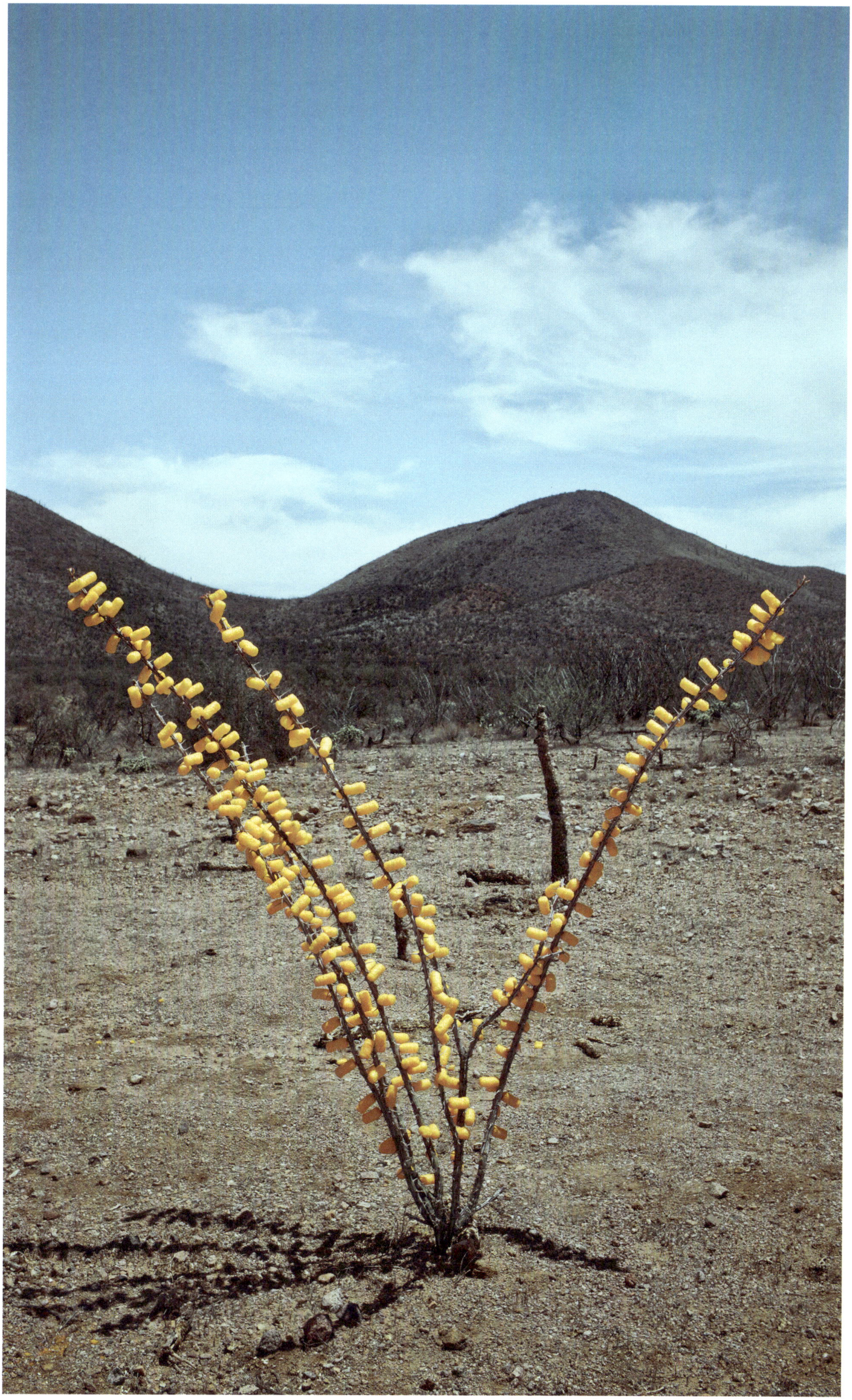

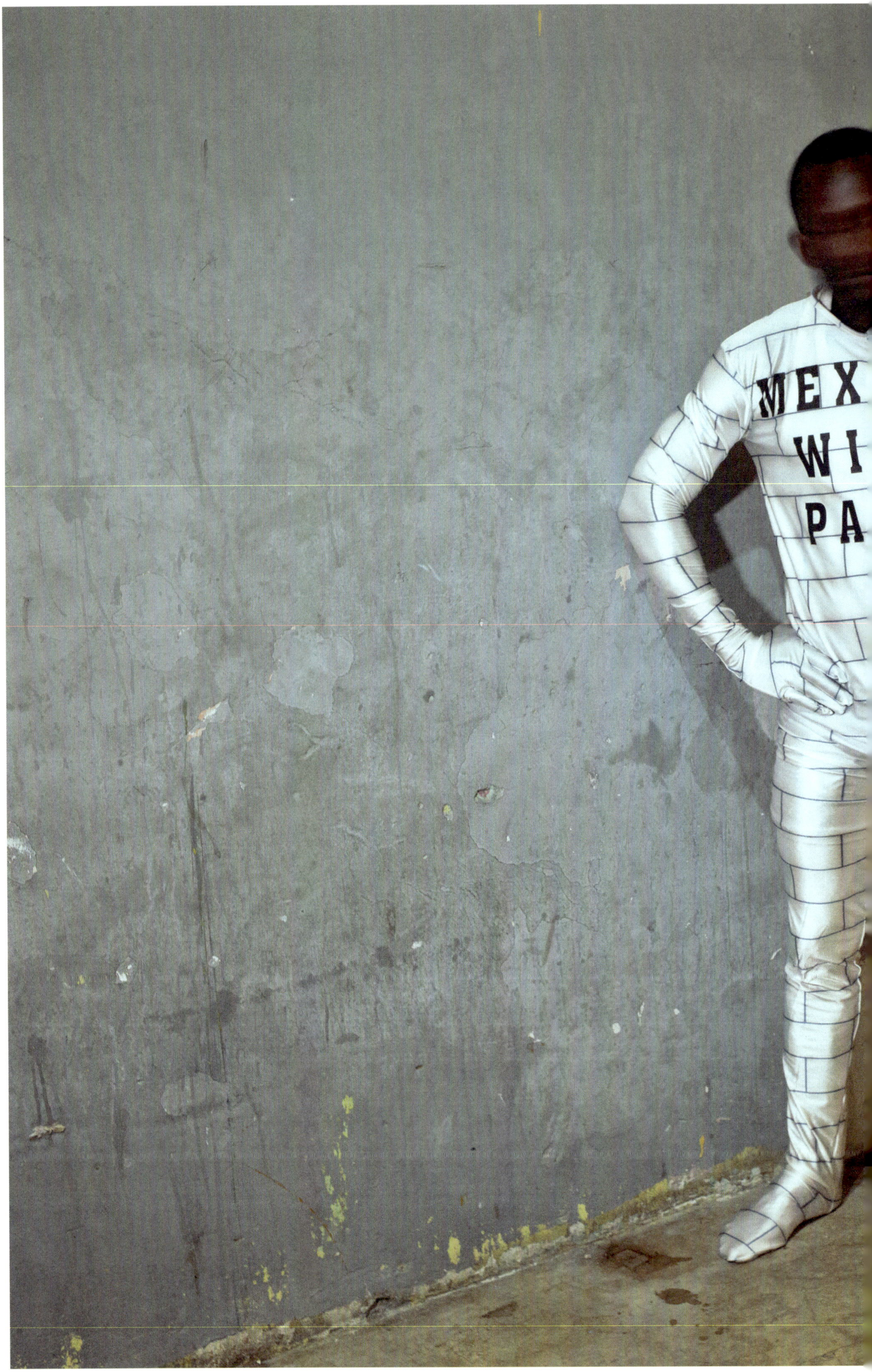
MEX
WI
PA

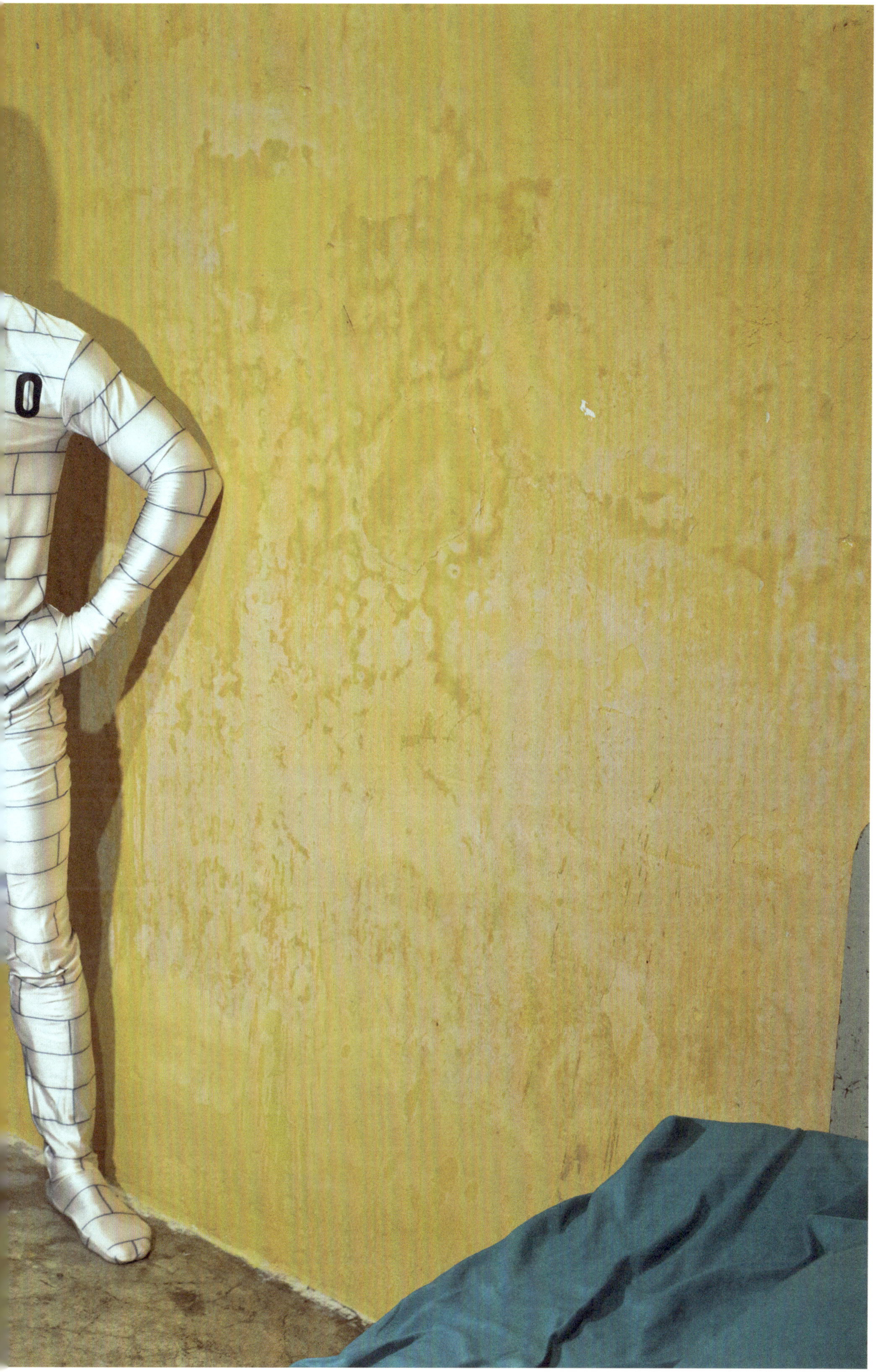

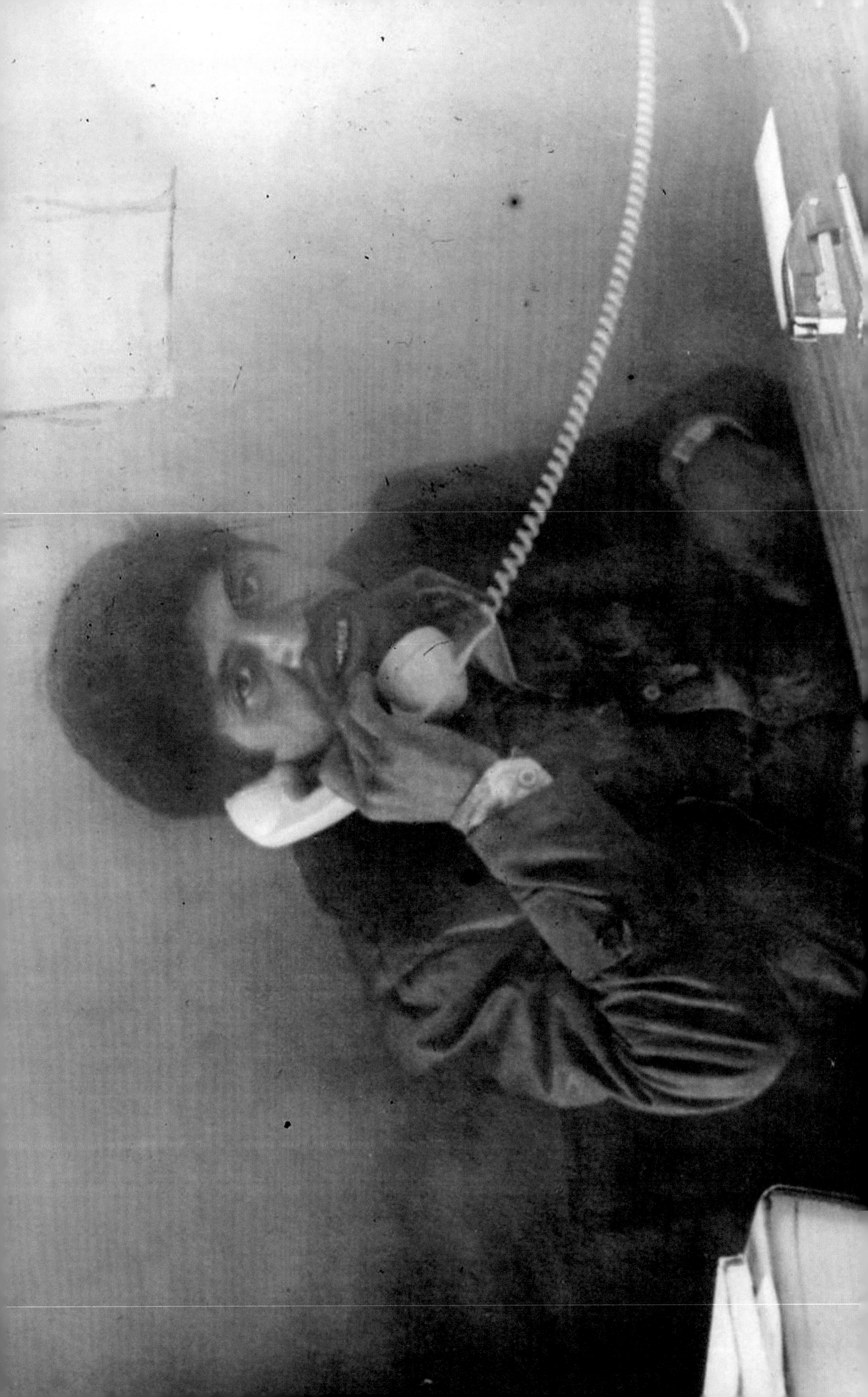

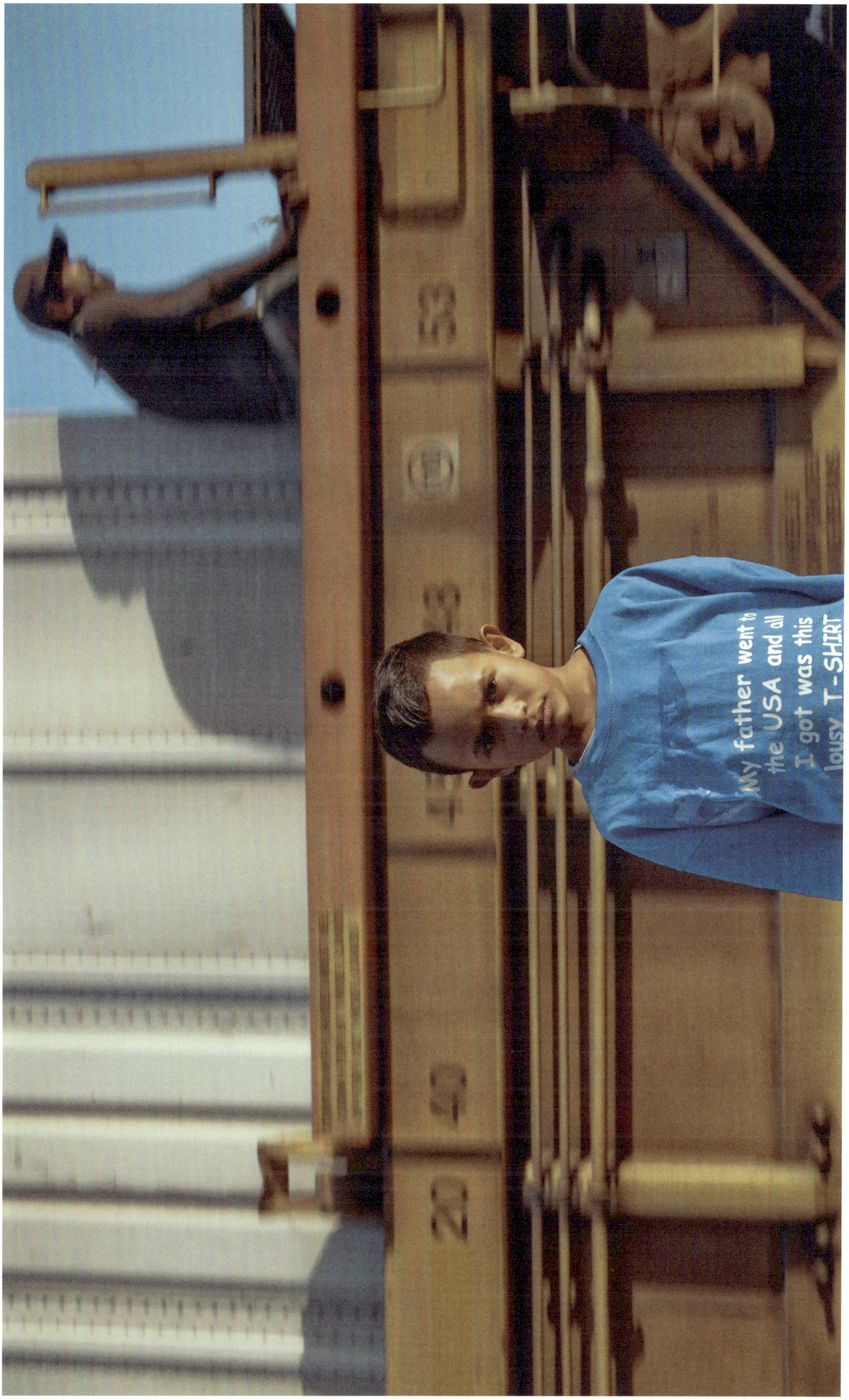
My father went to the USA and all I got was this lousy T-SHIRT

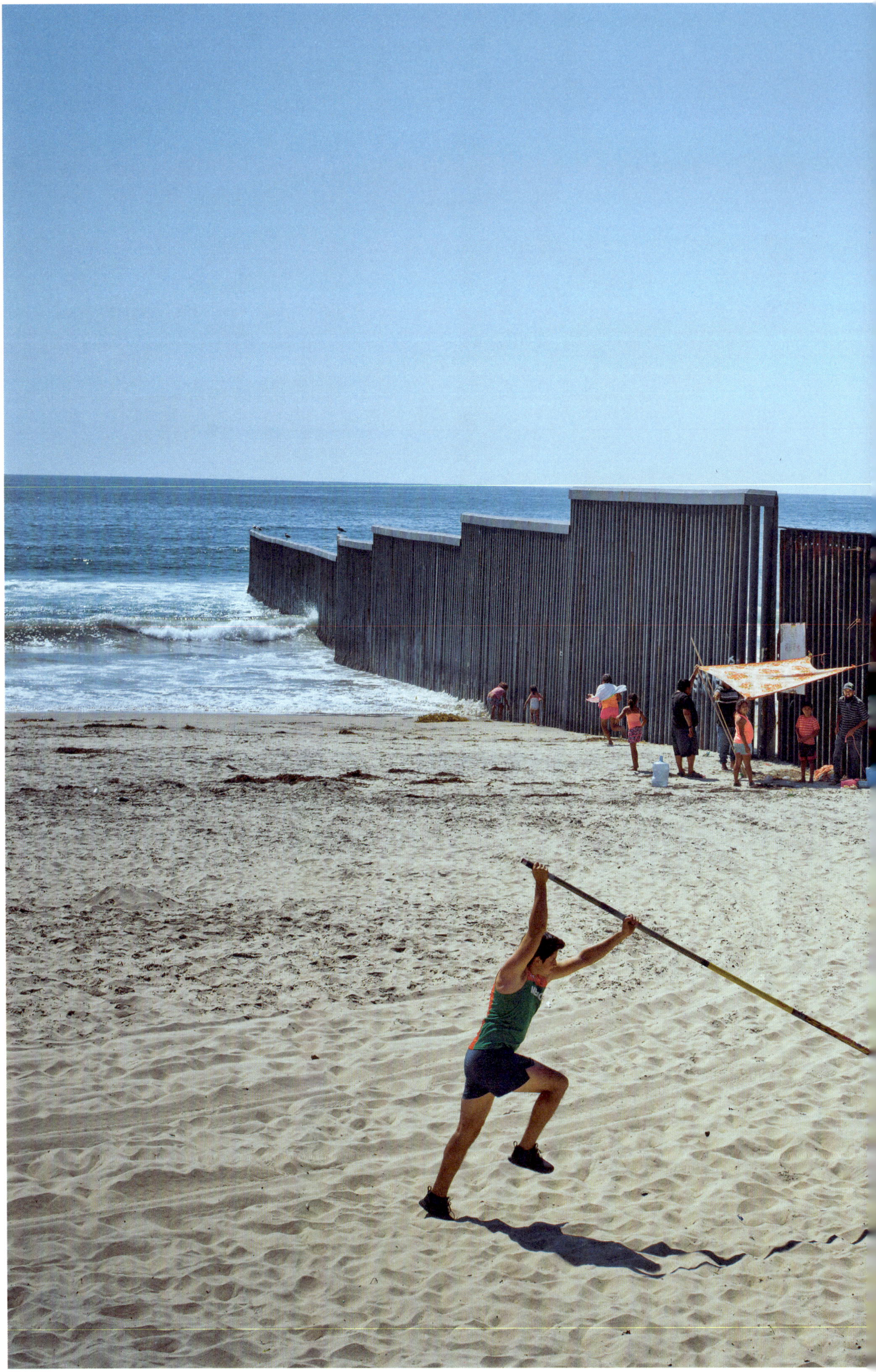

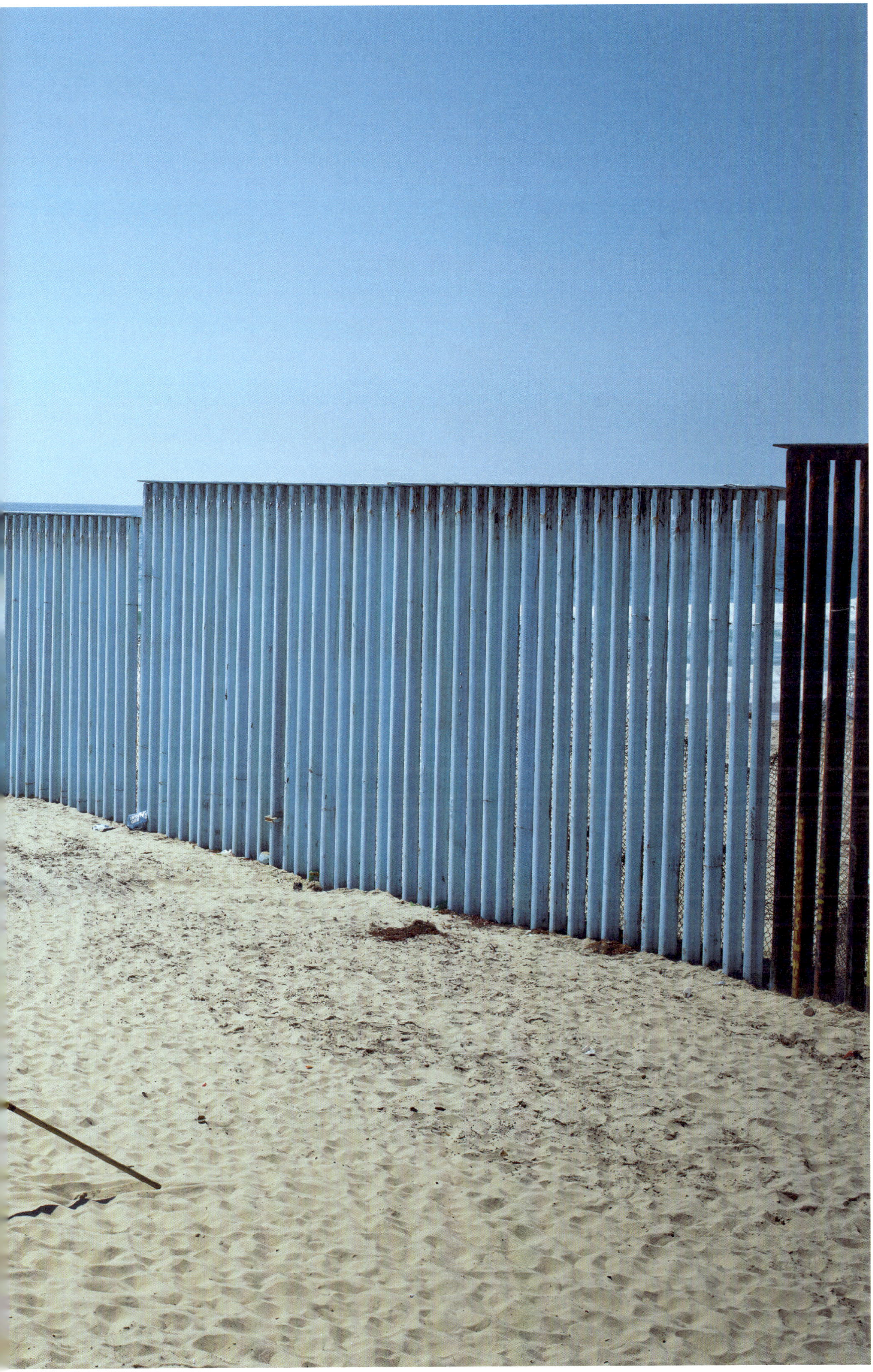

My eyes are fearfully bent upon the sea.

I dread to see one of these

monsters darting forth from its submarine caverns.

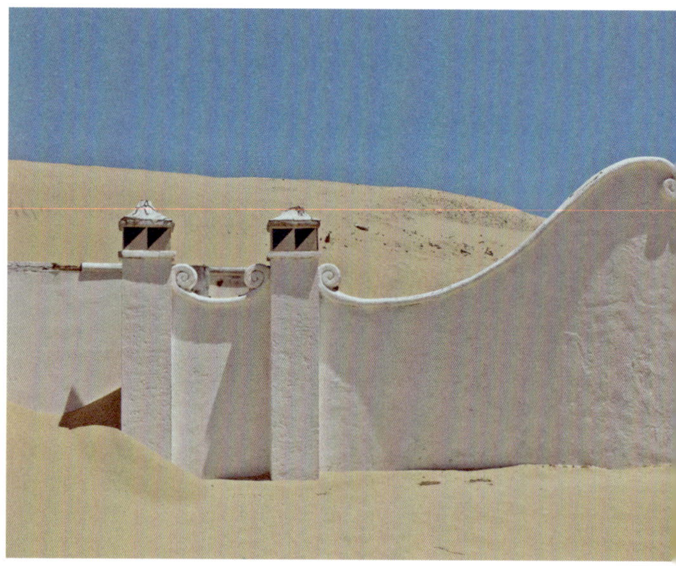

Mes yeux se fixent avec effroi sur la mer. Je crains de voir s'élancer

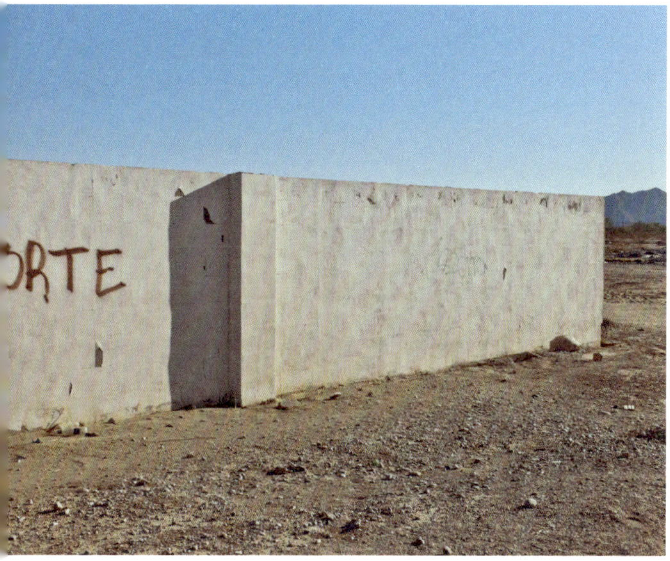

l'un de ces habitants des cavernes sous-marines.

Con terror dirigía la vista al mar. Temía ver salir a la superficie uno de aquellos habitantes de las cavernas submarinas.

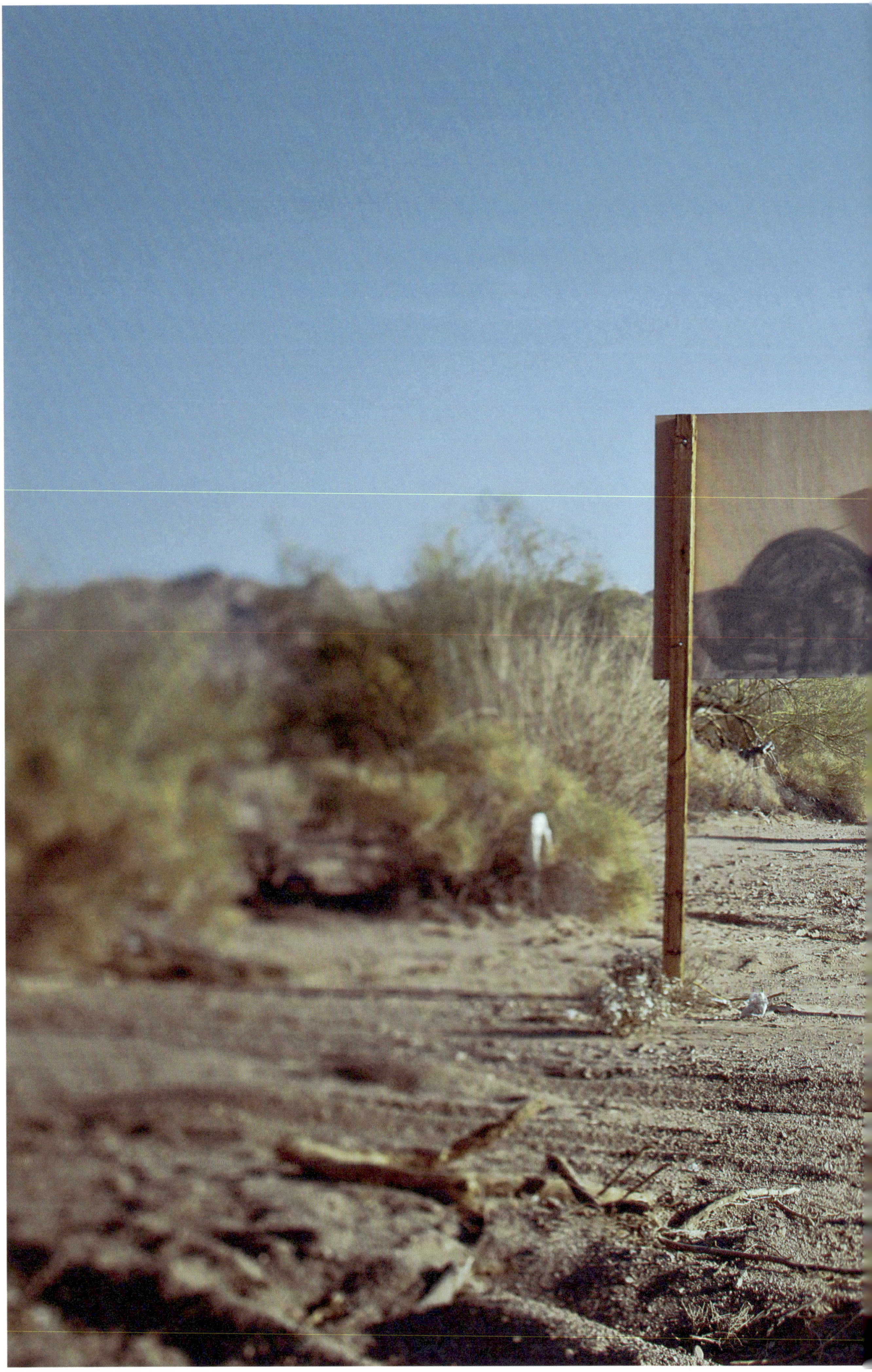

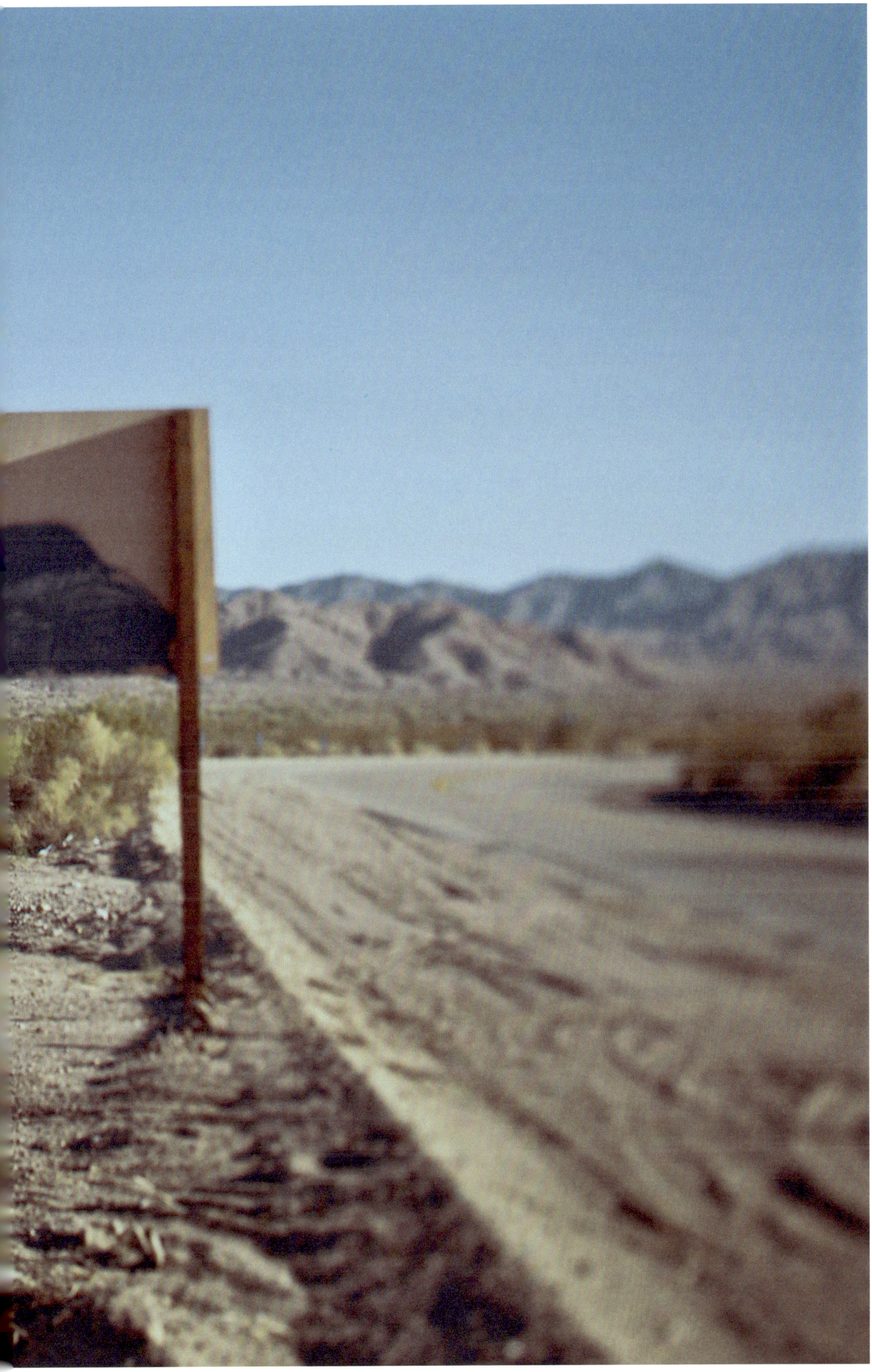

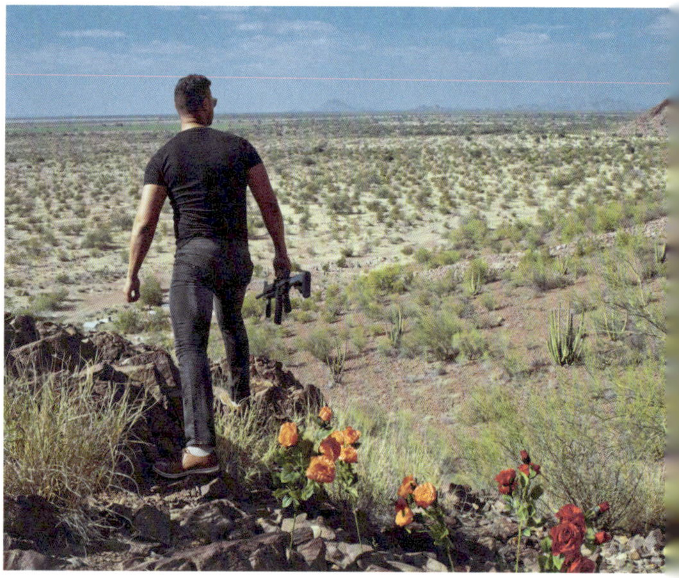

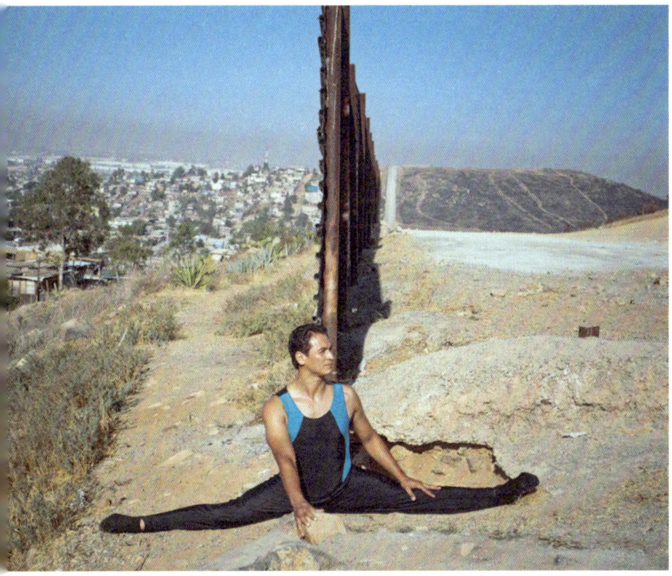

LIRIAN and YARIEL, CUBA

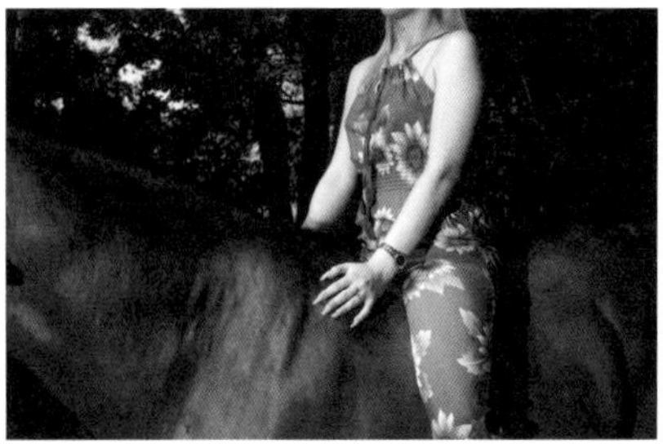

On February 1, 2019, I left Cuba with my husband for Panama. Upon arrival, we underwent checks at the airport. After a period of nerves and fear, we left and headed to a hotel in the city to spend the night. Early in the morning, we took a subway and headed to a bus terminal to reach the border. After spending almost a whole day there, we arrived, took a taxi, and went to a motel. From there, we crossed to Costa Rica since the countries are divided by a road. We got into a car and traveled on a rough road late at night. We were dropped off in a wooded area where a man awaited to take us to a farm. We walked 5 km. The journey was tough as we had to cross the river multiple times, climb hills, etc., all in the dark hours of the early morning. We were afraid because we only heard the sounds of animals in the woods. Also, when crossing the river, nothing was visible, and it had a current. When we reached the farm, we rested for three hours, and then we were picked up by a car to go to Costa Rica, still with a lot of fear because the driver was speeding and sometimes falling asleep. Also, there was always the fear that the police would stop the car as we were crossing illegally, and if caught, we could be deported to Cuba, rendering all our efforts in vain.

In the evening, we were taken to Nicaragua, left by the roadside, and had to catch a truck to reach the army camp. There, they took photos and conducted an interview. The army handed us over to immigration, where they also took photos, and we paid $150 for a safe conduct for one person. After spending a good while there, we were put on a bus with others, charged $30 each, and transported to the border with Honduras. We arrived at night and slept in a hotel near the border until the next day around 10 in the morning when we were picked up by a taxi and taken to where some men on horseback were to cross the river that bordered Honduras. We mounted the horse, crossed the river and a small wooded area, and headed to a hotel in Honduran territory.

There we were received and stayed for about 5 days to obtain the safe conduct, but it was not possible, so we had to leave illegally. We made several transfers until we reached Guatemala, and we were very afraid because passing illegally in Honduras is a big country to cross to Guatemala. We crossed a dangerous hill in the late hours of the night, in addition to crossing 2 fences and an open field where there were cows and donkeys, and we had to run because they wanted to hurt us. Finally, we skirted the entire immigration checkpoint and reached a gas station in Guatemalan territory. There we hid in a small bus for a few hours until they transferred us to a bus station to go to downtown Guatemala. When we arrived, we took another transport to the border with Mexico. On the way, we passed through several checkpoints and feared for our safety since we had no permission to be in that country. Already at night, we reached the border with Mexico, and they floated us across the river on rafts.

From there to Tapachula, where we spent more than three months waiting to go to the US border.

There we were around 20 days living on a bridge, enduring hunger and heat, and in the early mornings some cold and rain. When we surrendered, I was detained in an immigration detention center for 2 months. It is very difficult there because the people who are supposedly there to take care of you mistreat you physically and verbally. They see you as a despicable being, and you feel as if you have committed a crime and are imprisoned in that horrendous place serving a sentence. There is a lot of discrimination.

After spending 2 months detained, they released me, but sadly, my husband did not have the same luck. He was imprisoned in the US for 5 months, in Louisiana, which is a very racist state, and for that reason, he suffered a lot from physical and psychological abuse, in addition to hardly seeing sunlight. Only occasionally were they given 1 or 2 hours of sunlight, treated like criminals in an inhumane way, and many times the little food they provided had bugs; it was like waste. It truly was a great nightmare for both of us, and we never thought that a human being could be treated in such a way.

After 7 long and sad months, they deported him to Cuba with the simple reason that they do not want to accept immigrants. With the grace of God, he was able to leave Cuba again and went to Nicaragua, and from there, he traveled by bus to Honduras, where he was assaulted and left only with the clothes he was wearing. But we went through a big scare because he was physically mistreated and was pointed at several times with machine guns, and he thought they would kill him, but thanks to the Lord, it didn´t happen. Afterwards, with a lot of effort, he continued his journey, but with many more difficulties because he didn't have money and things became even more complicated because not everyone lends a hand without any kind of interest. Eventually, he crossed into Guatemala and then finally arrived in Mexico alive, but very psychologically affected. I didn't want to stay in the US without him, so I returned to Mexico to be with him, and that's what I did. Now here we are, both facing adversities together, but thanks to the Lord, we're together.

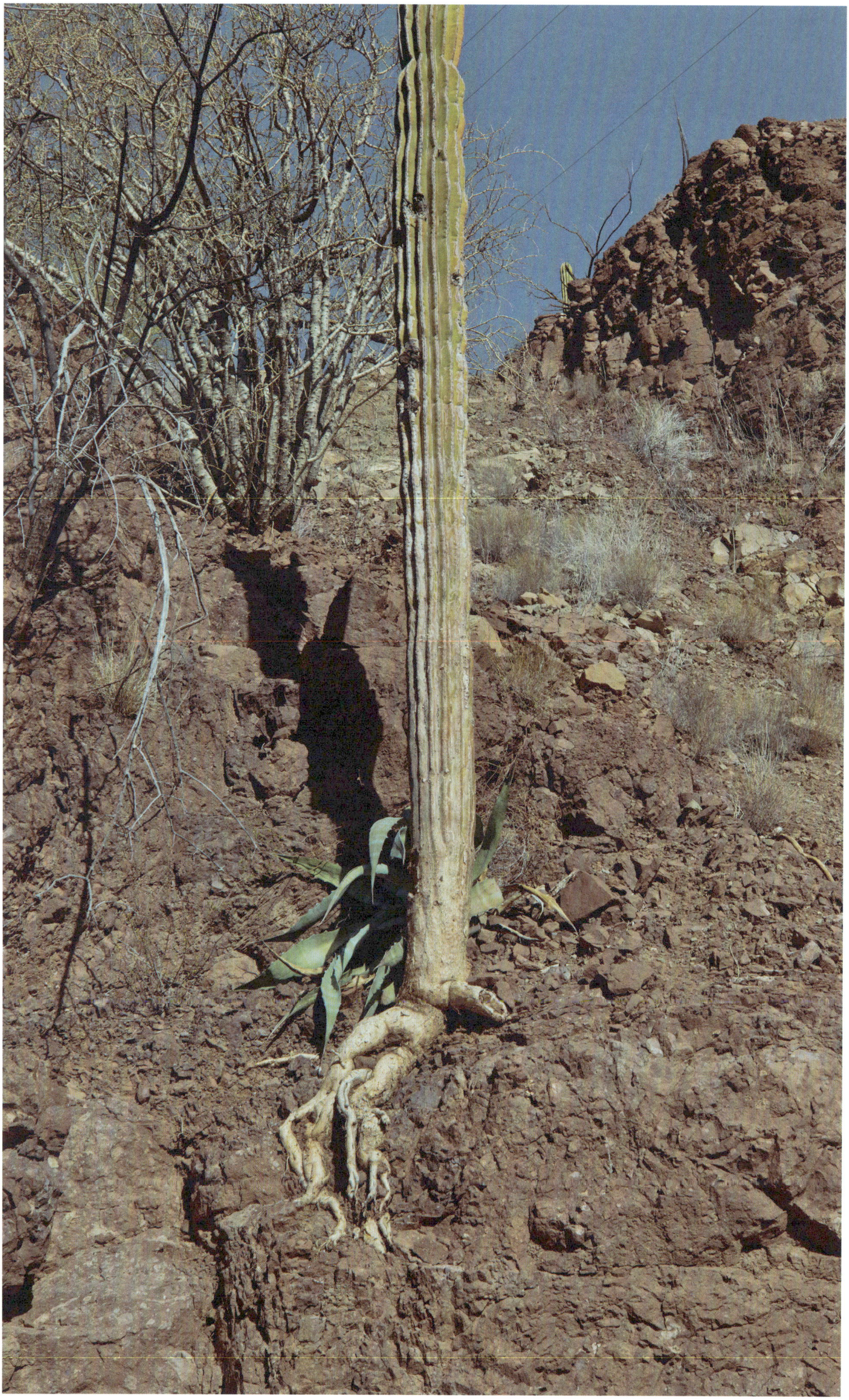

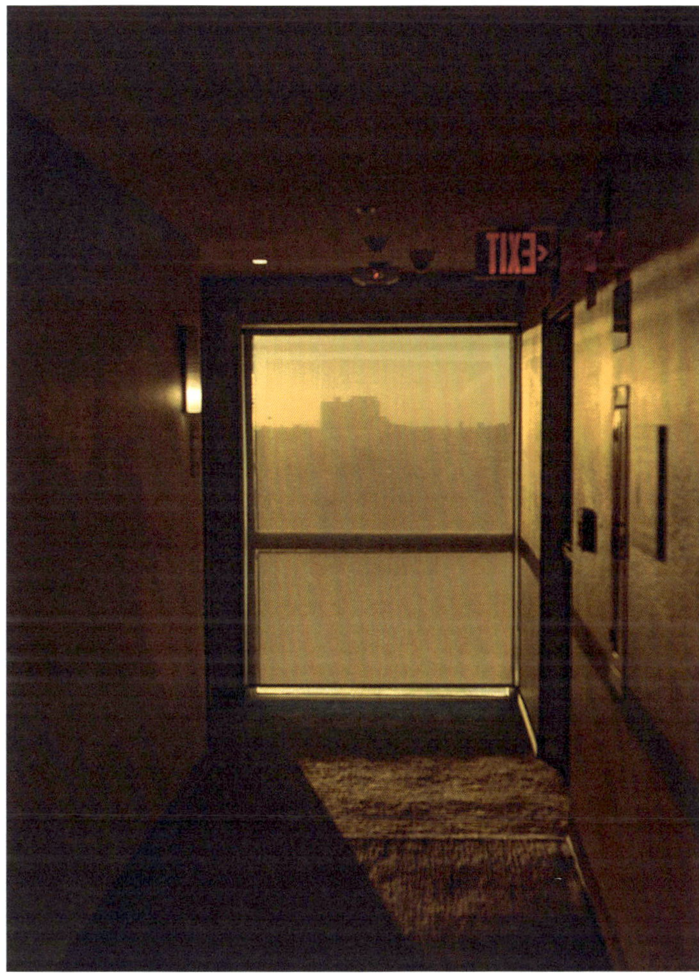

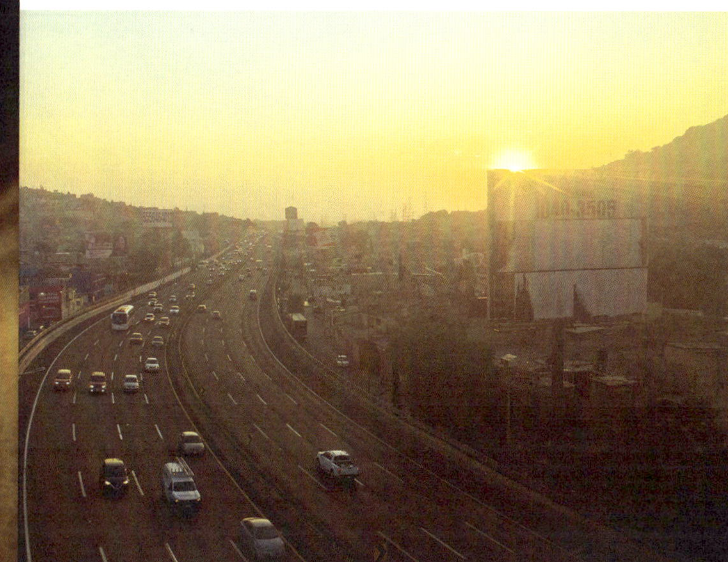

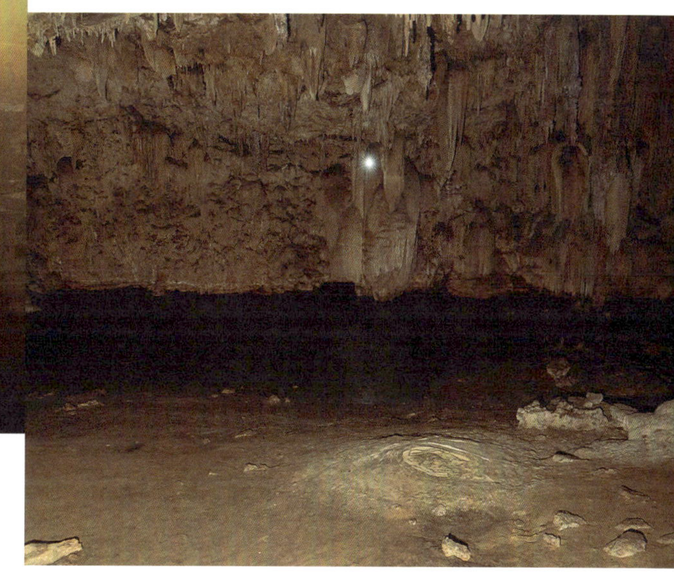

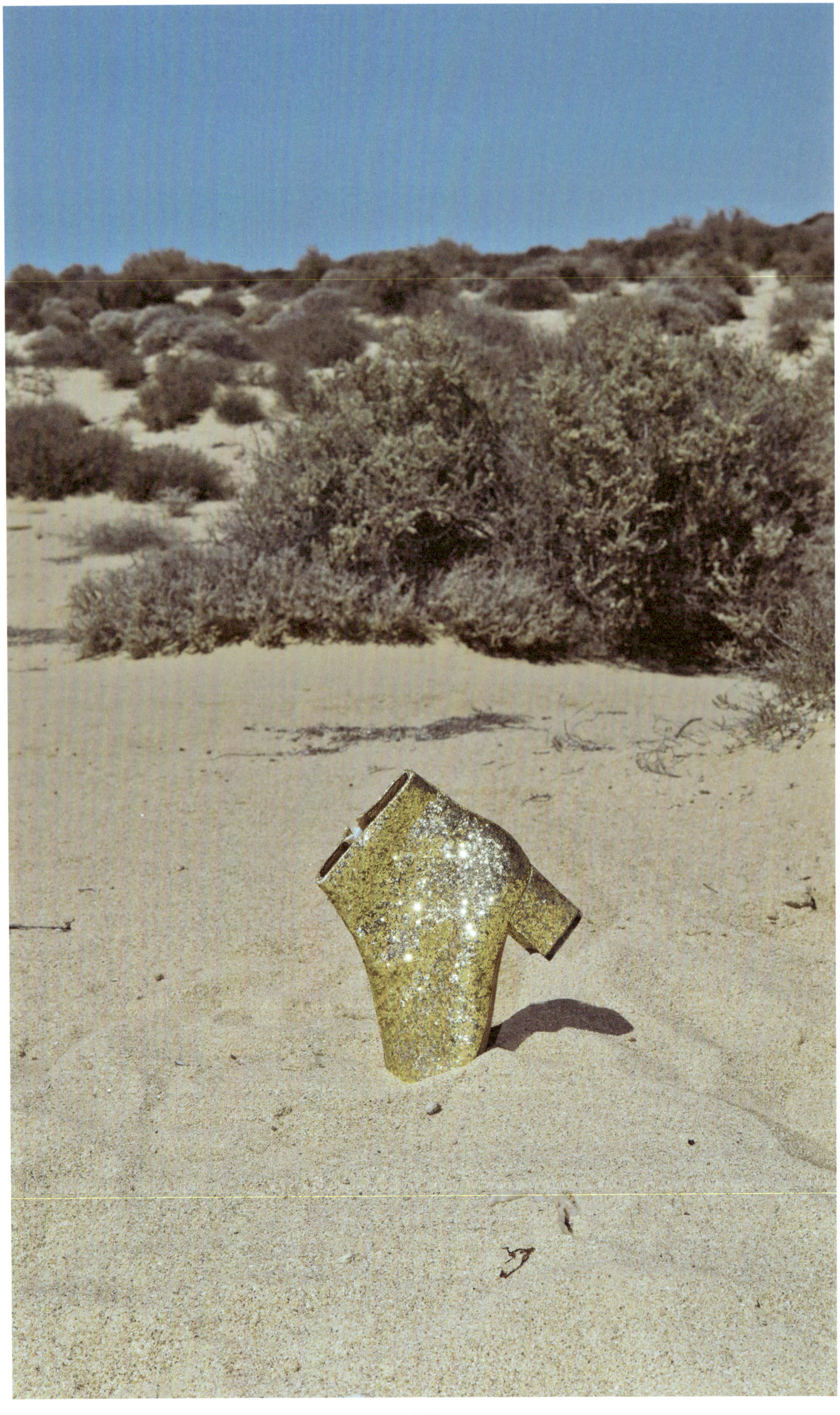

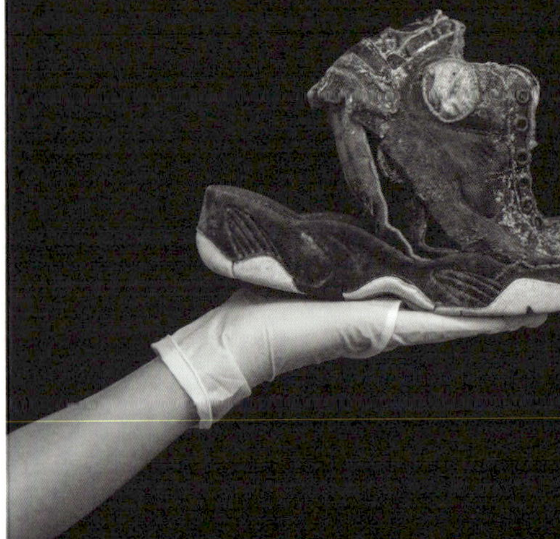

[51]

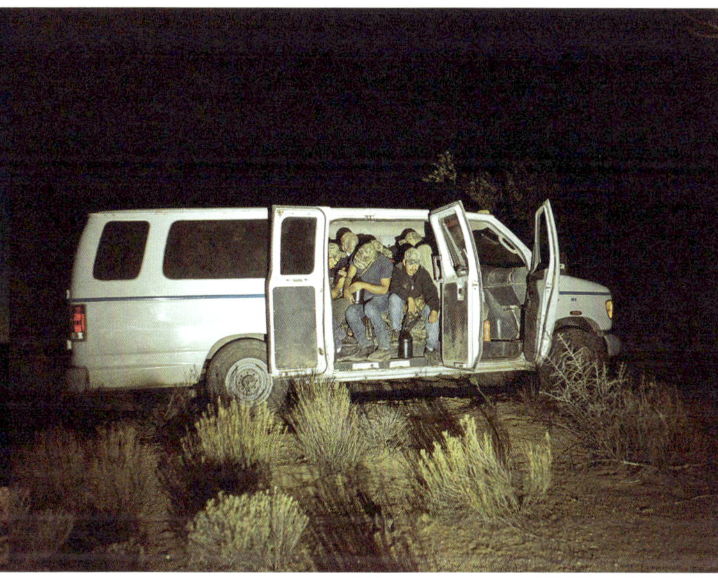

[52]

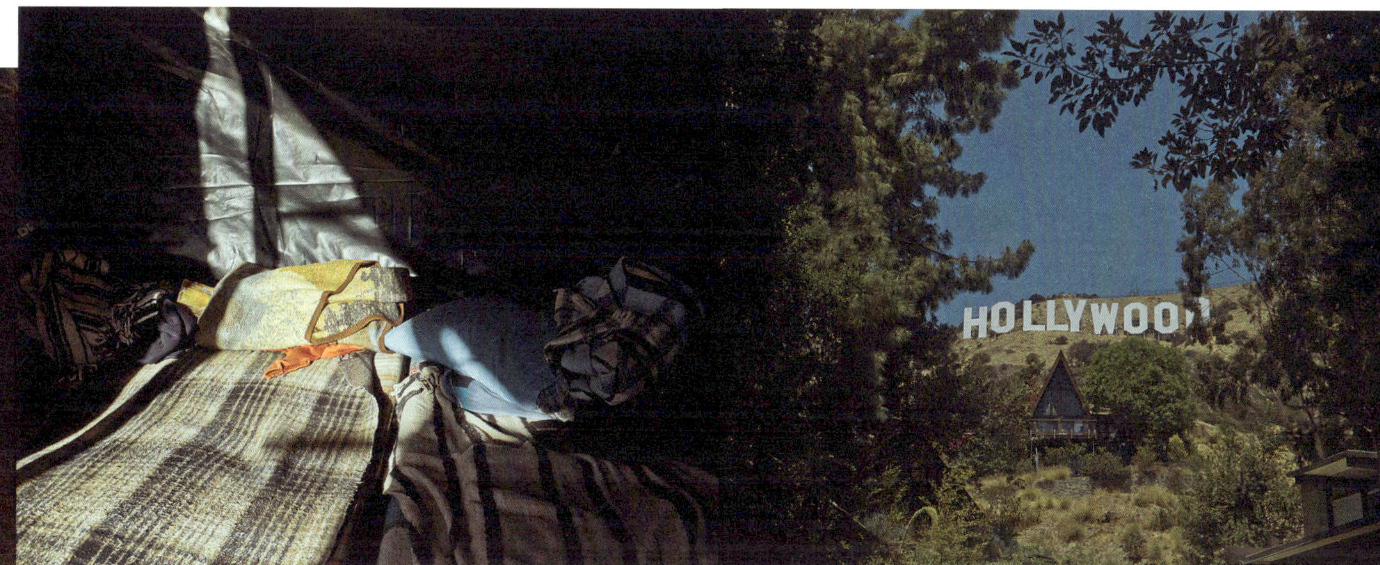

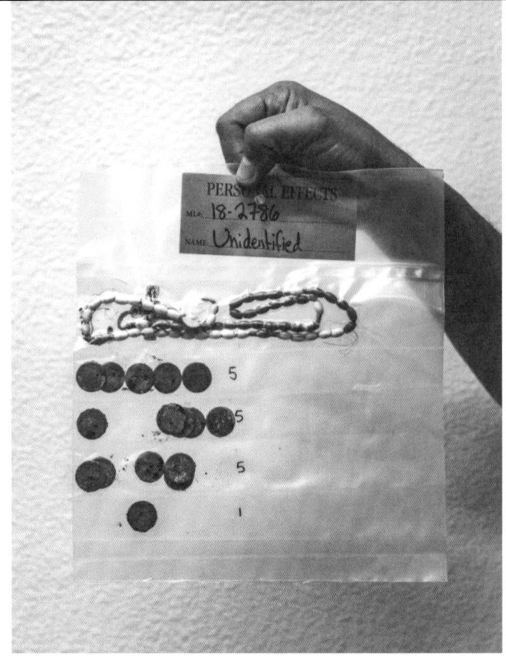

The Pima County Medical Examiner's Office in Arizona maintains an archive of objects found near the corpses of migrants within its jurisdiction in the Sonora desert. The Colibrí Center, an NGO in collaboration with the Medical Examiner's Office, employs forensic science to identify the remains of migrants who died during their journey, offering support and resources to affected families. In a study led by Jason De León from the University of Michigan, pig carcasses placed in the southern Arizona desert disappeared within six days, leaving only the objects as a trace.

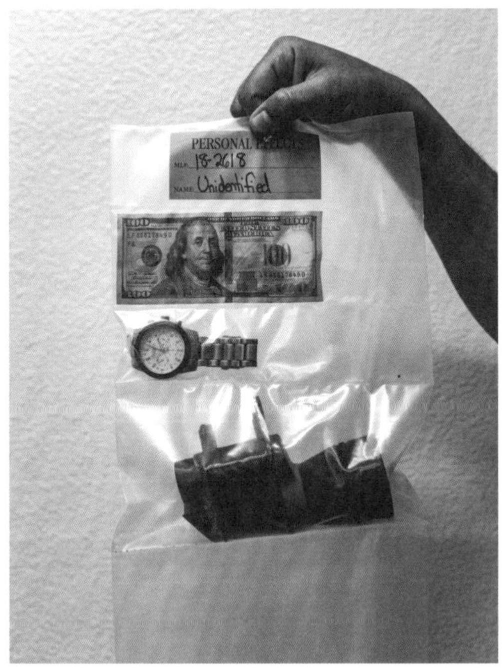

Given the staggering length and ruggedness of the journey, it is physically impossible for anyone attempting to cross the border on foot to carry enough water and food supplies to survive. In the words of Gerardo Campos, a humanitarian worker in remote parts of the border: "The migrants have an idea that they're going to be walking for just a couple of days, as they've been told by the coyotes to hook them and make their money. But they don't realize until they're into the desert that it's not two days. It's going to be about five, six, seven, ten days walking."

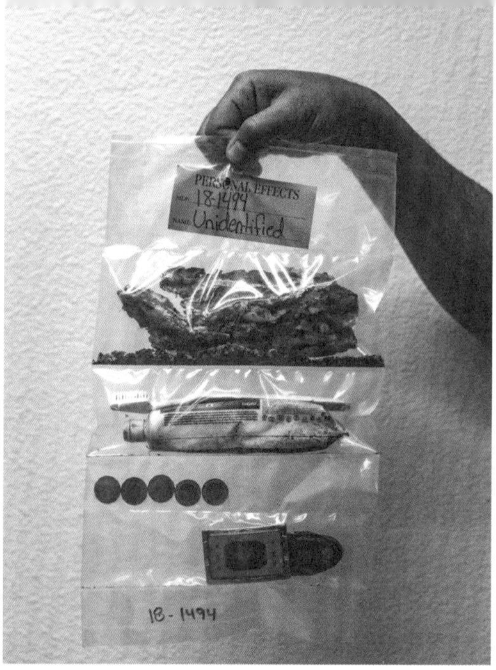

Mass death and disappearance result from a border enforcement plan that uses the Sonoran Desert as a weapon. Extreme temperature shifts pose risks, leading to dehydration in high heat and hypothermia in plummeting night-time temperatures.

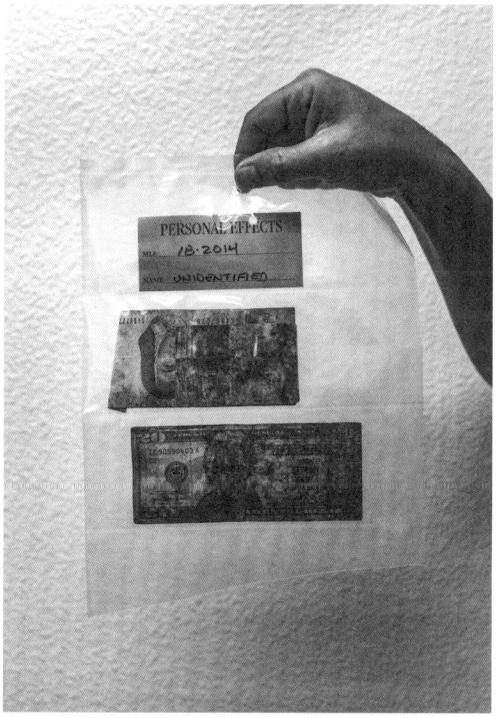

According to Border Patrol, most deaths occur as a result of dehydration. Many other migrants die after being left behind because of a simple, treatable injury. Migrants walk at night to evade detection, and rocky terrain makes broken bones a common occurrence. Even a bad case of blisters can cause migrants to be abandoned by the smugglers they pay to guide them, leading to almost certain death.

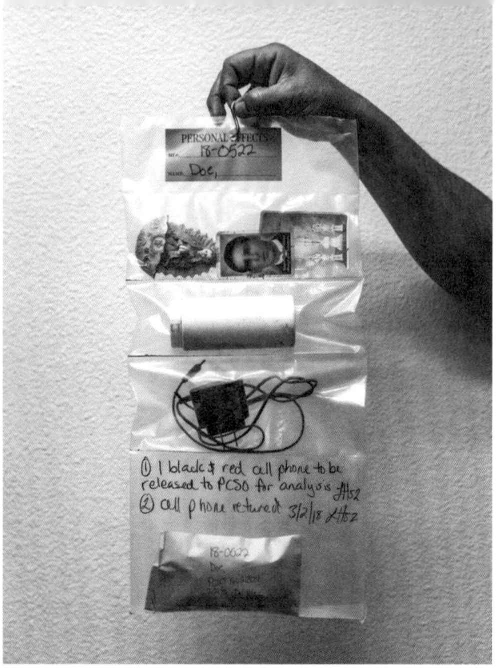

Scott Warren, a humanitarian aid worker with No More Deaths, faced charges in 2019 for providing food, water, and shelter to two migrants in the Arizona desert, leading to a highly publicized trial. The case sparked debates about the criminalization of humanitarian aid and the treatment of migrants along the U.S.-Mexico border.

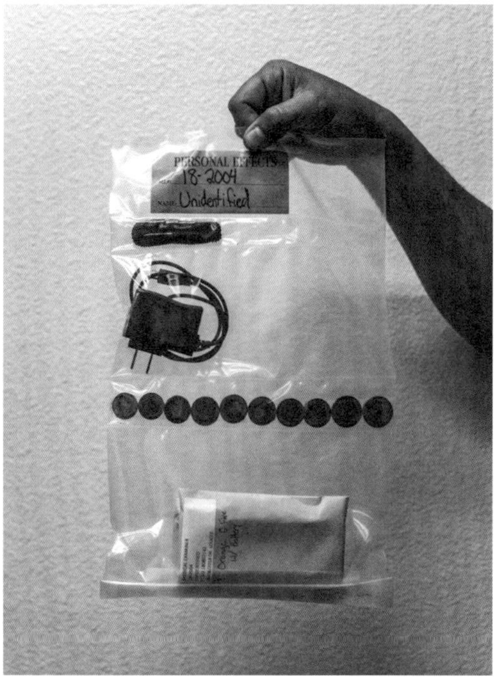

911 Dispatch: 911, where is your emergency?
Caller: No puedo hablar en inglés, señor, solo así en español. [I can't speak English sir, only Spanish.]
911: Uh… is there anyone that speaks English nearby?
Caller: No, no entiendo, señor, no entiendo. No hay uno que sepa hablar en español ahí? [No, I don't understand sir, I don't understand, there isn't anyone who knows how to speak Spanish there?]
911: Are you lost?
Caller: Solo en español, no puedo hablar en inglés… Inglés, no puedo… ya estamos muriendo, somos seis, señor. [I only speak Spanish, I can't speak in English, I can't in English… we are dying, we are six people, sir.]

— 911 Call, PCSD Ajo Station, 2015

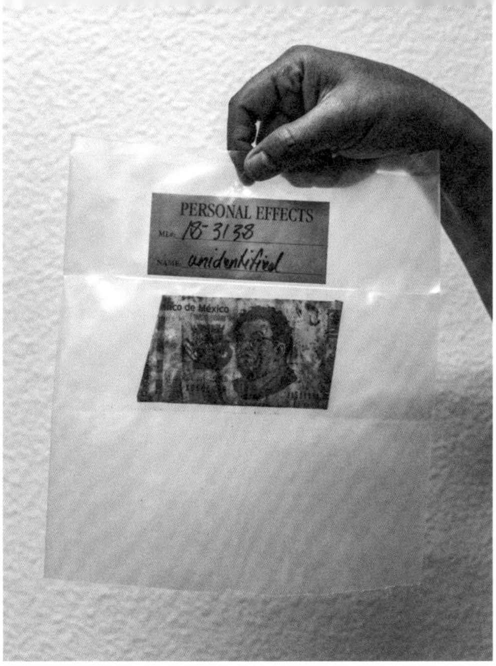

Between 1990 and 2020, the Pima County Office of the Medical Examiner examined 3,356 dead migrants. For 1,275 of them, the cause of death was "exposure or probable exposure" to extreme temperature conditions. In almost half the cases, the cause of death could not be definitely determined because the remains were too fragmented or decomposed. To these numbers must be added the corpses that were not found.

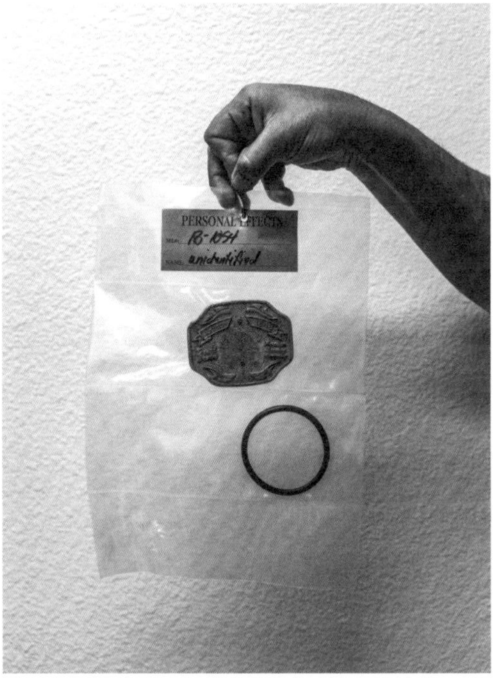

911 Dispatch: 911, where is your emergency?
Caller: Ayúdenme aquí! [Help me here!]
911: Pardon me?
Caller: Ayúdenme! [Help me!]
911: Do you need the police?
Caller: Eh? Ayuden… ya voy a morir. Ayúdenme… aquí estoy. [Help… I'm going to die. Help me… I'm here.]
911: You speak Spanish… You don't speak English?
Caller: Eh?
911: Do you speak English?

— 911 Call, PCSD Tucson Station, 2018

Je mangeai à peine, et je bus les quelques gouttes d’eau qui formaient ma ration. La gourde du guide à demi pleine,

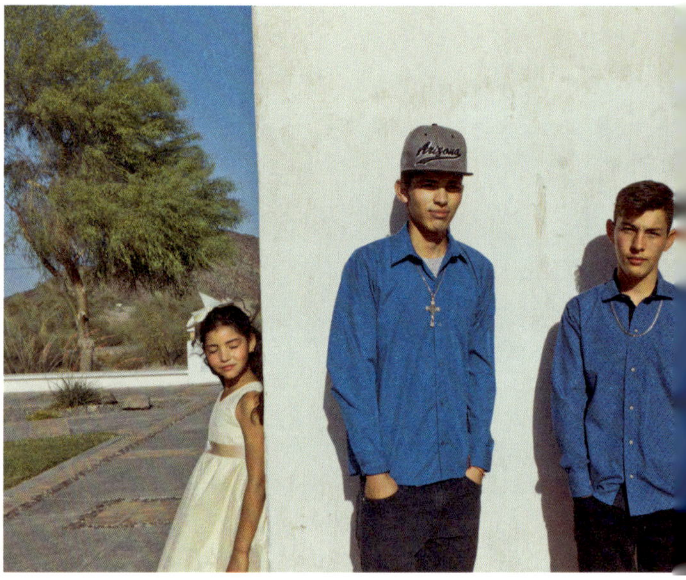

I scarcely ate, and I swallowed down the few drops of water rationed out to me. One flask half full was all we had left to slake the thirst of three men.

voilà tout ce qui restait pour désaltérer trois hommes.

Apenas comí, bebiendo en seguida las escasas gotas de agua que constituían mi ración. Lo único que quedaba para apagar

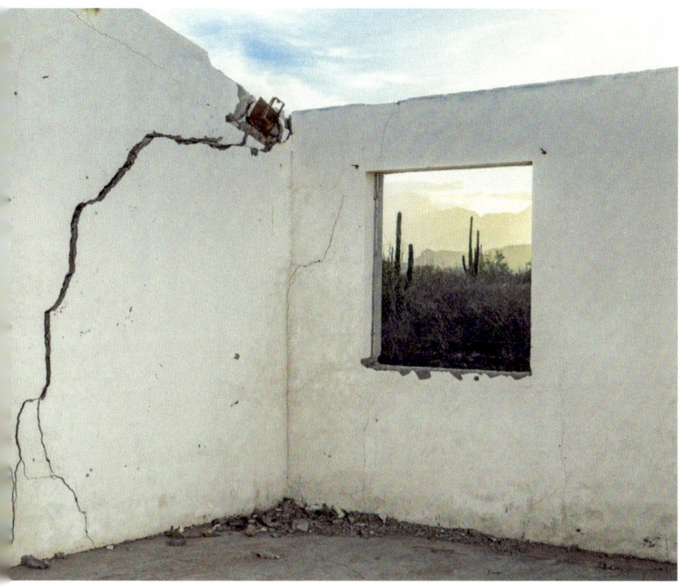

la sed de tres hombres era la calabaza del guia medio llena.

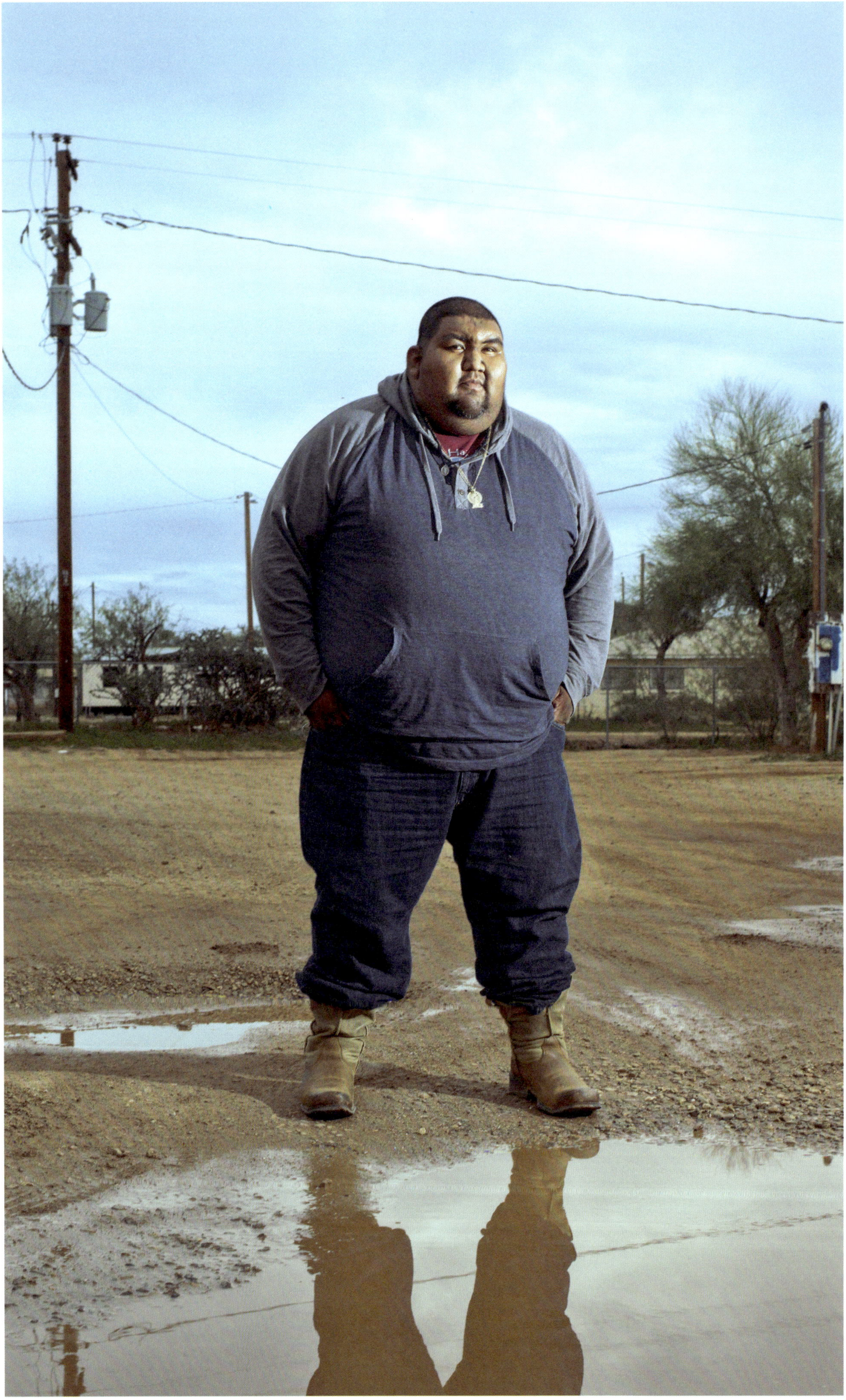

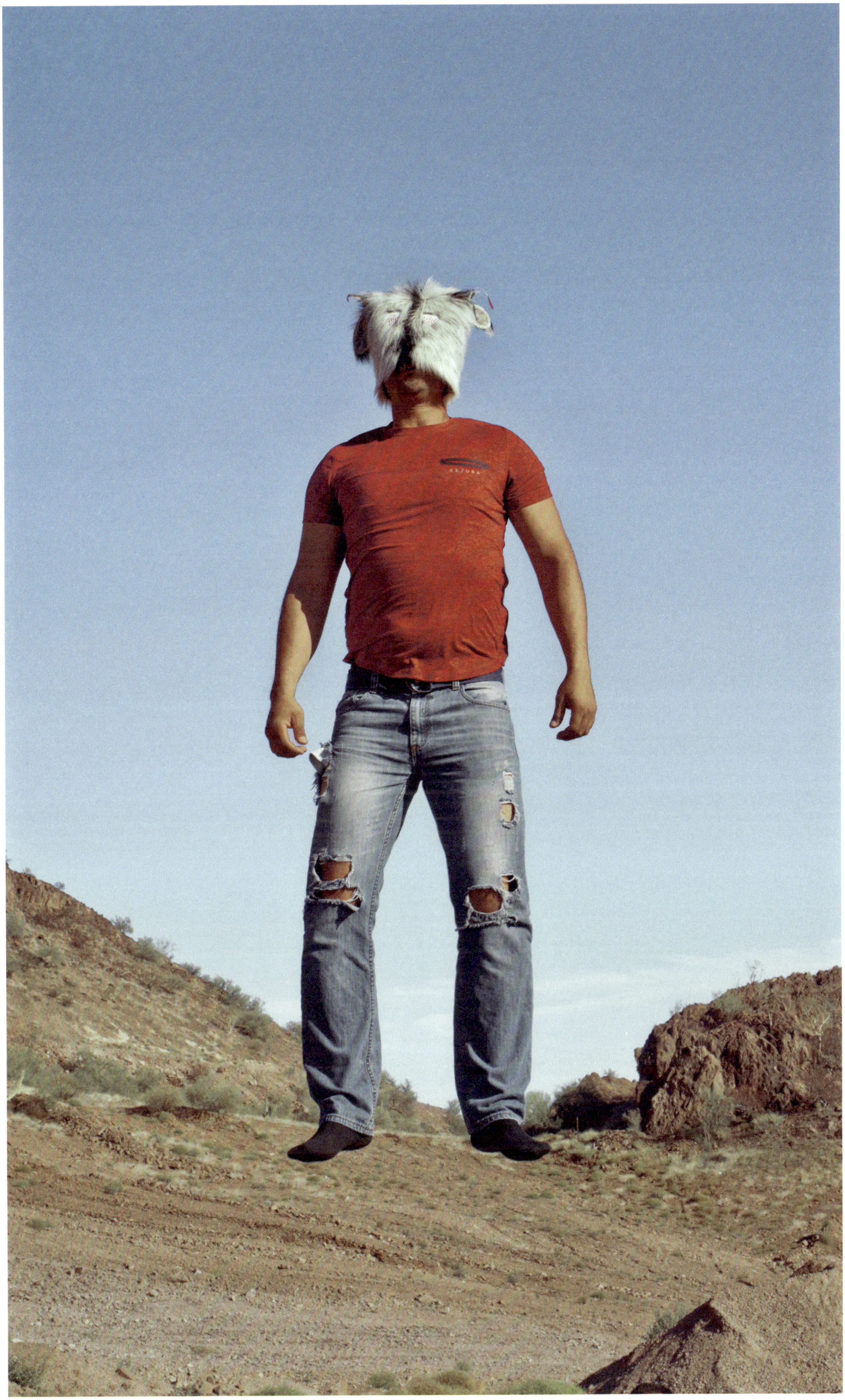

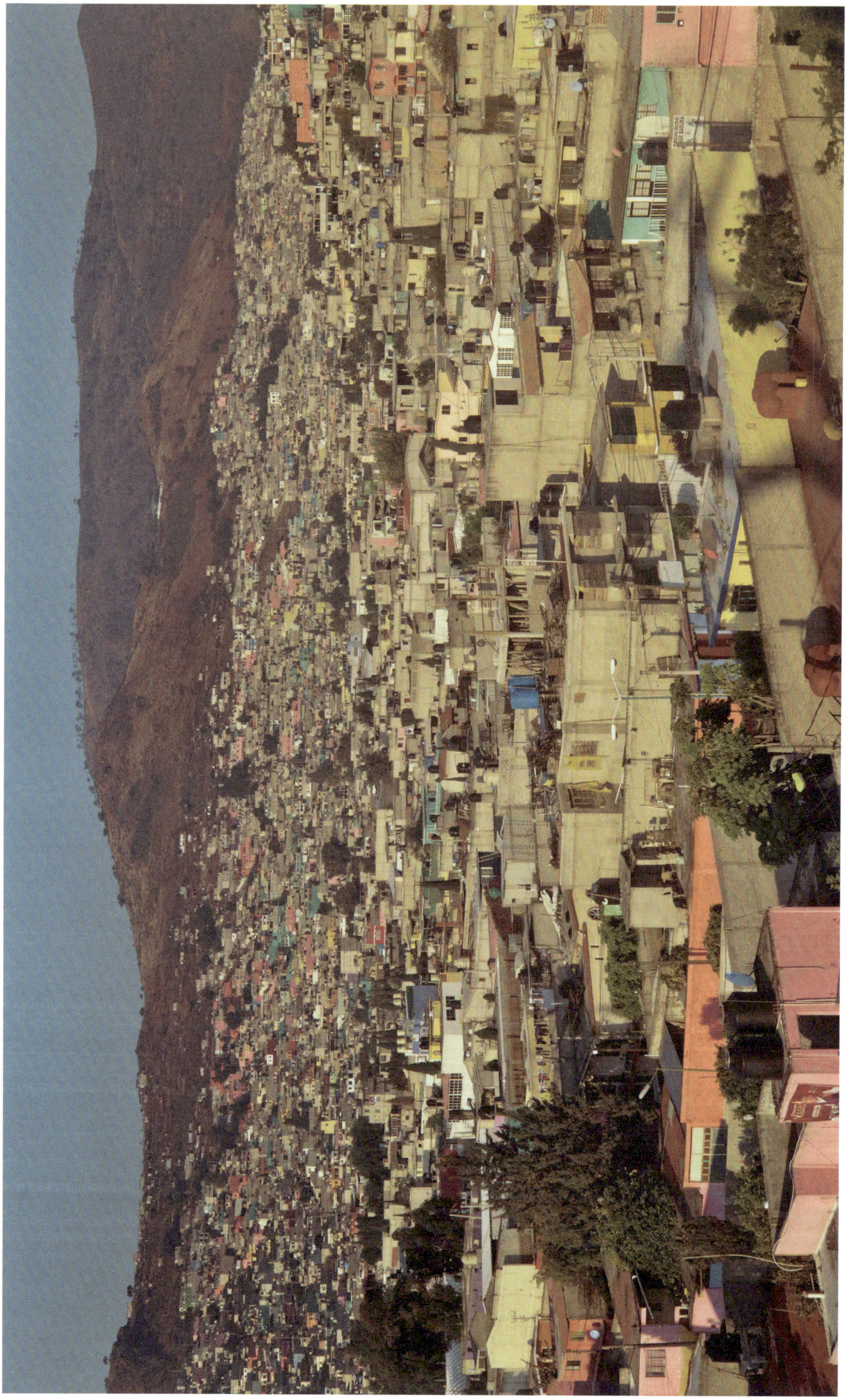

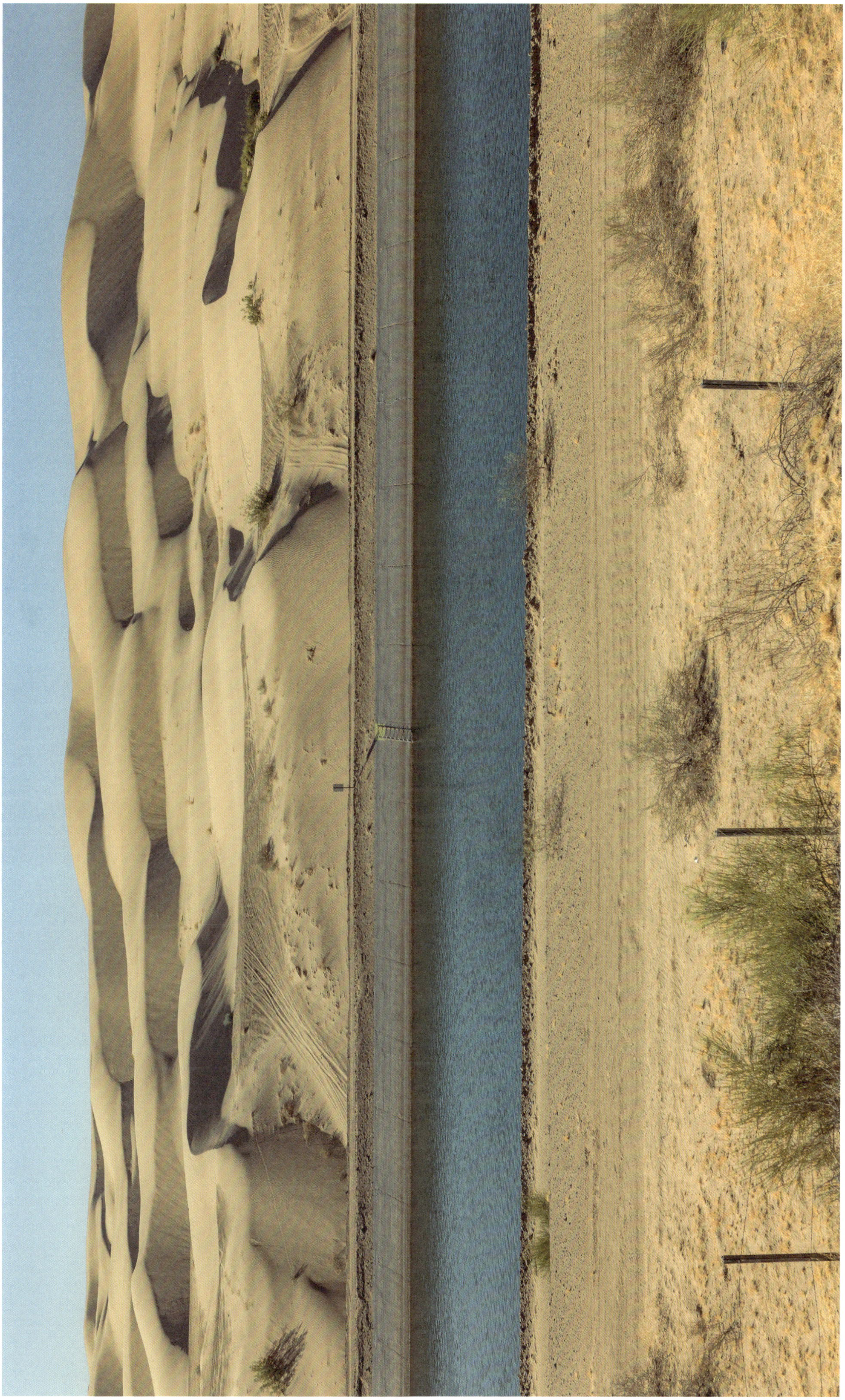

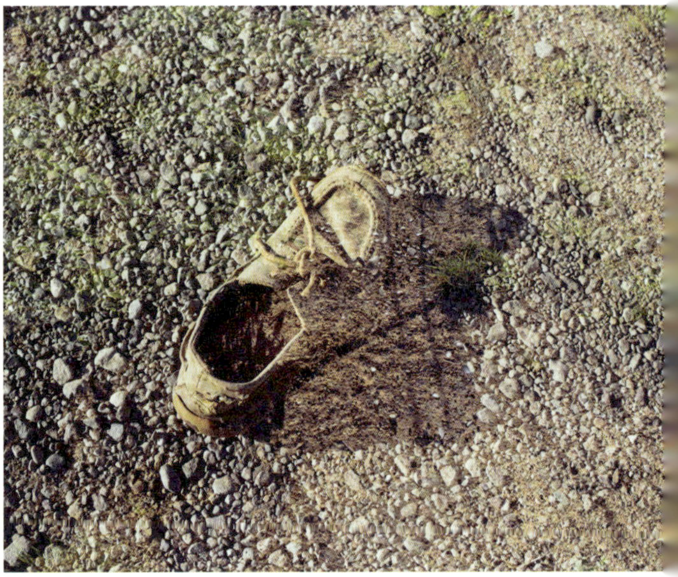

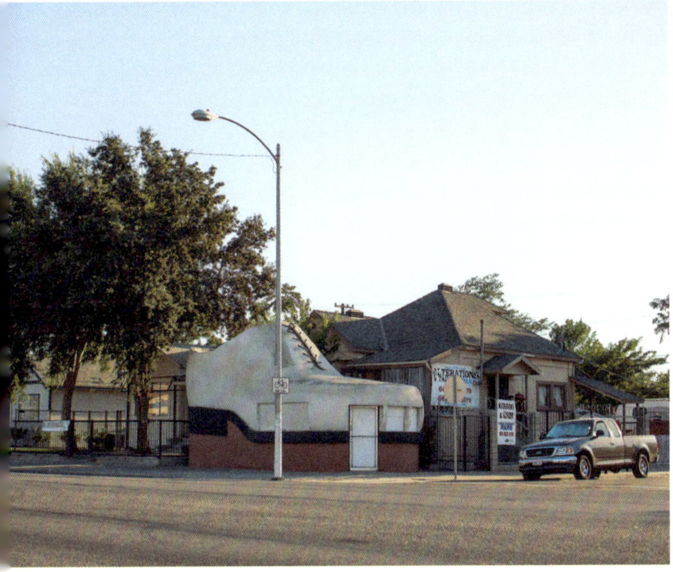
ALTERATIONS

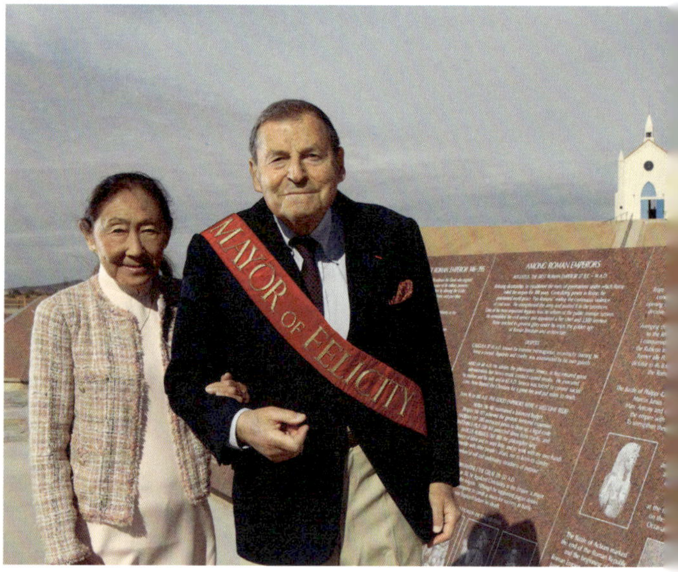
MAYOR OF FELICITY

FELICITY, CALIFORNIA, JULY 2021.

Jacques-André Istel is a challenging interviewee. I am not a particularly experienced interviewer and I tend to avoid confrontation, so he essentially leads the conversation while I try to sneak in a few questions, which he ignores completely. He's a very pleasant man – gallant, with exquisite manners. We are in his "bureau", the walls of which are lined with shelves of books in various languages. Further books are piled up on small tables near the sofa. Next to where I'm sitting he has placed a copy of *Around the World in Eighty Days* by Jules Verne.

Everything feels beige – the carpet, the curtains, the desert visible behind them, the bookshelves and the books themselves. Mr Istel is wearing beige trousers with a navy jacket and a sash that reads: Mayor of Felicity. He is in his 90s but looks sharp, and he knows it.

While I set up my equipment he explains how he founded the place, how migrants used to cross his land to continue their journey to the North, and how often he provided support to them. I obviously could not record that part of the conversation and spend the rest of the interview unsuccessfully trying to bring him back to these details, but it seems I missed that train.

The interview took place in July 2021, but it was not our first conversation. That took place in 2015 when I first arrived in Felicity. I'd been driving around the roads of southern California, killing some free time between assignments, and I decided to head to Why, a small town right by the border with Mexico and Arizona.

Just for the joke – why would you go to Why?

As it turned out, there was a reason. As I headed towards Why, I spontaneously took an exit I spotted on Highway 8 that read: Felicity, Center of the World.

How could I resist? That diversion in my itinerary triggered a project that would take me seven years to complete.

From the highway, all you can see is of Felicity is a group of standard brown buildings and a big sign that says "www.CenterOfTheWorld.us", but once you park you discover the rest – a pyramid, a huge flat structure made of corridors with granite walls, a maze, and a church on top of an artificial hill. An extremely long train moves slowly across the background, making the whole scene even more cinematographic and unreal.

The place was dusty and seemed empty, and I remember thinking that I may have been entering the headquarters of a cult, but I was too curious to give up. After some minutes wandering with my camera and knocking on a few doors, an Asian woman showed up with a broom. She welcomed me and asked if I wanted to know more about the place, to which I replied, "Of course." She took me to a room with half a dozen chairs, a TV and a VHS player, and pressed the Play button before leaving.

Alone in that room, I watched a 10-minute video which included stories of parachutes, dragons, deserts, granite, and the Center of the World. When the video finished I left the room, shaking my head in disbelief, and found an old man waiting for me at the door.

He looked at me and my camera and said, "Welcome to Felicity. Do you know you need permission to take photographs?" "No, but where can I get that permission?" I asked. "With me," he said. "May I have your permission to take photographs?" I asked, and he replied, "Yes." After a couple of awkward pauses, he spoke again: "Do you know Henri Cartier-Bresson?" to which I responded that I never had the pleasure but that I do, of course, know his work (I could not imagine then that six years later I would become the president of Magnum, the agency he founded). The old man then explained that he had discovered this place in California more than 40 years earlier when he was doing a road trip with Cartier-Bresson's sister. (I would later establish that he was in fact referring to another Magnum photographer, Marc Riboud, whose family he was very close to.)

The whole encounter felt quite surreal and I left the place feeling nonplussed, but fully understanding that this was the beginning of something.

Felicity lies just a few miles away from the Mexican border where a part of the wall is built on the desert, and if you climb up to the church Mr Istel built to preside over his monumental "History of Humanity in Granite museum", you can almost see it. I imagined the journey of the migrants and their arrival in the US, right at Felicity, right at the Center of the World.

The next thing I did was to secure a copy of Jules Verne's *Journey to the Center of the Earth*, a book I had read as a child and which to be honest had made little impact on me. A journey to the Center of the World, on the other hand, in which the migrants were the heroes in a classical adventure with the final destination being a hollow monument surrounded by a hostile desert, looked to me like the real face of the American dream.

Six years on, I am back in Felicity and asking the questions. Or trying to.

Cristina De Middel: Good morning, Mr Istel. Thank you for taking the time to speak with me today. You go to bed and wake up every day at the Center of the World. What does that involve?

Jacques-André Istel: Good morning! Well, I like to start my day with some physical activity, so I do 100 push-ups and 125 squats. After that I enjoy a swim in my lap pool, which I've tried to make as elegant as possible. Then I head back upstairs for a light breakfast in bed, a habit I've had since my boyhood in Paris and which I respect wherever I am, not only when I'm in Felicity, where I only spend half of my time.

CdM Your life story, Mr Istel, is quite fascinating. You were born into a prominent family in Paris, and your journey is full of remarkable twists, turns and adventures. Can you tell us about some of the many different occupations you've had?

J-AI Certainly. I was born in 1929 in Paris, the son of a distinguished financier, André Istel. My childhood was marked by strictness and discipline, with corporal punishment for any misbehavior. When the Nazis occupied Paris during World War II my family managed to escape on diplomatic passports and eventually settled in New York in 1940. We thought we had lost everything, but the kindness of friends and strangers helped us rebuild our lives. I was a difficult student and my parents tried everything until I eventually made it. I am now 92 years old and so far I have sold an entire forest in Vancouver, I have been a soldier, an airplane pilot, I invented modern parachutism, I have been a teacher for skydivers and hold the world champion title for skydiving, and now I manage the Center of the World and make a living out of tourists who want to know more. There may be more, but I cannot remember all the details.

CdM How did you come up with the idea of creating the Center of the World? How serious was the endeavor and what did you want to prove?

J-AI Felicity was borne out of a desire to create something special and meaningful. My wife Felicia and I built this town on 2,600 acres of land in the desert, and it's been our home since 1986. We've added several buildings, including the Church on the Hill, inspired by a chapel in Brittany, and the 21-foot tall stone and glass pyramid which marks the exact Center of the World, at least in our playful interpretation. The idea of the Center of the World can be quite abstract, given the Earth's spherical nature. But I managed to persuade the Board of Supervisors to embrace the humor and designate Felicity as the center of everything. Now there's a plaque marking the spot, and visitors can enter the pyramid there for a small fee. It's a testament to the power of imagination and a bit of absurdity. In practical terms, I wrote a fairy tale and presented it to the Board of Supervisors of Imperial County, California, to approve the creation of the official Center of the World in Felicity. Now you can imagine five local politicians when they received my request...I appeared in white tie and tails as an ambassador, and brought with me three trumpeters from a local high school to make it even more formal.

CdM I love your sense of humor and definitely see myself in your team for that, but beyond the display of absurdity, Felicity is built in quite a strategic place. Right at the border and in the middle of the desert. I guess it is not an innocent choice. You mentioned that Felicity used to be a stopping point for migrants heading further North. How was your interaction with them? What did they think of the place?

J-AI I chose this place because I love the desert and the quietness of it. I am lucky to have a wonderful wife, Felicia, which is also the reason why this place is called Felicity, by the way. She brings joy to my life and I do not need much more. Just a quiet place to work and develop my ideas. I fell in love with this desert many years ago and wanted to share this fascination by getting people's attention. Making the Center of the World in a remote place is for me a statement that speaks for itself.

CdM As a migrant yourself, and married to an Asian woman as you are, do you consider yourself an example of success in the run for the American Dream?

J-AI I am a migrant. That is true, but...

At this point my camera stops recording and the rest of the two-hour interview is lost. I only discover this unfortunate lapse about a year later, when I start transcribing the material gathered through the seven years of the project.

What I remember of the missing part is that Mr Istel told me about his numerous patents, and his project to start selling shares in Felicity to investors. He didn't want to see the project of his life become an abandoned roadside oddity. I promised to help in spreading the word, but I got too busy. I also did not know how to do it.

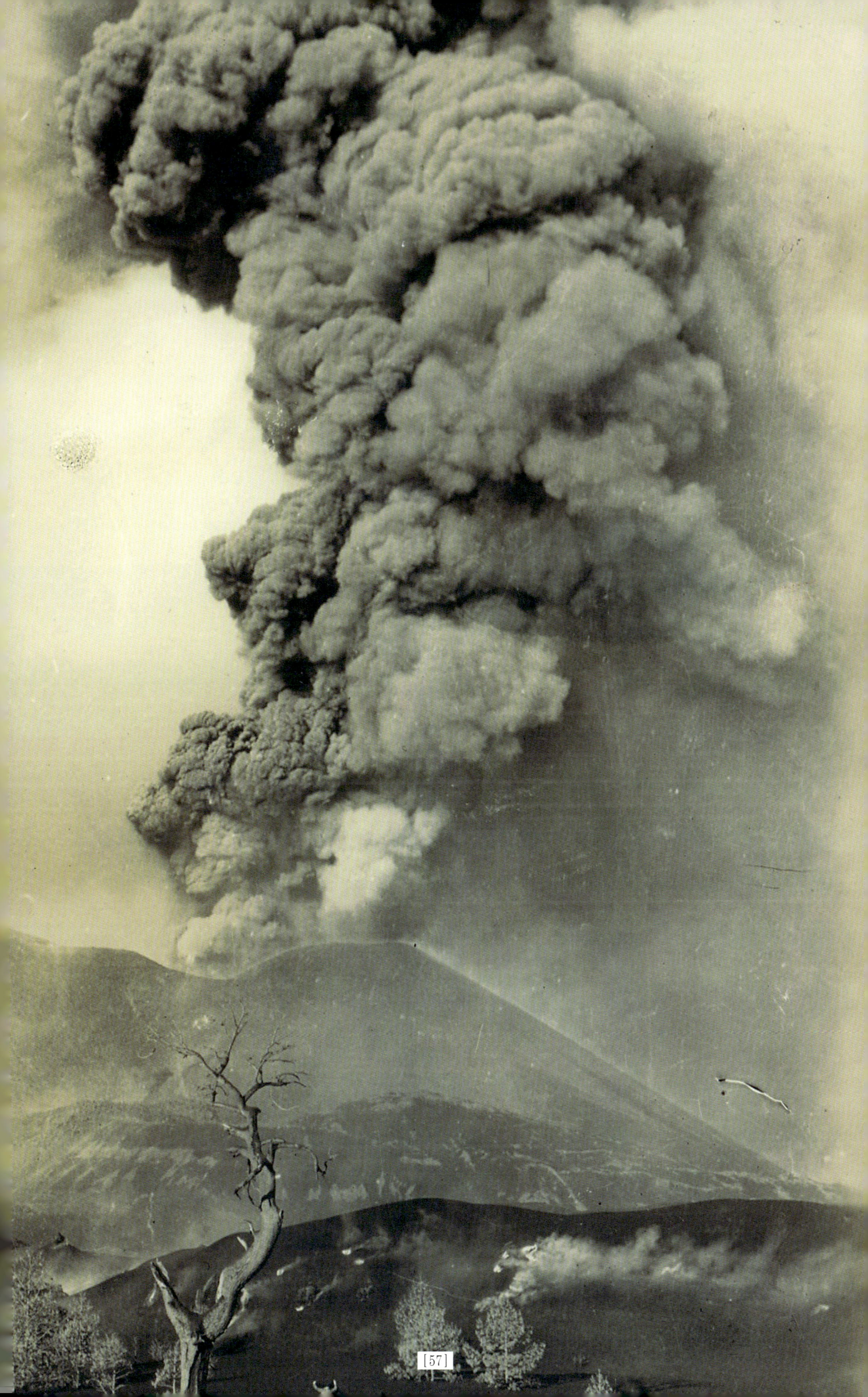

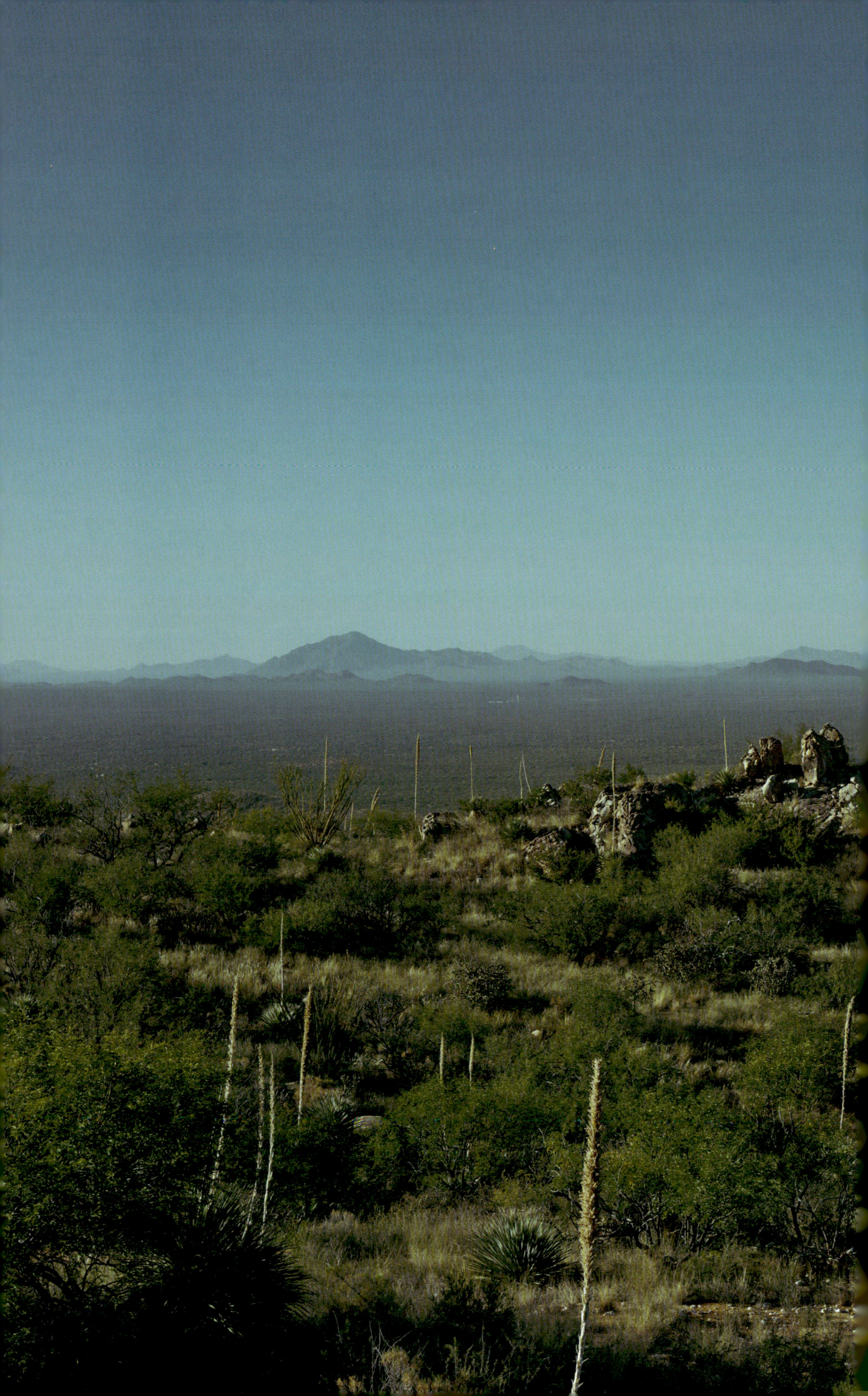

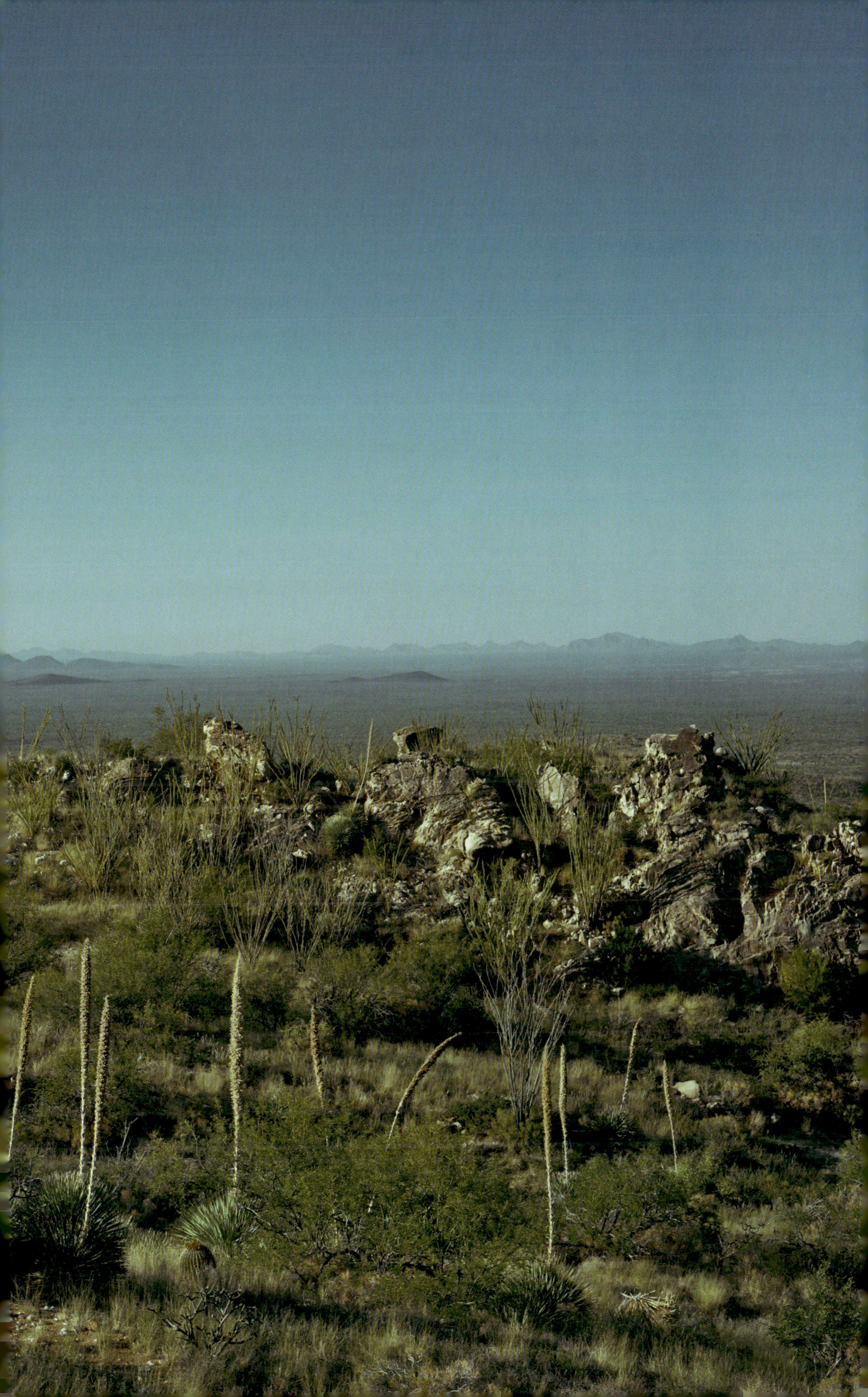

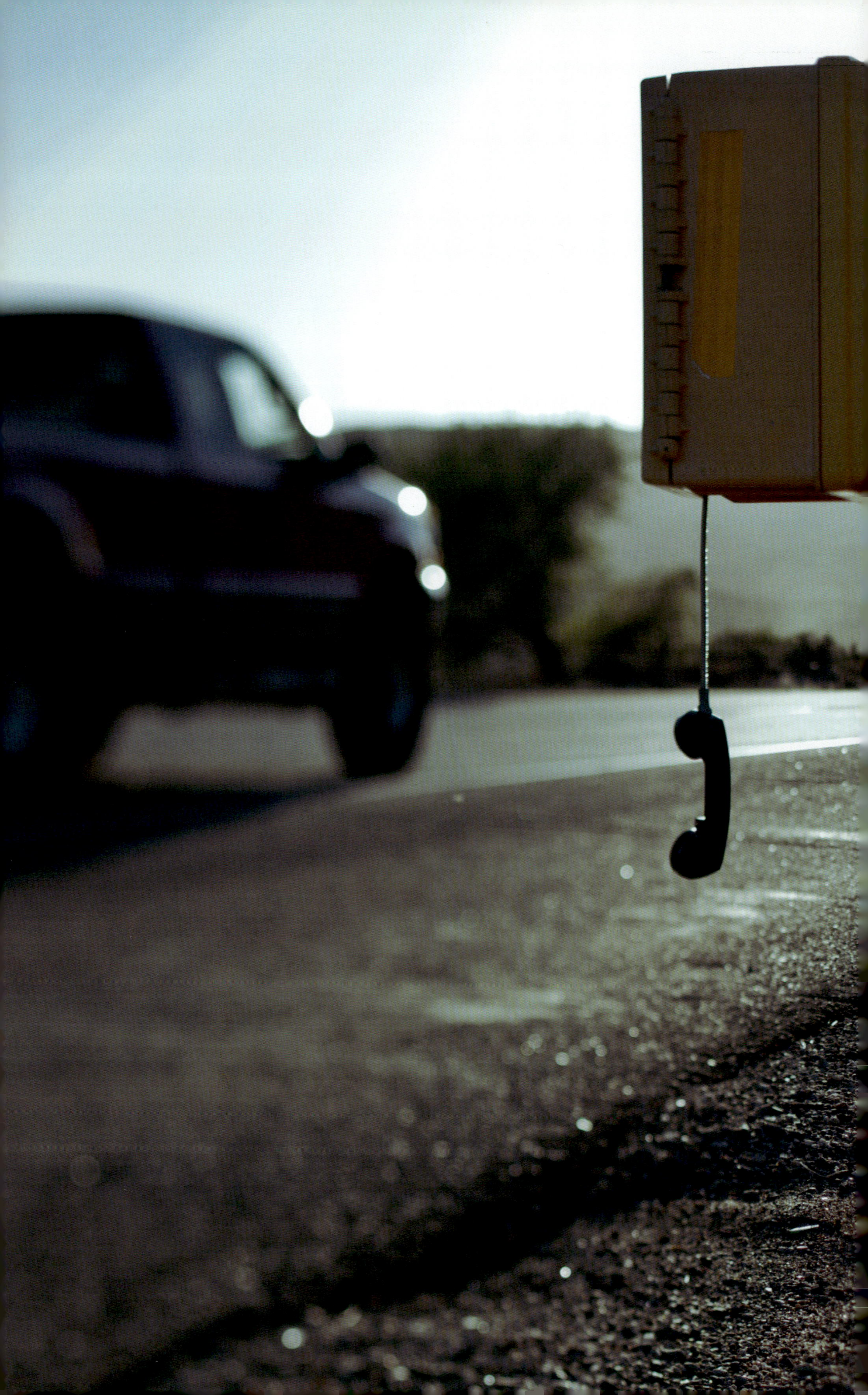

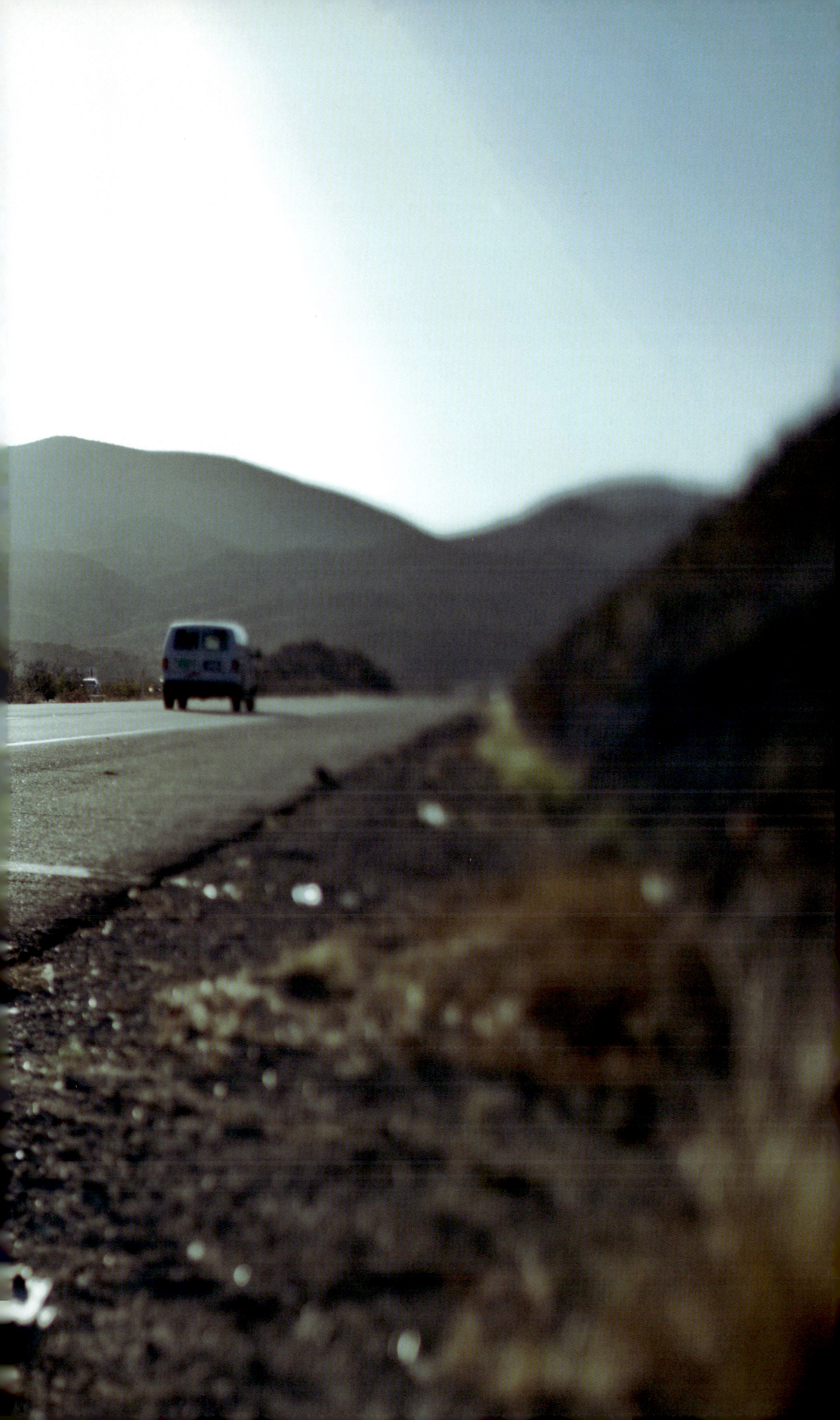

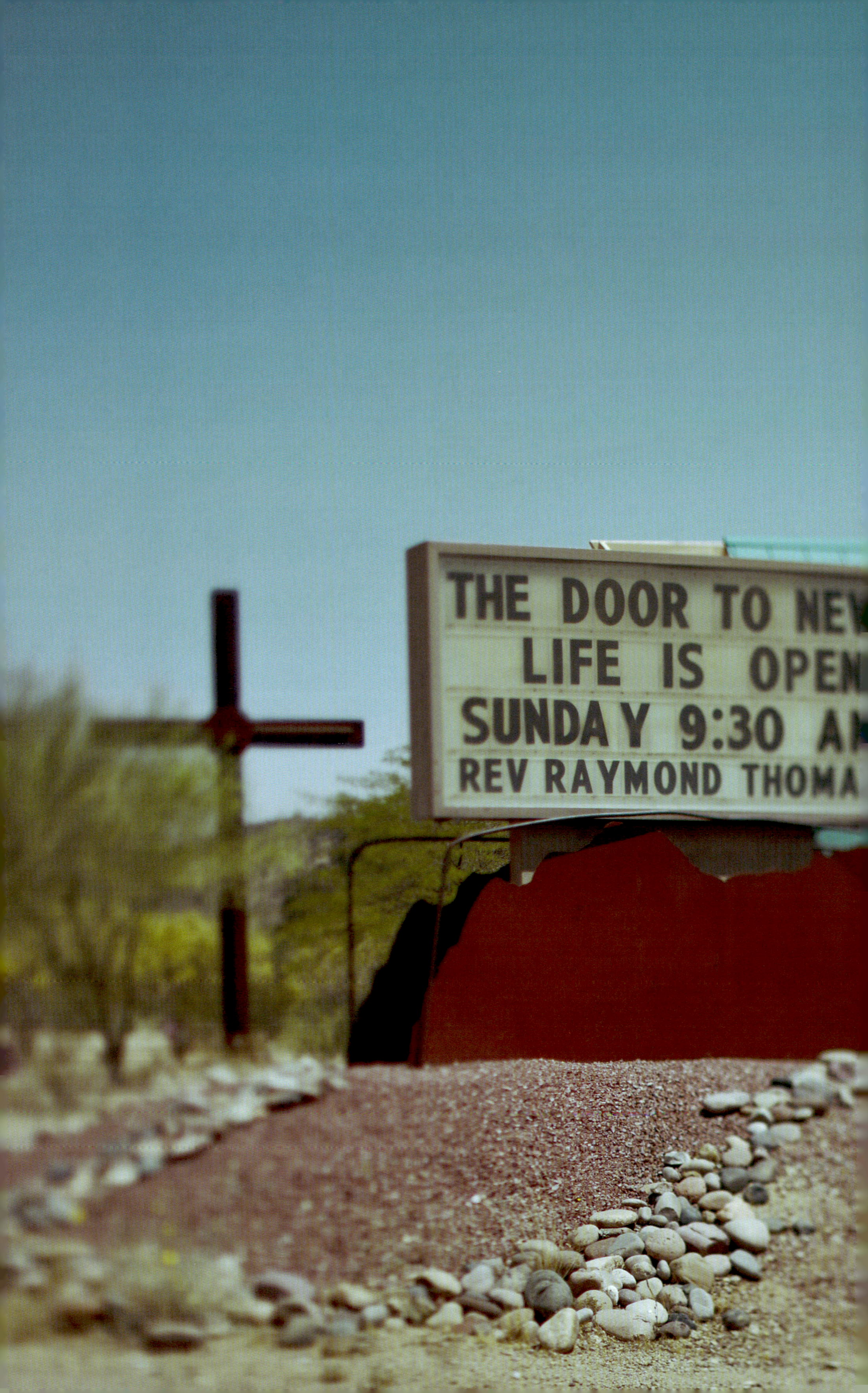
THE DOOR TO NEW
LIFE IS OPEN
SUNDAY 9:30 A
REV RAYMOND THOMA

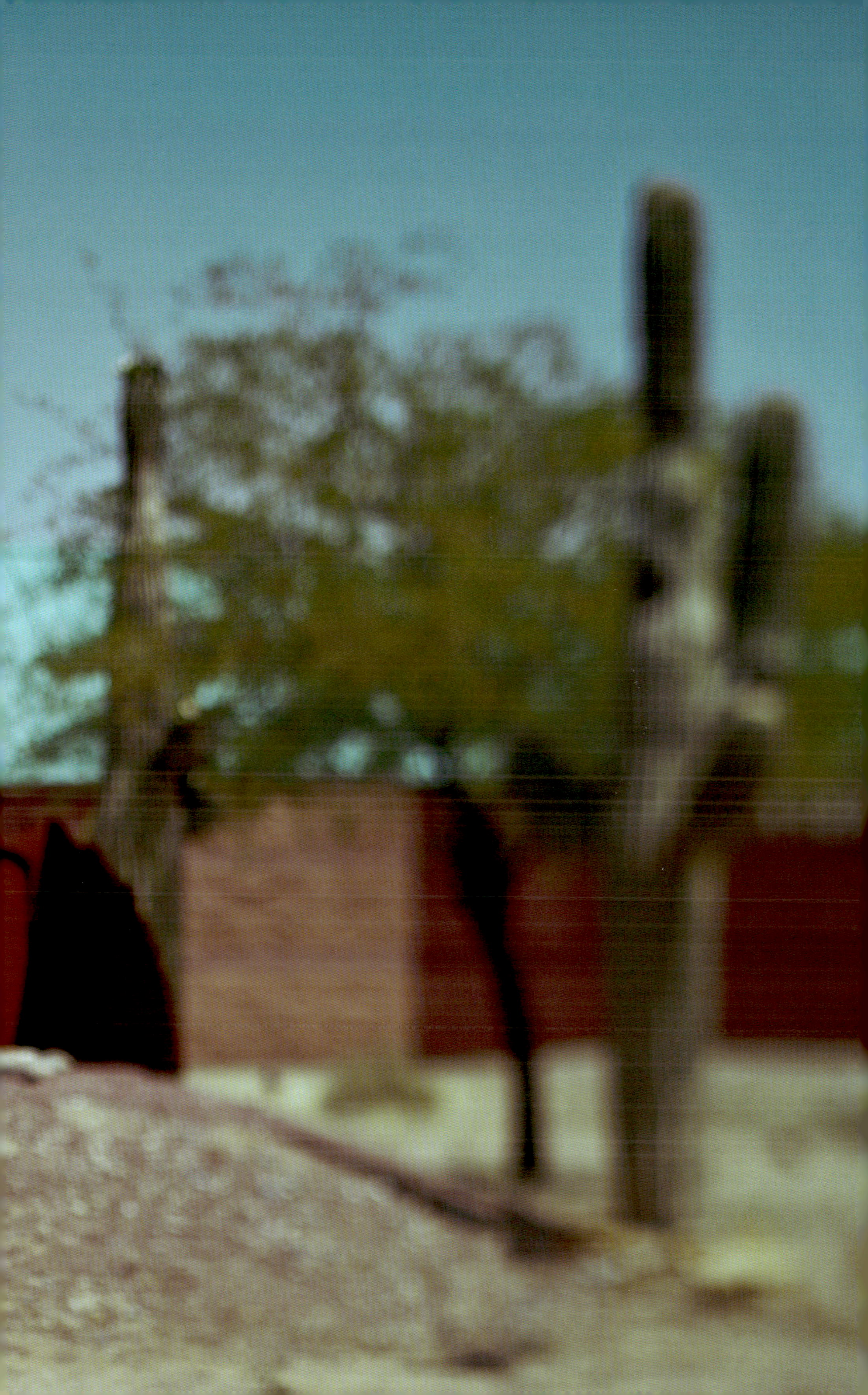

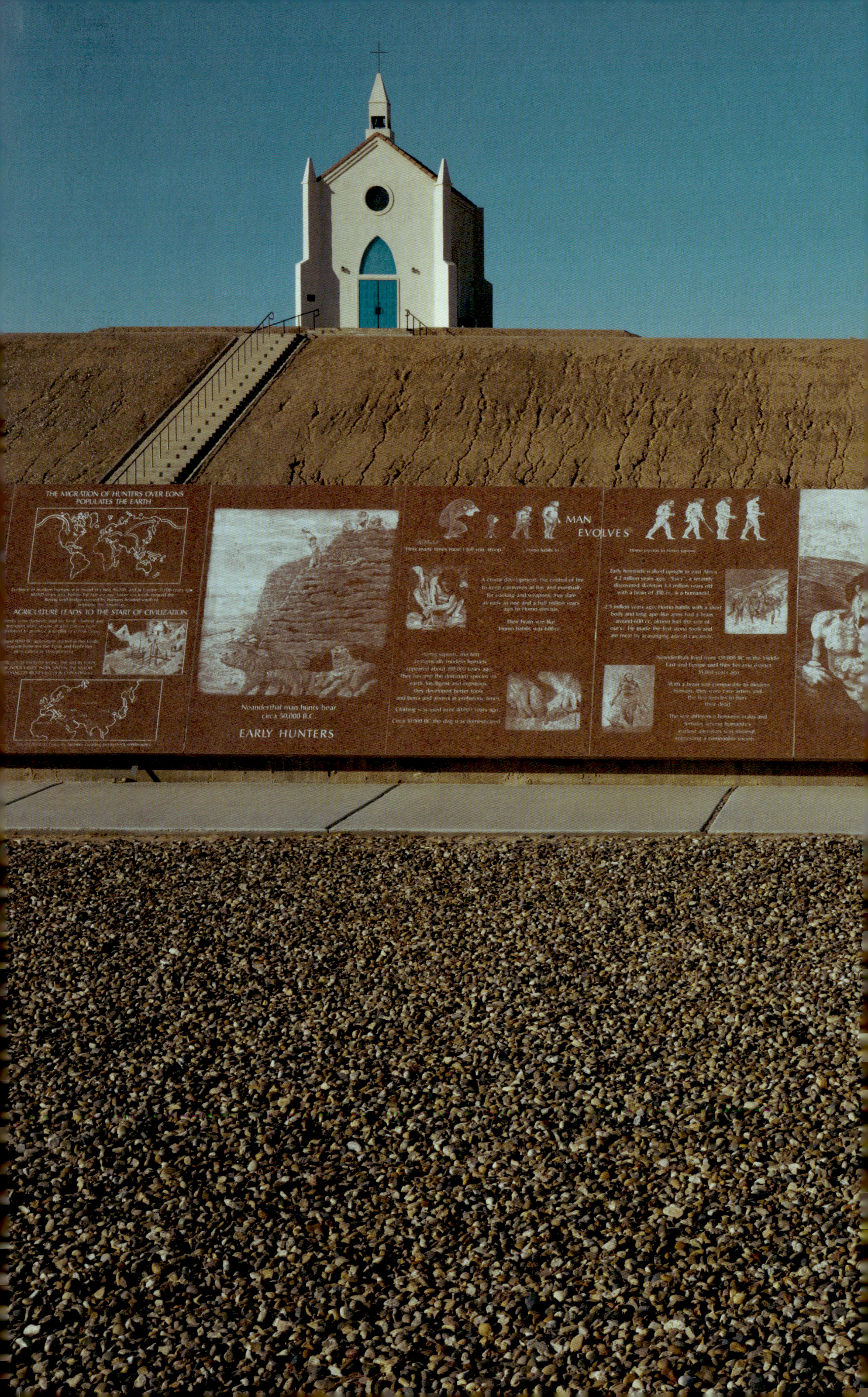
THE MIGRATION OF HUNTERS OVER EONS
POPULATES THE EARTH
AGRICULTURE LEADS TO THE START OF CIVILIZATION
Neanderthal man hunts bear
circa 50,000 B.C.
EARLY HUNTERS
MAN
EVOLVES

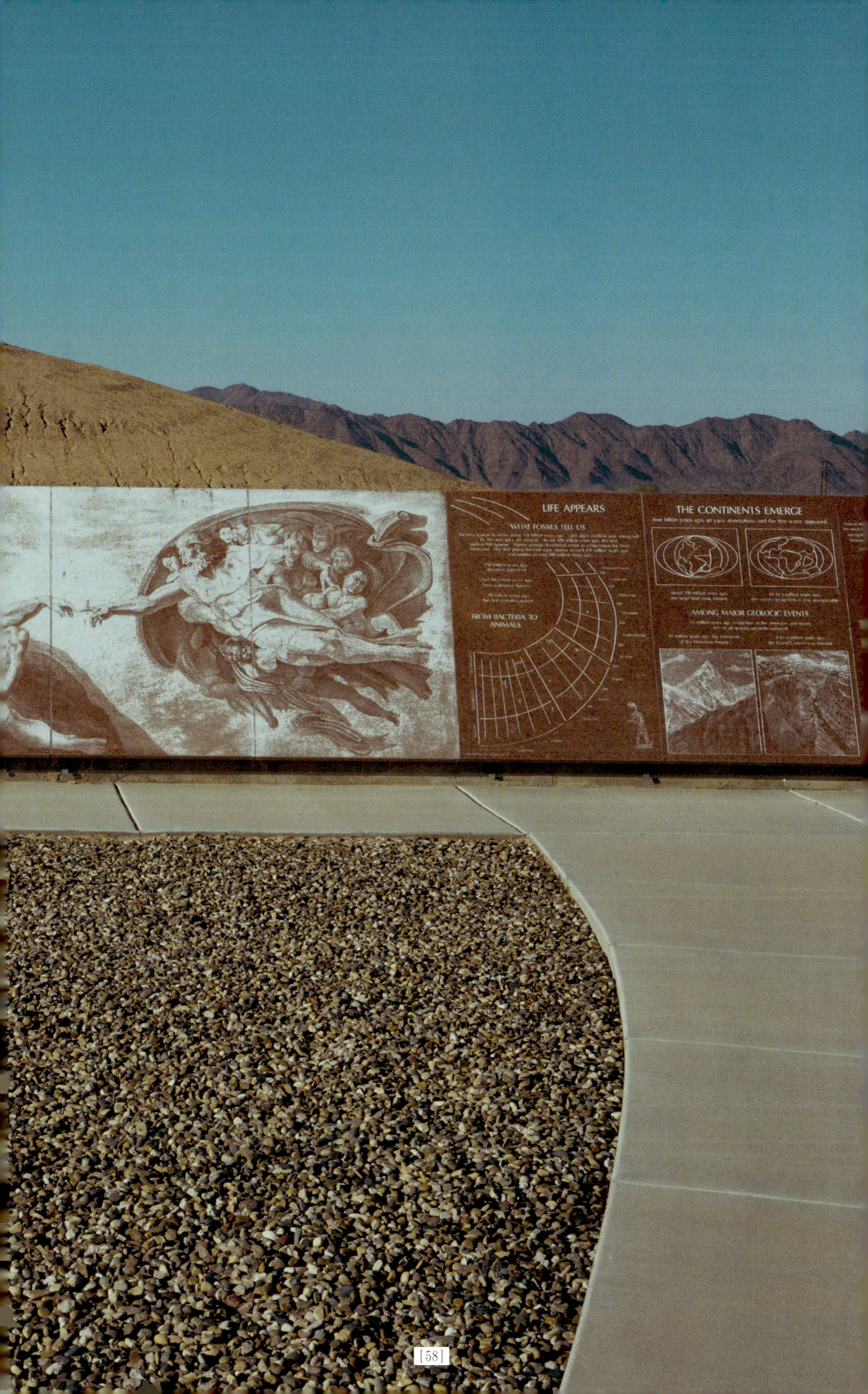
LIFE APPEARS
WHAT FOSSILS TELL US
FROM BACTERIA TO ANIMALS
THE CONTINENTS EMERGE
AMONG MAJOR GEOLOGIC EVENTS

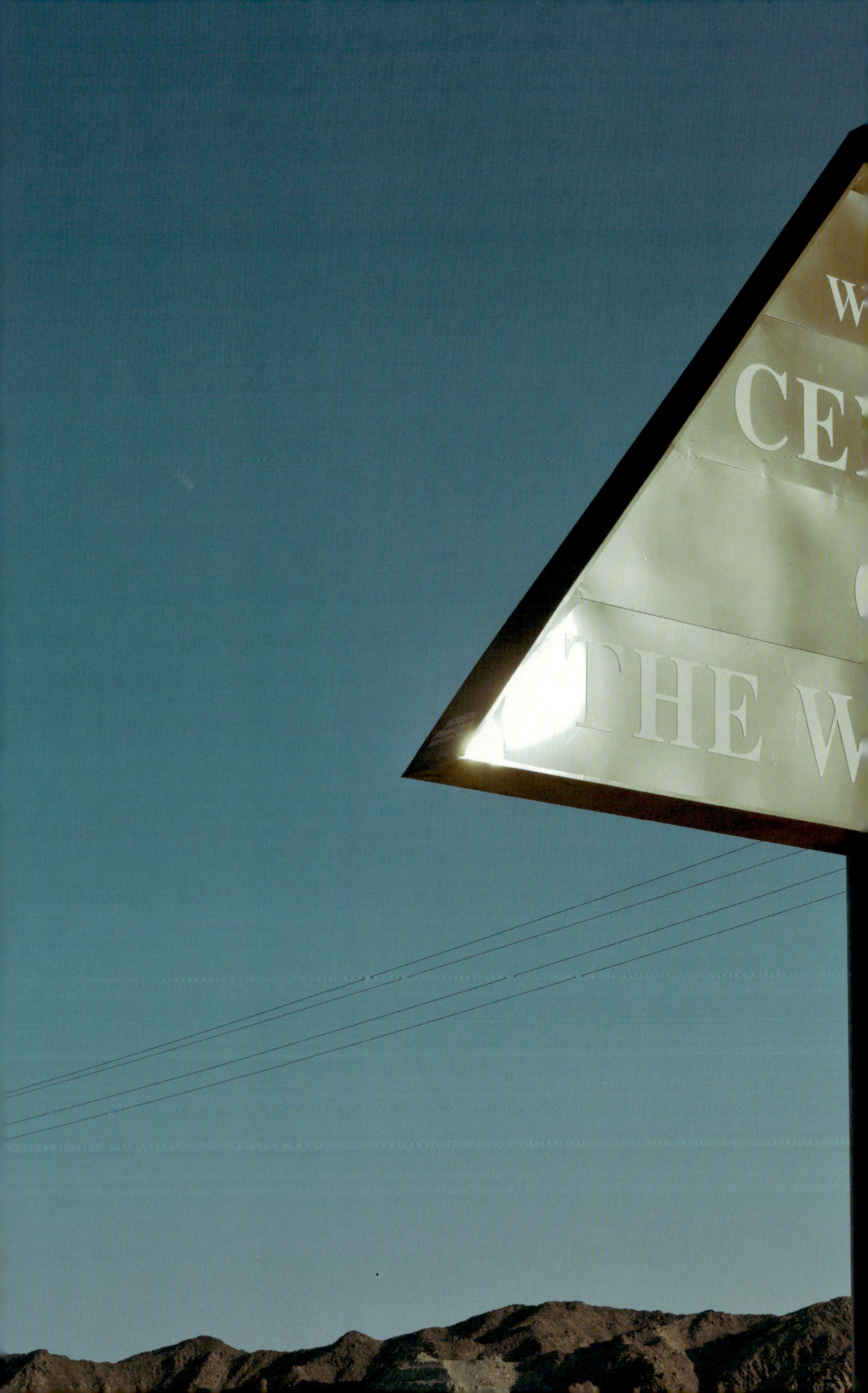

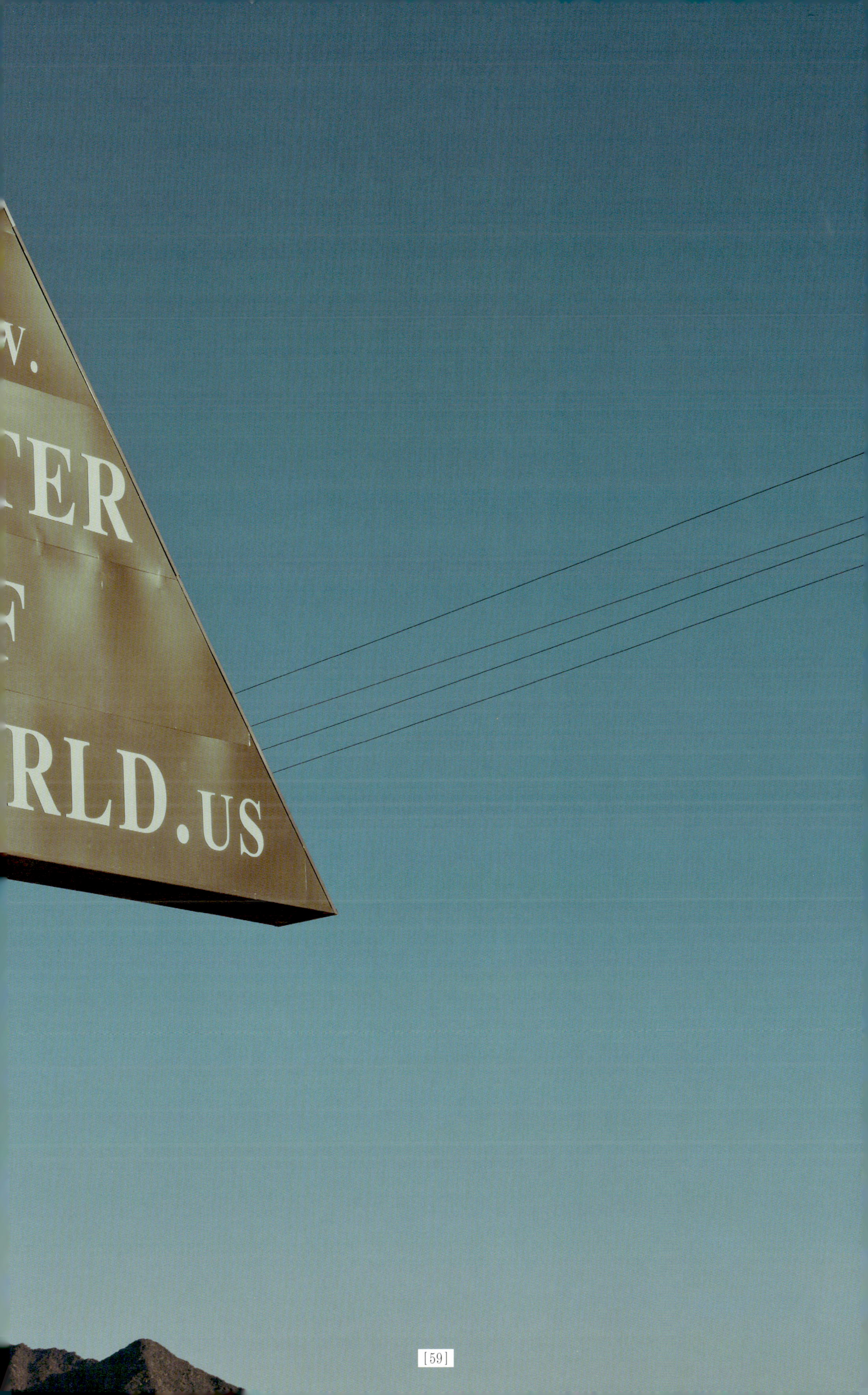
W.
TER
F
RLD.US

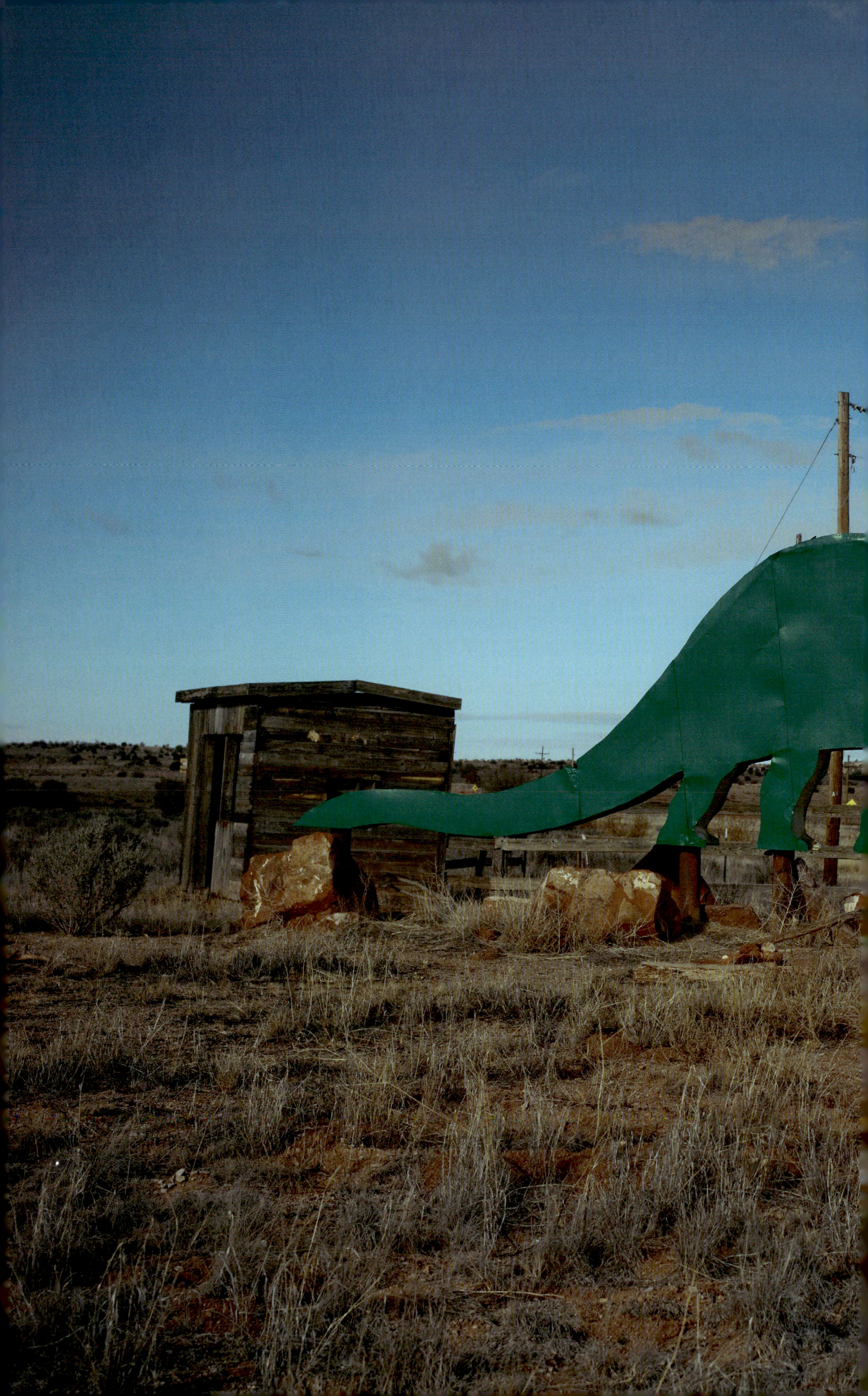

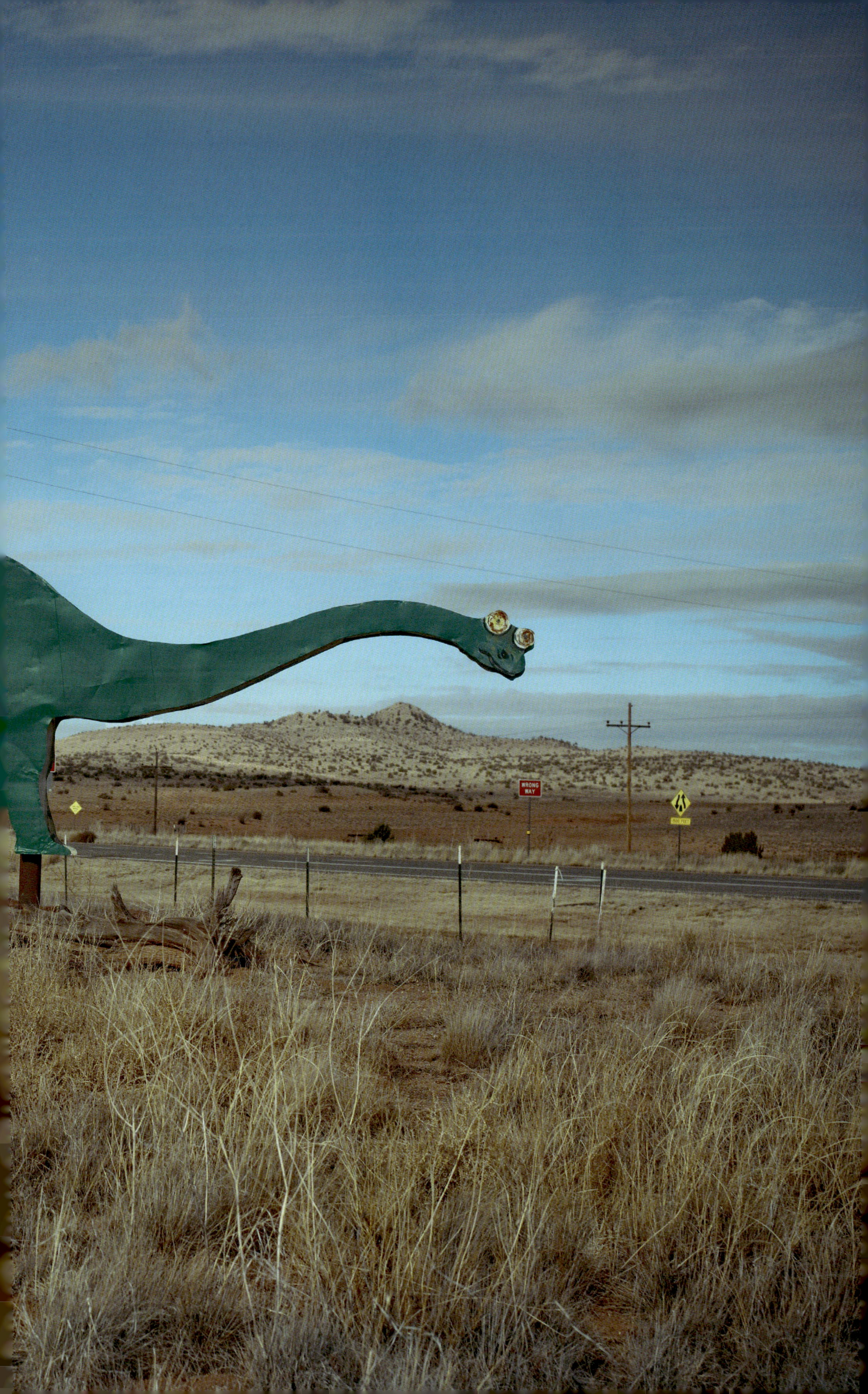
WRONG
WAY

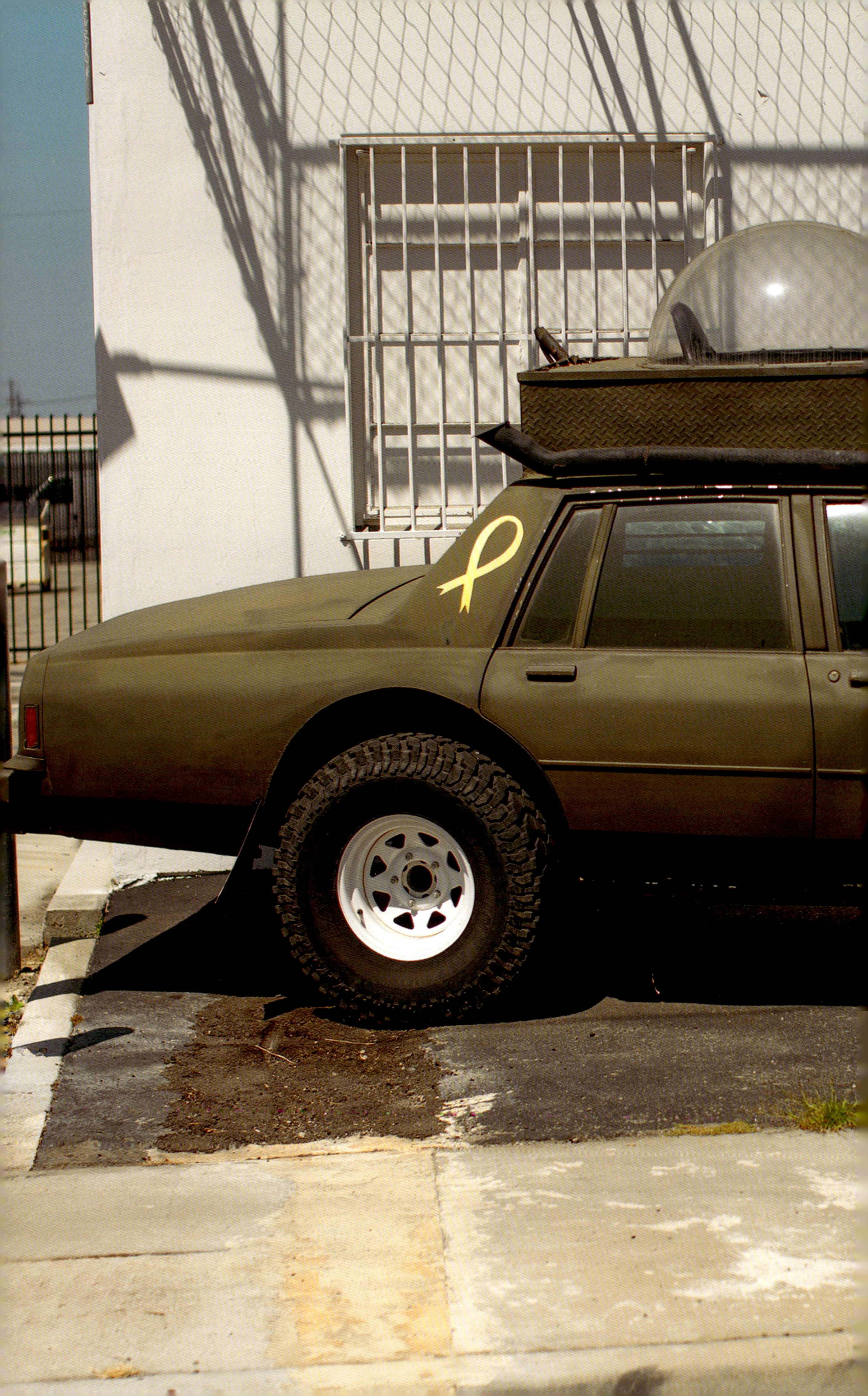

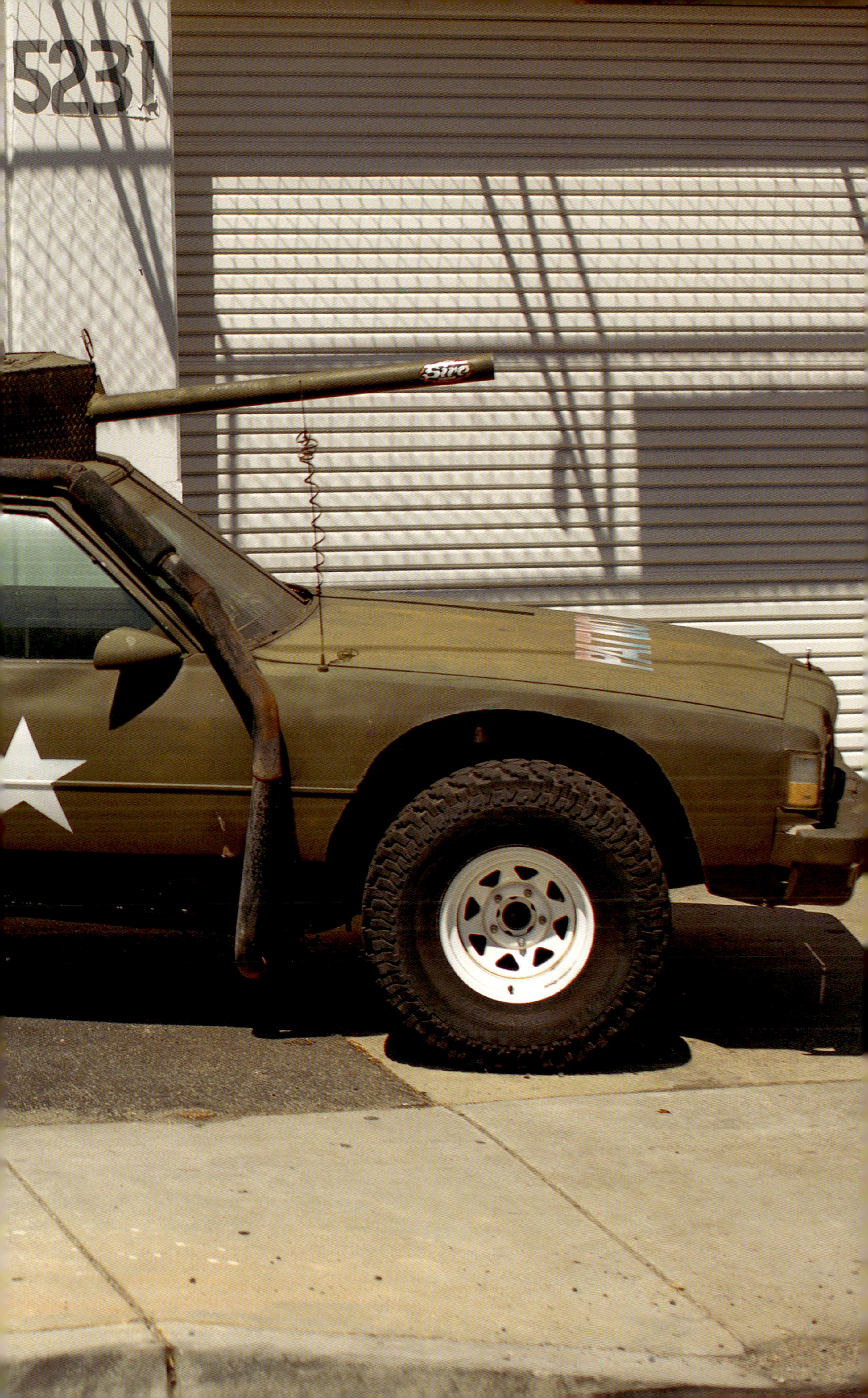
5231
Sire

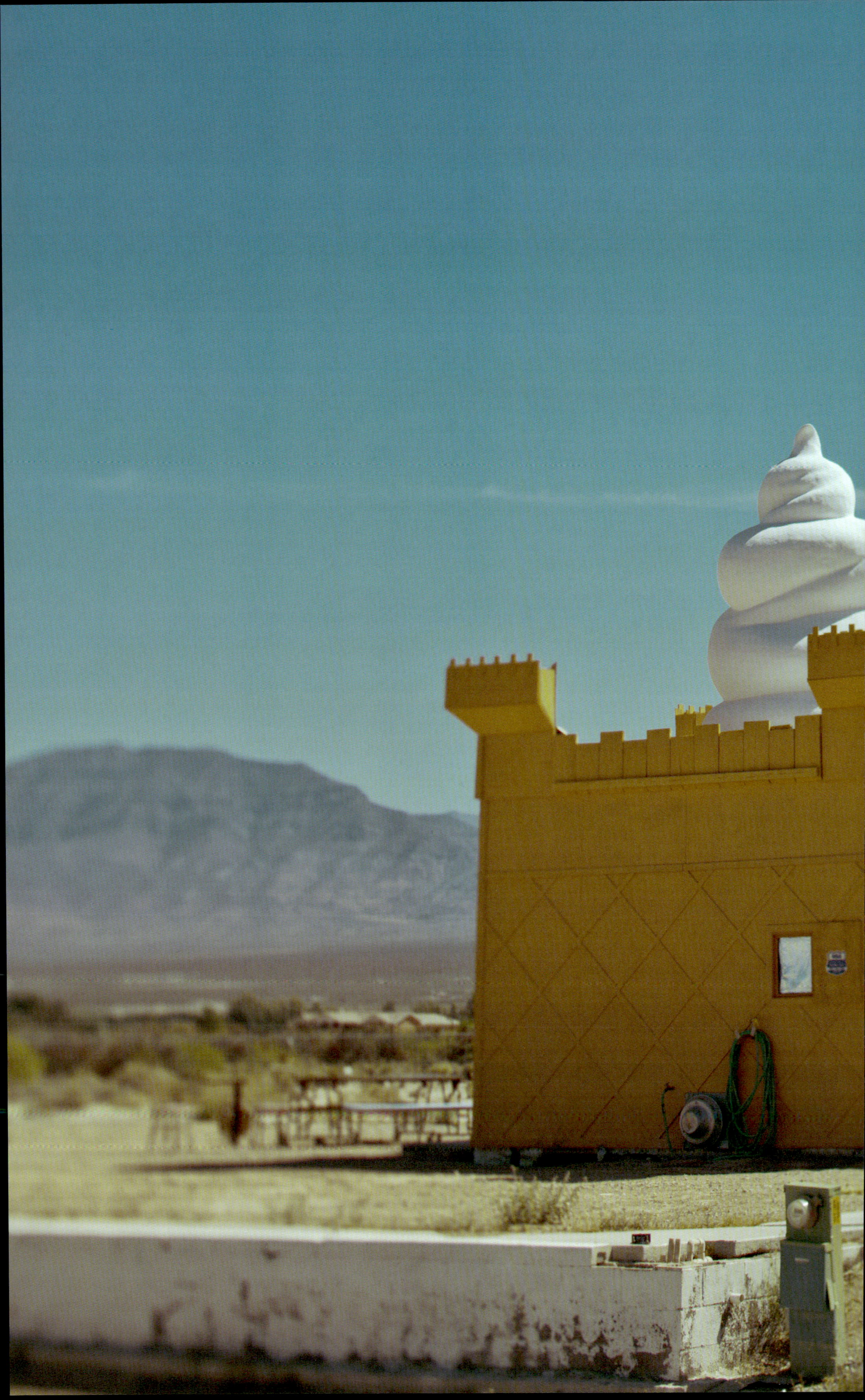

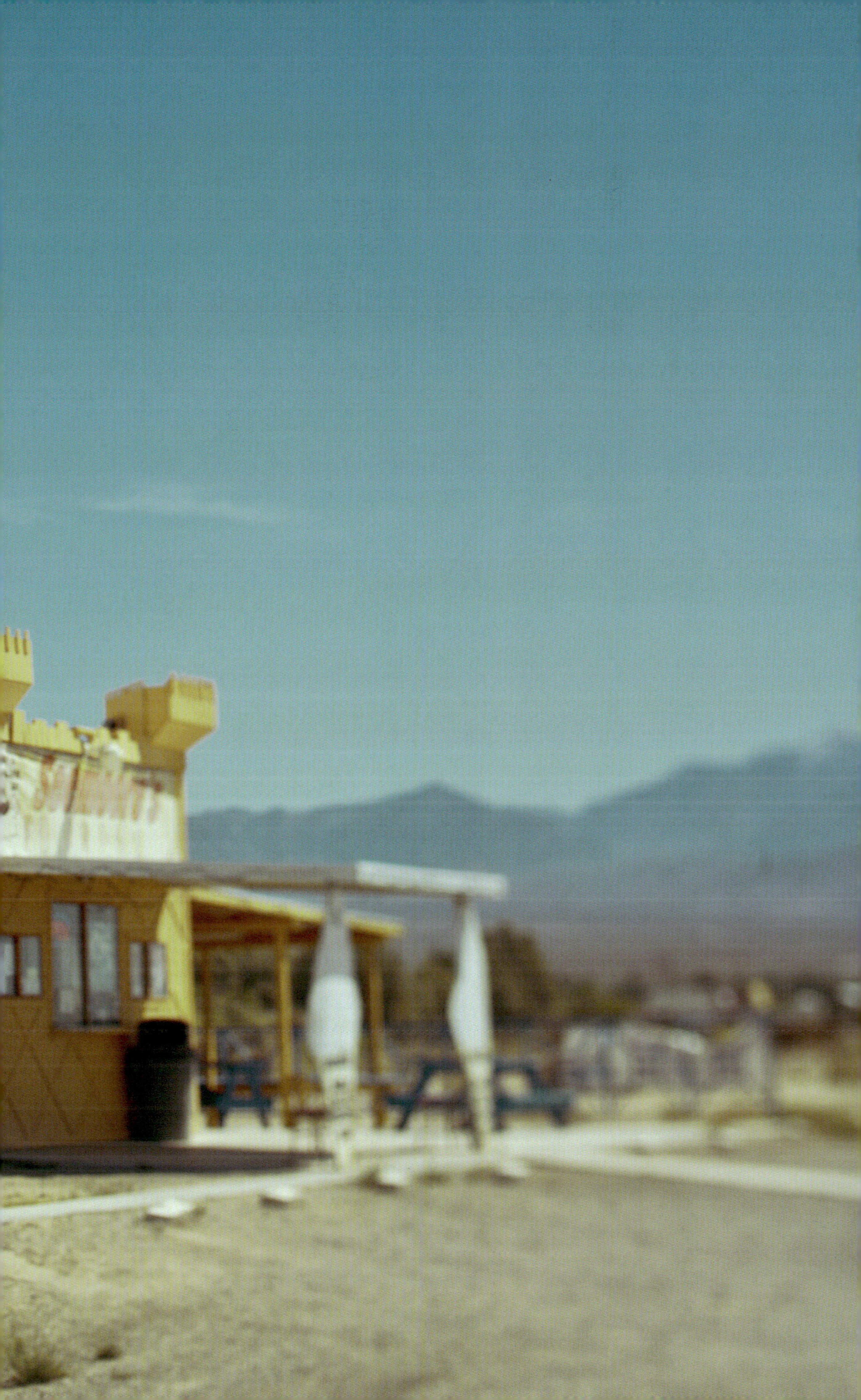

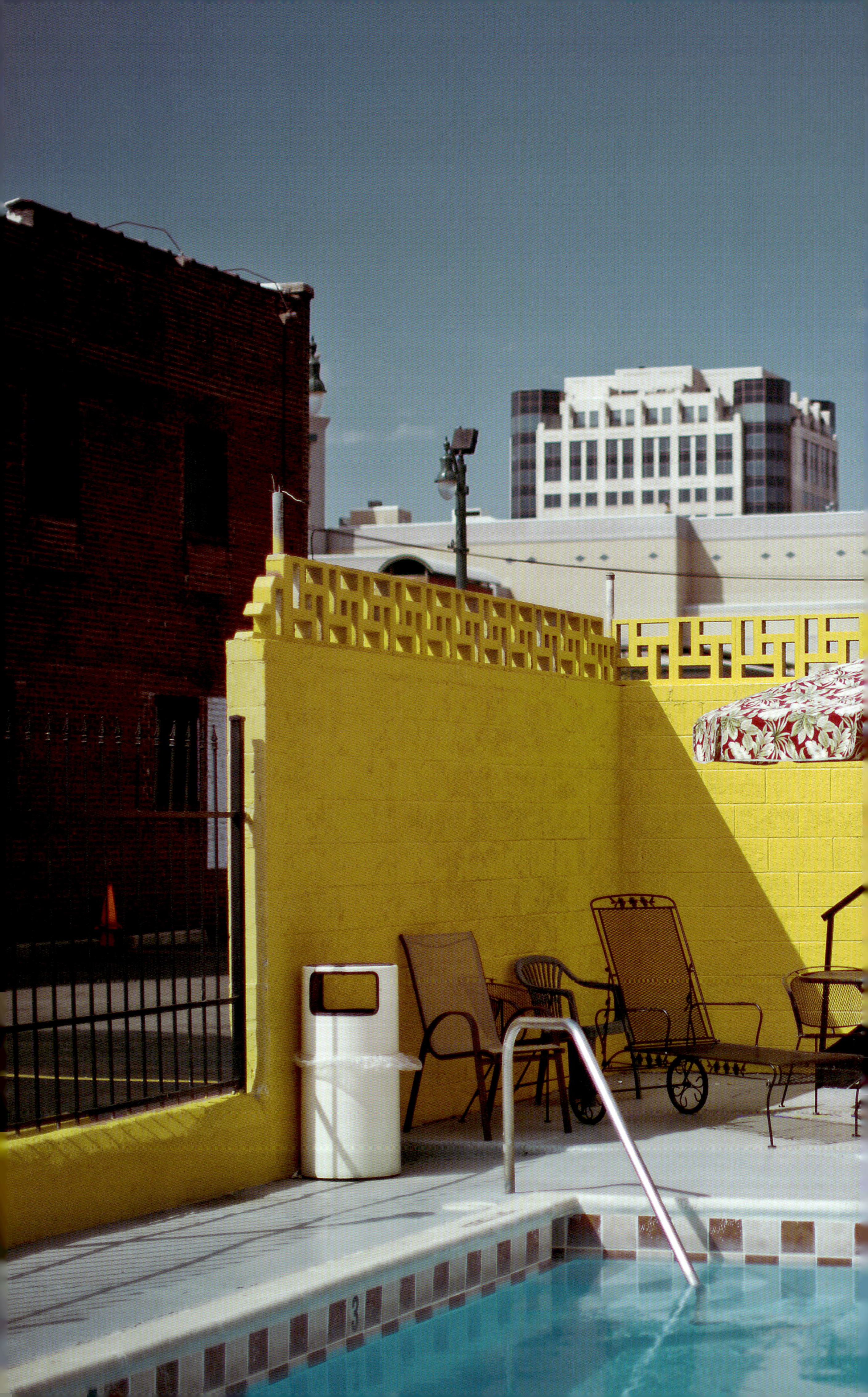
3

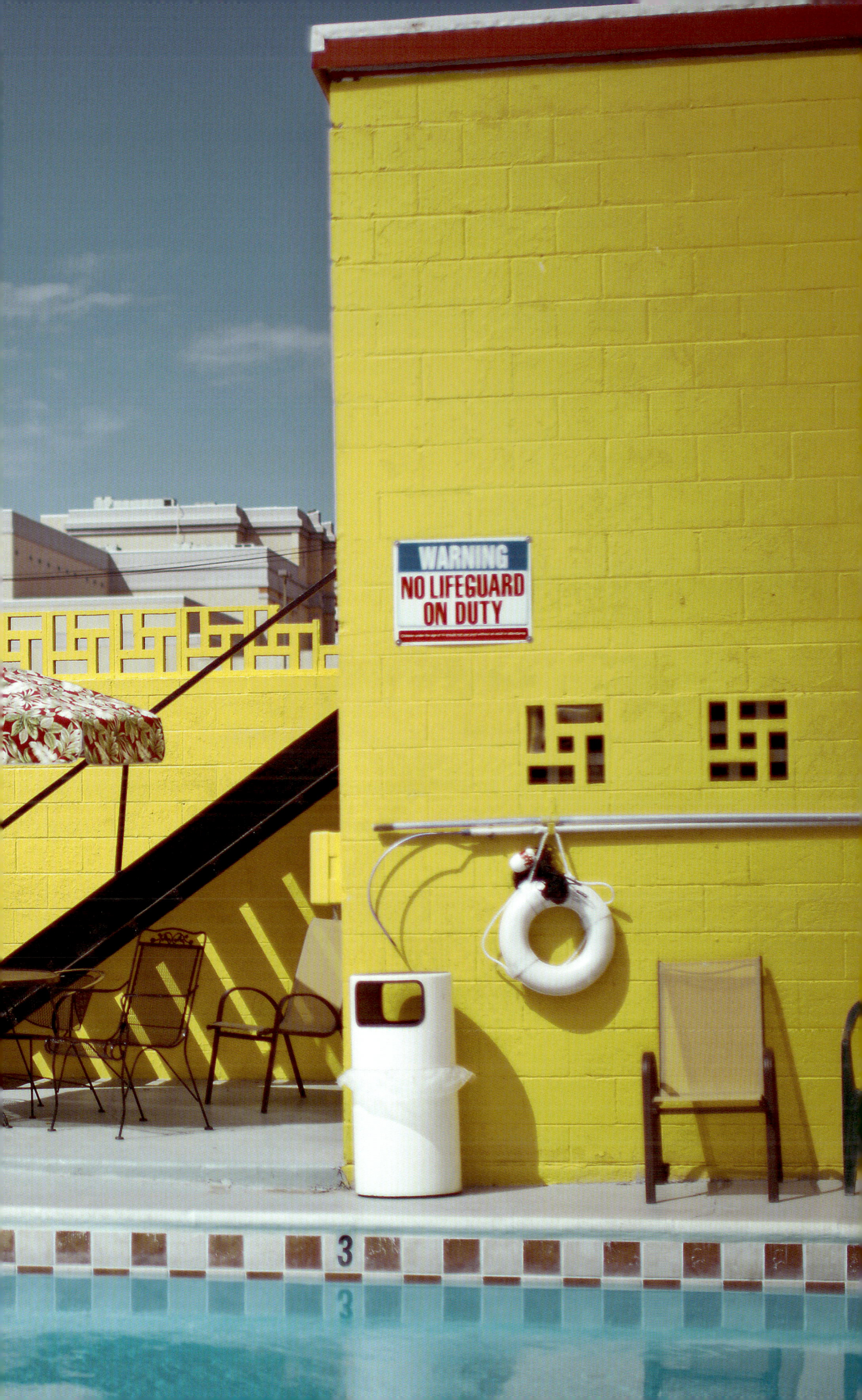
WARNING
NO LIFEGUARD
ON DUTY
3

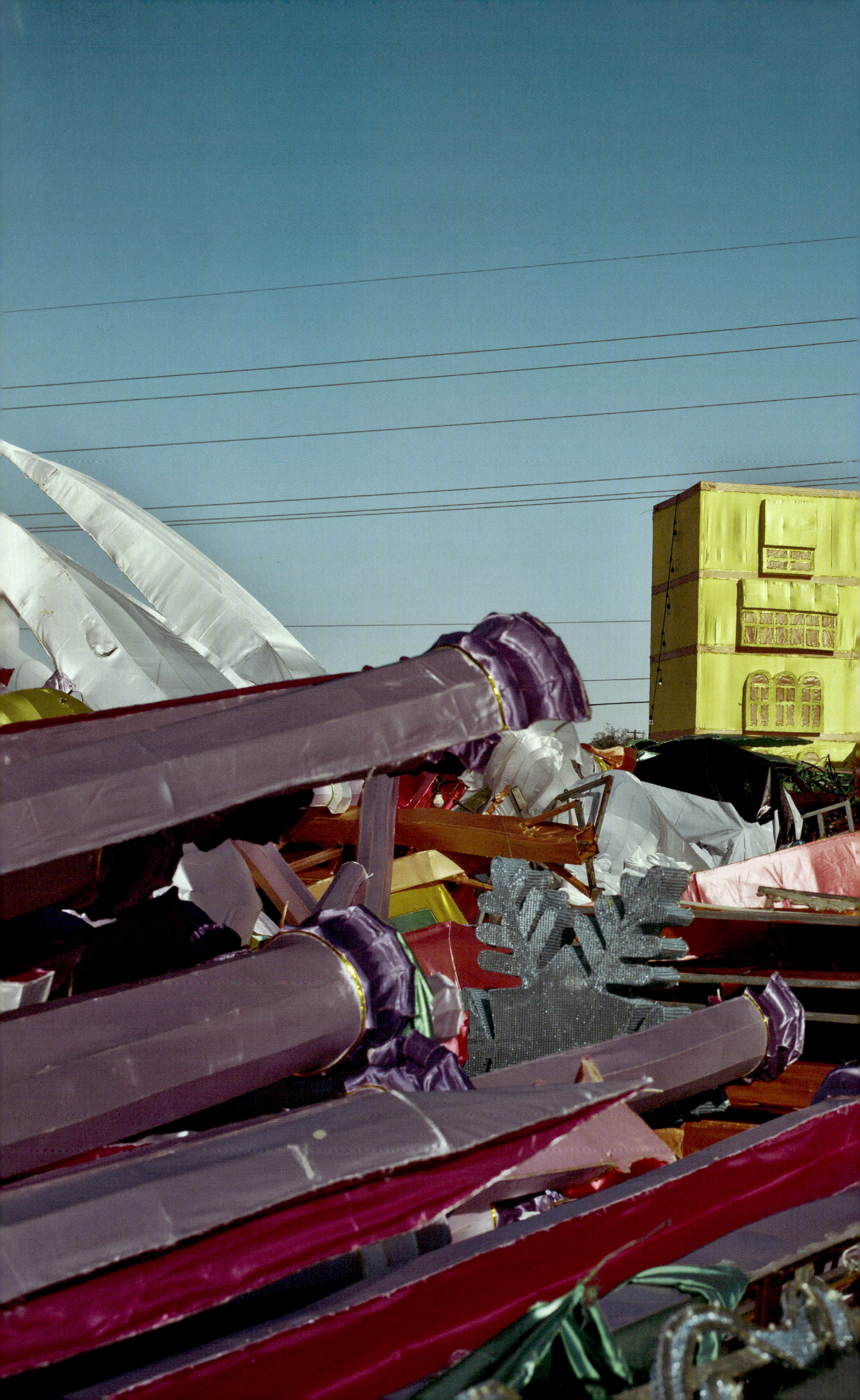

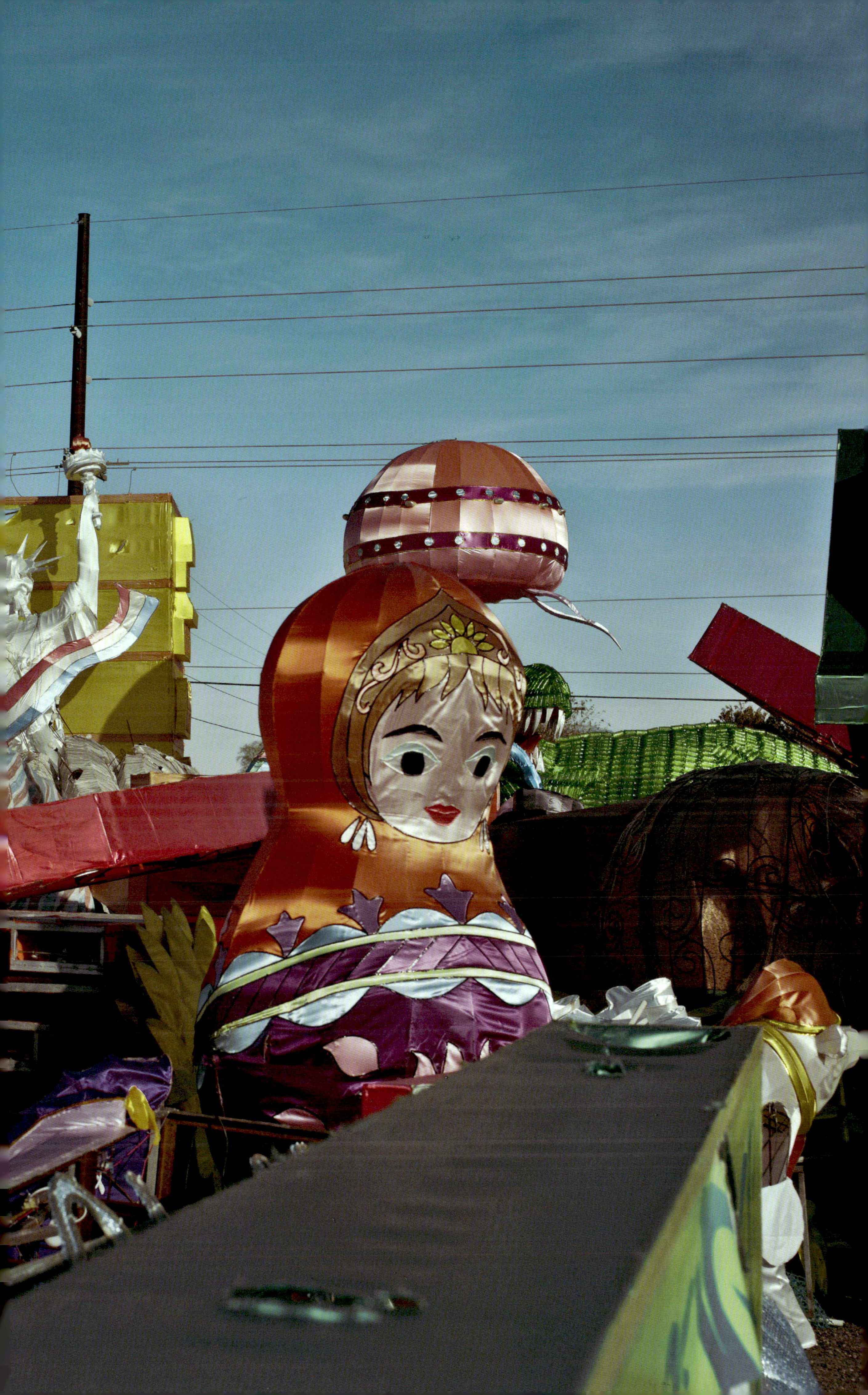

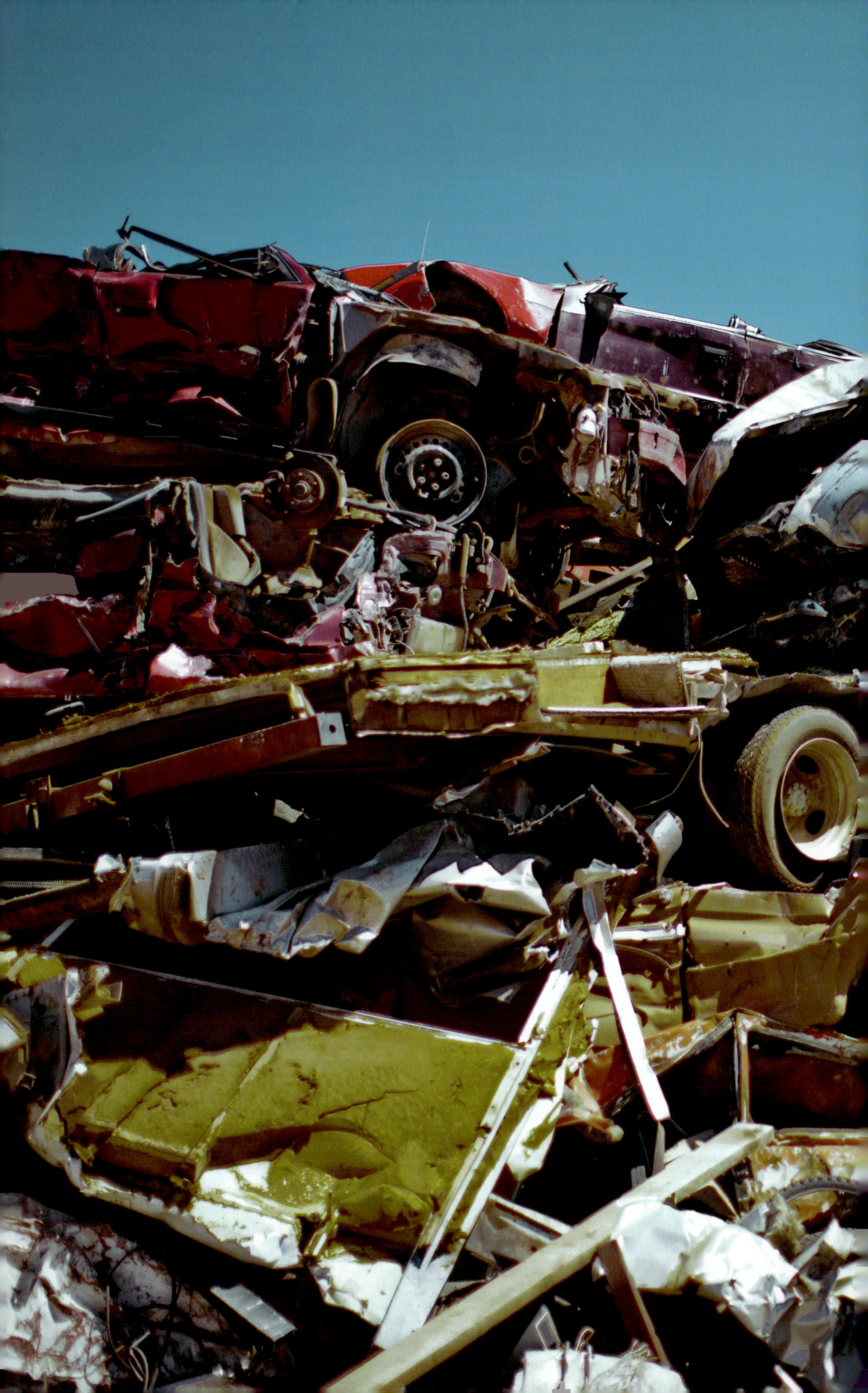

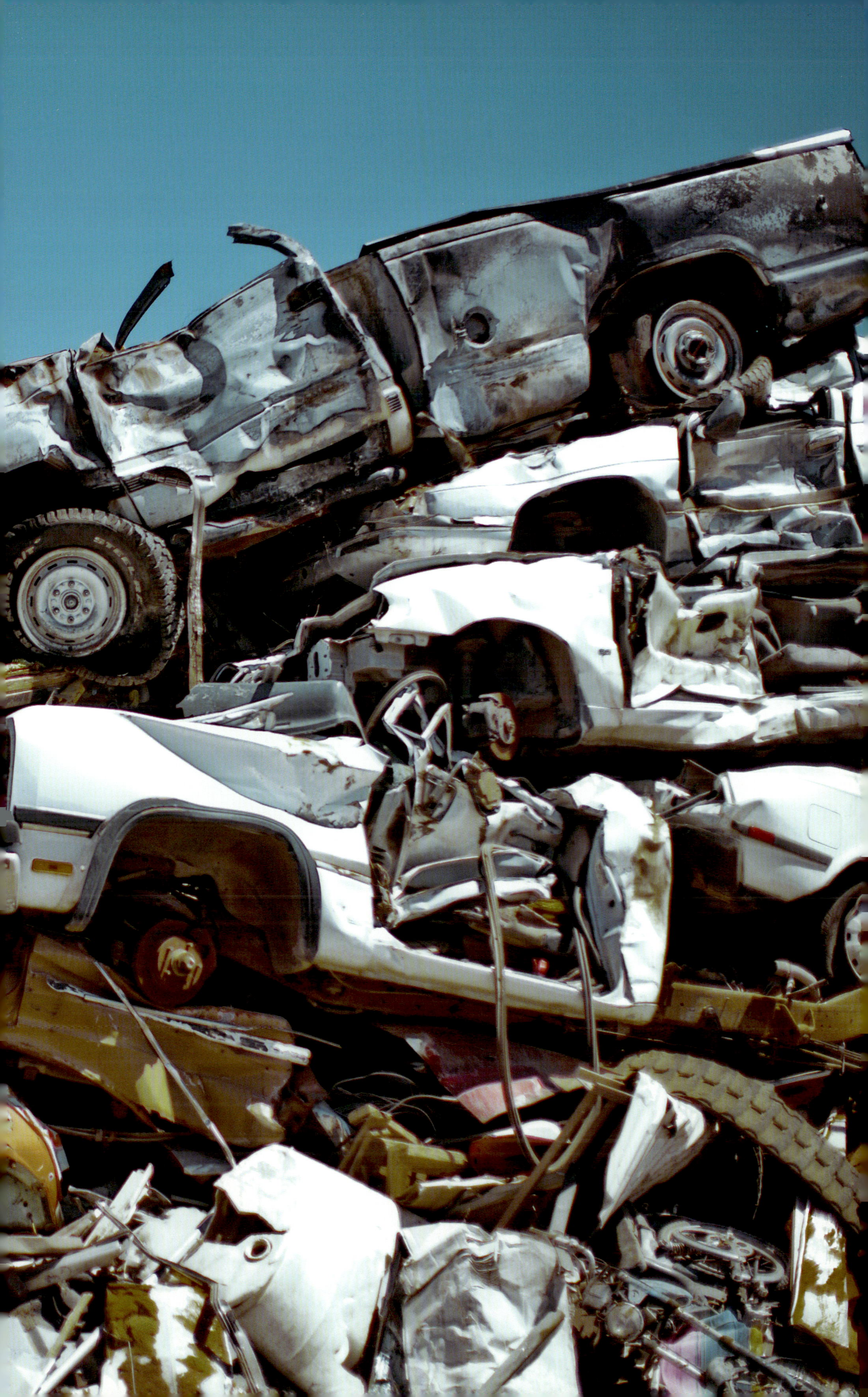

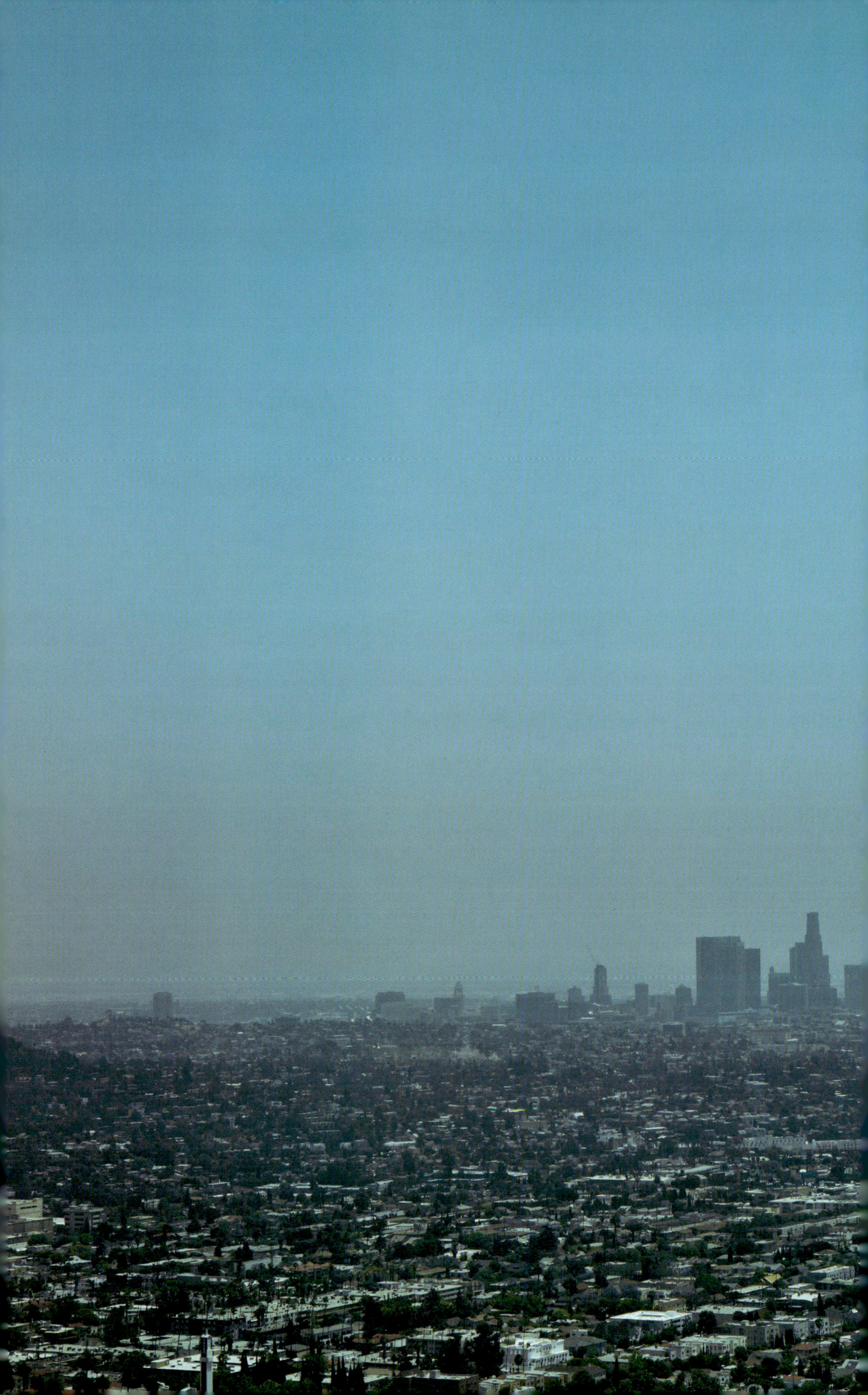

PEDRO ANZA,
JOURNEY TO THE CENTER

I

The chilly dawn wind won't let her sleep. Lying face up on the back of "The Beast", she rests her gaze on the night sky above the Sonoran Desert. Riding train cars, or in small clandestine vans, she has already traveled across thirteen states of the Mexican Republic. The sky seems endless, and gazing at the stars calls up memories of her journey through the Panamanian jungle. In the darkness as she moved away from the rest of the migrant group to relieve herself, she remembers seeing the eyes of a black jaguar: two motionless spheres staring back at her, reflecting the moonlight in the dense foliage of the jungle night. Fear had shot through her and she'd leapt to her feet. The two orbs vanished with a sound of rustling branches that faded into the depths of the jungle.

"That's good luck. The jaguar is a good omen," said an Ecuadorian migrant who was boiling river water in a rusty pot. Her name was Carmen, she came from an indigenous region of Ecuador, and she spoke broken Spanish because her mother tongue was Quechua.

Any portent of good fortune, whether the ominous presence of a wild animal watching her urinate or the friendly hand of a stranger, made her feel at peace on that deadly path full of poisonous snakes and frogs, bandits, and the fast-rising rivers that claimed so many lives. But one had to cross the Darién Gap, the mass of jungle that acts as a natural border between Colombia and Panama, in order to traverse Central America, reach Mexico, and cross the border into the United States. From 2021 to 2023 alone, more than 85,000 migrants from different countries and continents had entered the jaws of the Darién in search of that dream.

The decision to make the journey had not been an easy one. Others in her country with worse financial circumstances than hers had not subjected their fates to the trials of the arduous journey. All of her neighbors had heard close accounts of at least some tragedy: rape and murder in the Panamanian jungle by *indios* and bandits, abuse and sexual harassment by authorities in Guatemala... And worse still: in Mexico, police violence and the constant persecution of the immigration authorities were compounded by extortion and kidnappings by bands of criminals, or having their limbs severed by the angry freight trains they nicknamed "The Beast", which had to be boarded to reach the US border if they wished to avoid being sent back from the immigration checkpoints to their homelands.

And two months later, there she was, moving along gazing at the skies as she lay on the iron back of the beast. They had had to leave. Her son Johángel was about to turn seven, and she was sorrowfully contemplating a future of misfortunes for him should he stay in his place of birth.

"It's just a dream. Do you think it's worth it? Life there is hard, *chama*, it's not like people tell you, like you see in the movies, he'll have to work two or three jobs, his son will be schooled by the *gringos* and you won't even have time to see him. Not everything in life is money...

all that glitters is not gold, *chama*," her grandfather insisted, trying to persuade her to drop her idea.

Leaving everything around her – her neighborhood, home, family, environment, friends, everything she knew. Before she made the decision, the United States had merely been a comforting idea. Her sister and brother-in-law, who had gone there four months ago, insisted that they make the journey and that they were waiting for them in Denver, Colorado, where Johángel could go to the same school as his cousins.

Once she finally made up her mind and the preparations for the journey began, she felt a piercing sensation inside her, a strange vibration in her belly, a constant feeling that had accompanied her on her way through all the countries. Today, as the train chugged its way through the last kilometers to its destination, she couldn't shake it off, but instead felt its tremors more sharply.

"Was it a warning, perhaps?" she thought to herself, troubled, two days before leaving. A warning from God telling her that leaving meant losing her center?

After all, her center was there, in her homeland. It was, in fact, exactly in the yard of her house, where the midwife had persuaded her deceased mother to bury the umbilical cord of her newborn child to root the baby to her place of origin, her territory. But today, thirty-seven years later, facing chronic economic difficulties and raising a son alone in a neighborhood that grew more violent every day, she found the mere idea of staying was overwhelming. If the center had anything to do with sanity she was going to have to look for it elsewhere, because she felt that sanity was abandoning her there. She was determined: she would set off on her journey in search of a new center for herself and her son.

II

In the river where they drank water that night, on the second day their walk through the jungle and now on the Panamanian side, they saw three corpses. She saw only two, though she perceived the first one by its smell, as she heard another walker protesting as he recorded the scene on his cell phone:

"Just what we were all afraid of," bewailed the young man, "a corpse, *huevón*, a dead *hijueputa*."

Still stricken with fear, she hadn't wanted to turn around. A few hours earlier on the last stretch of the path to the point where they rested, as they were crossing a narrow, muddy trail on the edge of the river, they saw a pregnant Haitian woman lose her footing and slide down the slope into the rising water. The woman was one of a group of about four hundred migrants they had left with a day earlier from the small town of Acandí in the Colombian Chocó. The husband was out of his head and howled unrestrainedly, banging his head. According to a young Haitian who'd been walking a meter behind the deceased woman, as she fell the woman had her last few words, as if to herself alone: "God forgive me." The sight of the other two corpses was impossible to avoid. Beached in a gorge, the naked, pale, putrid bodies lay a few meters apart from each other. But there was no other water to drink than the river's. Water of the dead. Drink it or be one of them.

That night, after drinking the deathly water, a young migrant named Kevin, originally from Cauca, Colombia, shared a can of tuna and half a pack of cookies with her and Johángel. Kevin told her he was fleeing Colombia because of the violence. He'd received threats. There were seven shots in his torso and two in his left leg. Over the next two days of walking through the jungle, Kevin, who was going slowly because of his weak leg, came to her aid and carried Johángel when he cried out from exhaustion on the steeper slopes.

It was now two months later. On the roof of the train more than four thousand kilometers away, having been through so many different countries, all of that seemed like a bad dream, and in the starry Mexican sky she tried to hold on to the memory of the good omen in the jaguar's stealthy gaze, and to push away the rest of the impressions the route had sculpted so intrusively into her conscience.

Still searching the skies with her gaze, she wondered about the fate of Carmen and the rest of the group of several different nationalities that had crossed the jungle with her. She wondered if, like her, they would be on the edge of slumber, and if the road would also be sheltering them from danger somewhere in the vast desert surrounding her.

Reaching the desert hadn't been easy. For the undocumented migrant, Mexico was a tortuous journey from which few emerged without some mishap or a hint of tragedy to recount. *"Mexico lindo, tan lejos de Dios y tan cerca de Estados Unidos,"* ("Mexico, so far from God, so close to the US"). she'd heard a Mexican migrant sing on her first day on the train.

In Mexico she'd felt more disoriented than ever. Upon arrival, she cut loose from the group with whom she'd crossed the jungle and Central America. She'd last seen Carmen and her family in Tapachula, and had lost track of Kevin long before, in Honduras. Then, alone with her son, she'd continued along the five hundred kilometers separating Chiapas from Oaxaca, where she'd joined a small group of Guatemalan migrants and two young Senegalese men who'd been her companions since then. Before moving on to Huehuetoca, the town where they would board the Beast, just over 500 kilometers from there, she'd spent five days sleeping in the open area of a park in the center of the Oaxacan capital. The migrants crafted makeshift homes out of cardboard and tarps they'd scavenged, or been given by passers-by or citizens' and religious associations. She remembered the streets of downtown Oaxaca, vibrant and picturesque, with many parades and dances. A brief pause, a haven of tranquility before she continued on along the uncertain migrant path. Tourists thronged the streets, strolled by, ate in restaurants and took photographs of passers-by. While resting on a bench with Samba, one of the Senegalese men, she saw Johángel talking to an American couple. When she went up to scold her son and apologize to the tourists, the woman asked her smilingly where they were from.

"We are Venezuelans, he's African, from Senegal."

"We haven't been to Venezuela yet, but we were in Senegal and we really liked it," replied the man in gringo-accented Spanish, meanwhile handing Johángel an American coin and gently tousling his hair. She wondered if all Americans would be as pleasant as that couple when they reached the United States. She also wondered if, like her, they traveled seeking their center, feeling the constant sense of loss in their belly, running from inevitable disaster with a simultaneous suspicion of not being where they should, and not possessing the slightest certainty about the future.

Johángel put his new coin, one more for his collection, into a worn yellow plastic bag. He now had a total of seven coins, one from each country he'd visited since leaving his home in Venezuela: Colombia, Panama, Costa Rica, Nicaragua, Honduras, Guatemala, and Mexico; now the eighth, from the United States, their destination. As she watched her son count the coins, she hoped that the quarter they'd just been given would augur well for their future destiny. If there was anything she needed on this journey it was good omens, divine auspices, signs from God, or something intangible, a force to help her stand firm. Yet along her journey she'd been met with warm support by other migrants, men and women who embarked on the journey driven by the most varied reasons and circumstances, although the common denominator of the migratory impulse usually conjugated the perceived impossibility of overcoming the harsh socioeconomic conditions to which the place of origin seemed to condemn them, and the irreconcilable violence of their marginal Latin American home environments, rural or urban. Few in this odyssey were traveling; almost all were escaping.

III

The metal skin of *La Bestia* feels like ice on her back. The machine makes a lot of noise but is soon to reach the United States, and that comforts her. Next to her, crossing through that vast desert horizon which makes her feel so tiny, lies a Honduran man no more than forty years old whom they'd met in Nayarit before boarding the train they were now traveling on. The man had just come out of a kidnapping, and two purple lines still framed his eyes. He'd been tied up hand and foot, with his eyes blindfolded, in a small room with other migrants until his family in Tegucigalpa could gather the 2,000 dollars that were being demanded for his life.

She'd been lucky, at least compared to other migrants she'd met on her journey through Mexico. In the more than 3,000 kilometers since she'd crossed the Suchiate River, on the border between Guatemala and Mexico, the only setbacks she'd encountered had been two thefts. The first one on a stretch of road approaching Arriaga, Chiapas; the second in Juchitán, Oaxaca. In Arriaga, two police patrols had stopped the combi she was traveling in, forcing her, her son, and the rest of the undocumented migrants to get off. They demanded 500 pesos from each of them, children and adults, to to continue their journey north, albeit on foot. Reluctantly, the officers accepted the 750 pesos she offered for herself and Johángel; she had no more. Later in Juchitán, other uniformed men – they never knew whether these were policemen or bandits – used the same procedure. Again, the alleged policemen had to settle for less than they desired; they'd just been stripped of all their money and their pockets were empty. But one of the migrants, a Venezuelan, had a relatively recent cell phone model in good condition. That, along with 800 pesos gathered by the rest, cheered up the masked men with guns, who allowed the group to continue onward.

"I'd rather cross that *hijueputa* jungle a thousand times than than go through Mexico again," complained the young man who'd handed over his phone as they walked along the road. The same statement, expressed in many ways, summarized the general feeling of migrants passing through Mexico. A sudden movement returns her to the immensity of the desert landscape. The train slows down, it seems to be stopping. The sky begins to lighten. There are no more stars in the sky, just a very white cloud drowsing in stillness high in the sky. She closes her eyes. The wind is still cold. God willing, they're coming into Caborca, the train's last stop. There, with the rest of the travelers, she will cross to Altar, a town with 8,000 inhabitants, where the coyotes await them to cross the Sásabe Desert.

IV

The desert, paradoxically, strongly resembled the jungle. It was a giant and indecipherable landscape where you had to beware of both venomous snakes and armed men who roamed its makeshift paths waiting to find a wanderer to steal whatever few belongings he might still have. It had been at least five hours since they got off the van which had transported them from Altar, Sonora, to some remote place in the desert, a point lost in the middle of a night so dark that it made any object a slight distance away impenetrable to the sight. They were forbidden from turning on their cell phone lights. Only the *coyotes* had flashlights, and their instructions were clear: keep walking, keep your mouth shut, and be alert to any of their indications. They had to pay close attention to the sound of footsteps to avoid tripping over the other walkers. There were a total of thirty migrants. Three men led them, all three carrying a gun at their waists and a second, unholstered one. Further ahead, two others led the way by turning their lights on and off, sending silent signals to the rear. Water was scarce; they had to conserve the few liters they'd dared to carry, not knowing how long they'd still be walking. The coyotes didn't give any information; they had only warned them, before getting on the van, that anyone who fell behind the group could pretty much consider themselves dead; the best thing that could happen if so was to be found by the US border patrol, arrested and deported. But such a fortune did not usually embrace any stragglers.

"If the pumas don't eat them, they get bitten by vipers and then eaten by the coyotes. And if not that, then the rancher gringos shoot them or the thugs on this side find them and take them. But no one gets out of this desert alive."

The first time she saw the *coyotes*, in the safe house in Altar where they'd been locked up all day waiting for the evening to fall before they boarded the van that would carry them into the desert, she felt very scared. Along the route she'd been hearing stories about clandestine graves in the desert, and the betrayals of the coyotes who, once they'd got their hands on the undocumented migrants' money, would leave them to their fate or hand them over to the criminal gangs in the area, who would demand money for their rescue. But her sister and brother-in-law, who had crossed that inhospitable desert themselves, had assured her that she could trust the coyotes, and that eased her fears a bit. The sinking feeling in her belly had increased, but she was close to crossing the border, and close, too, she hoped, to finding her center. She decided to trust. For a moment she felt as if no-one had ever set foot on that land, and the immensity of the space made her feel tiny again, as small as the grains of sand the wind lifted from the still-warm ground and blasted into her face. The lights of the two coyotes walking ahead are two glowing spheres in the darkness; they remind her of the eyes of the jaguar in the Panamanian jungle. Johángel is clutching onto her hand. The group stops abruptly. The flashlights go out. For an endless minute, everyone is still and silent. Voices can be heard in the distance. She thinks the worst, that the voices belong to a rival group disputing the desert with the coyotes or that they belong to border patrol agents who are surrounding them and about to arrest them. Cupping his mouth with both hands, one of the coyotes mimics the sound of a bird. Five lights flicker on and off in the distance.

"They're ours," murmurs the coyote, who turns his flashlight straight back on and resumes the group's march. "Everyone nice and quiet, please, and only me nervous," says the man with renewed spirits, pointing to a spot on the nearby horizon, "That over there is the US."

The above narrative, featuring a Venezuelan migrant woman traveling north through the continent on a train with her son, is based on testimonies from migrants at various points along the migrant route between northern Colombia and northern Mexico. The sighting of the jaguar in the Panamanian jungle, the pregnant Haitian woman who falls and dies in the river, the Honduran man recently released from kidnapping aboard the train, etc., are based on direct, individual migrant testimonies; although such situations and many other similar experiences are recurrent and normal on the Latin American migrant journey.

AUTHOR'S NOTES

[1] For the past 30 years the Mexican border town of Ciudad Juárez, in the Mexican state of Chihuahua, has been marked by the tragic phenomenon of women and girls dying or disappearing. This grim story began three decades ago when the bodies of two girls were discovered in the city, initiating a horrifying series of more than 2,300 murders of women to date.

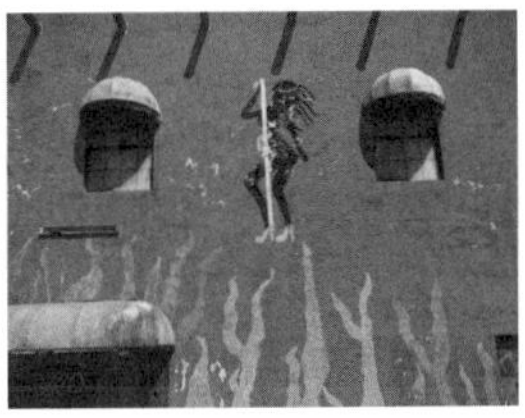

[2] Detail of a migrant's bed at the Casa del Migrante in Caborca, a shelter founded in 2015 which has assisted over 8,400 undocumented individuals heading to the United States. During interviews, migrants refrained from divulging details about their border-crossing plans, citing the need for a low profile. Caborca experiences ongoing cartel conflicts for control of the human and drug trafficking businesses, and has the highest homicide rates in the state of Sonora.

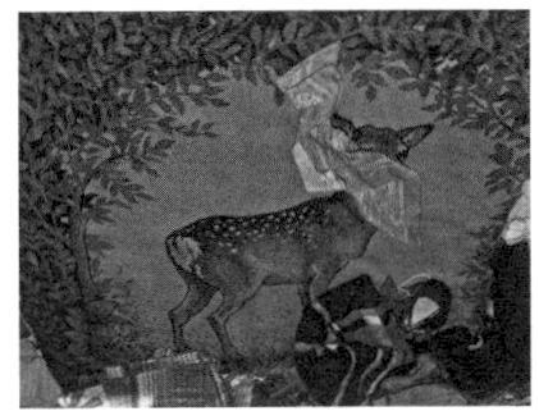

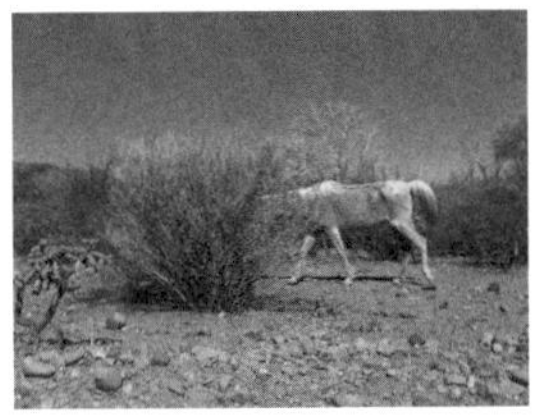

[3] The distance between Tapachula, near the southern border with Guatemala, and Caborca, a common crossing point in the state of Sonora, is 2,077 miles (3,325 km). Walking this distance would take around 750 hours. Depending on a migrant's budget, the journey can last days, weeks, or even months. In the picture, a wild horse wanders in the desert-like landscapes of the state of Sonora.

[4] The Caverns of Cacahuamilpa in the Mexican state of Guerrero are among the world's largest cave systems. This "live" cave system continues to receive groundwater, contributing to ongoing formation growth. The system contains 90 large "salons", only around 20 of which have yet been fully explored.

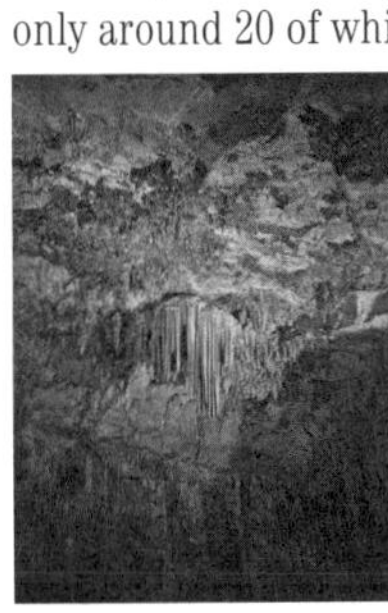

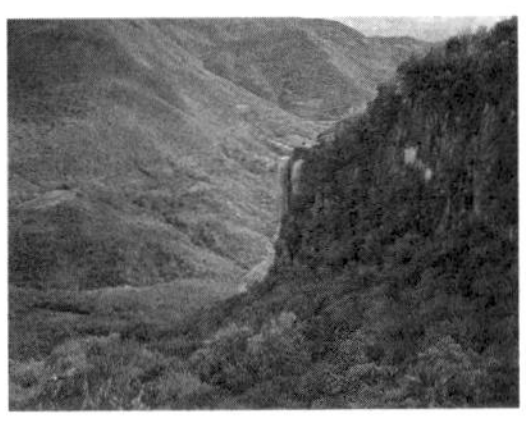

[5] Hierve el Agua is a rock formation and mineral water spring in the mountains of Oaxaca, now a tourist attraction but around 2,500 years ago a sacred site for the Zapotecs. In 1990 two artificial pools were constructed to enhance the appeal of this confirmed archaeological site, known for one of the world's oldest irrigation systems. Ongoing conflicts among local communities persist over the right to exploit this attraction in one of Mexico's poorest areas.

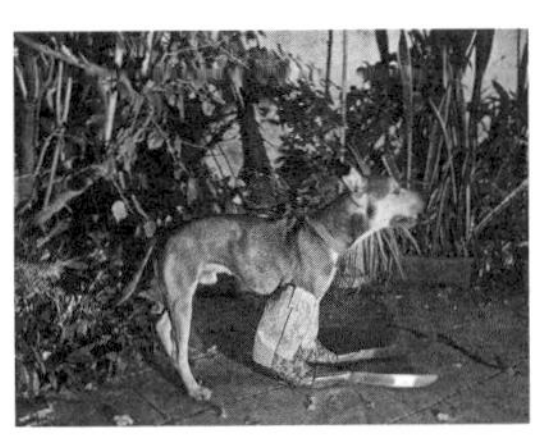

[6] The drug war in Mexico is characterized by intense cartel conflicts, and significantly impacts the nation's economy and society. But despite rising crime rates and escalating violence, the tourism industry in Mexico is flourishing, having increased by 11% in the past year. The two industries, tourism and organized crime, have a comparable business size, each generating an estimated $30 billion annually. The picture features a dog wearing machete-point cowboy boots created by the artist Bárbara Sánchez-Kane.

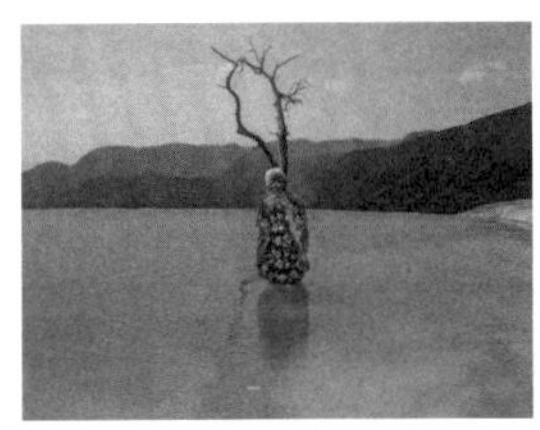

[7] The second time I went to Hierve el Agua I found the place empty with just a couple waiting by one of the pools. The woman started walking into the water and I ran to take a picture, but my camera would just not work. After trying everything I could to fix it, I had to give up and decided to sit next to the man to know more about them. The man told me they were borhers and that the place was sacred. He asked me if I wanted to take pictures and I replied that my camera was not working. He then told me to try again, that after our talk, it would work. And it did.

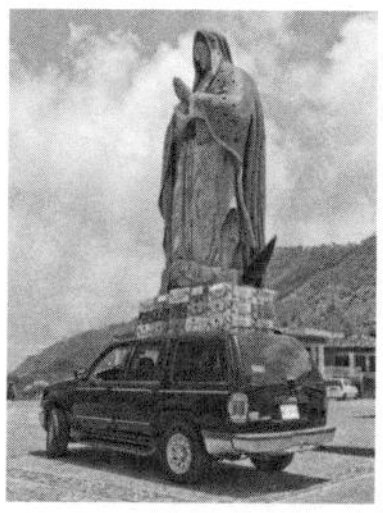

[8] The village of Xicotepec, Puebla, is home to one of the tallest statues of the Virgin of Guadalupe, the patron saint of Mexico.

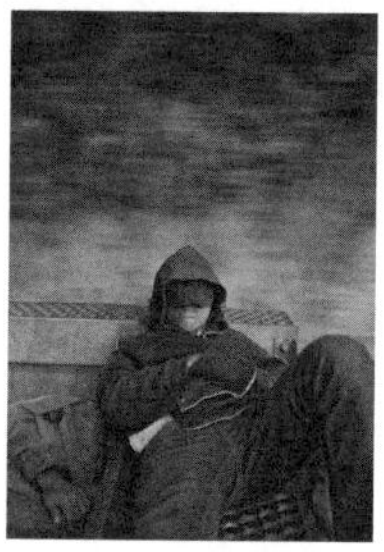

[9] Each year an estimated 400,000 to 500,000 migrants, mainly from El Salvador, Guatemala and Honduras, ride atop Mexican freight trains to reach the United States. This network of trains is known as La Bestia (the Beast), named for the dangers inherent in the journey. In the picture, migrants reach the end of the train journey in Caborca, Sonora, from where the remaining distance to the border will be covered on foot across the desert.

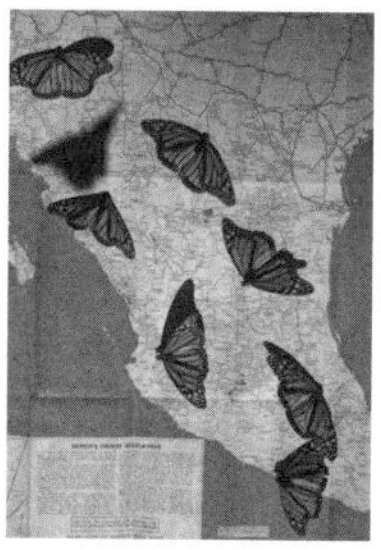

[10] Each year many millions of monarch butterflies migrate from the central and eastern Canadian provinces and the eastern and midwestern United States to the mountains of the Transvolcanic Belt in central Mexico. The offspring of those that overwinter in Mexico are known as first-generation monarchs. Each successive generation travels farther north, reaching the northern United States and Canada in three or four generations.

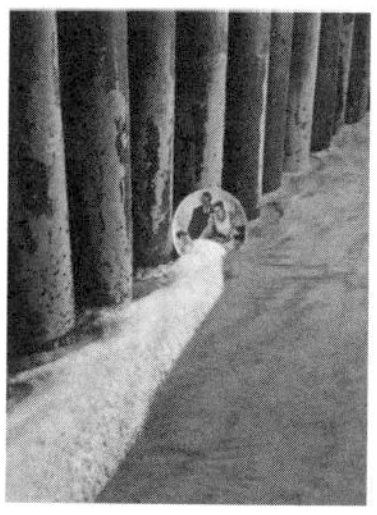

[11] The Trump administration's "Zero Tolerance" policy, introduced in April 2018, mandated criminal prosecution for adults entering the US unlawfully, and resulted in the separation of families, since children could not be held in criminal detention facilities. The policy faced criticism, leading to an executive order in June 2018 to halt family separations by detaining families together. In the picture a plate with a Thanksgiving scene painted by Norman Rockwell is placed beside the border fence at Tijuana Beach, in Baja California.

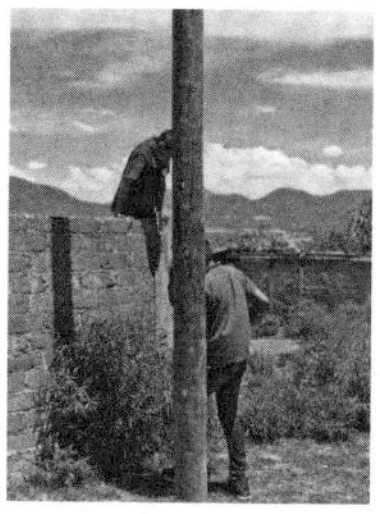

[12] Since 1993, the US Border Patrol's budget has surged more than tenfold, from $363 million to nearly $4.9 billion. The number of Border Patrol agents has tripled, with 85% being assigned to control of the border with Mexico.

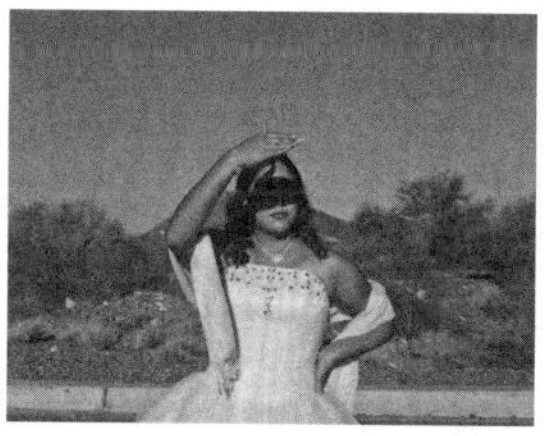

[13] In Mexican culture, a quinceañera is a celebration of a girl's 15th birthday, marking the transition from childhood to womanhood. Families typically spend an average of $20,000 and prepare for the celebration for years. For this image, I followed Flor during her official photo session with a local photographer in Caborca, one of the most violent towns in the state of Sonora. In December of the same year, a group of gunmen stormed another quinceañera celebration in the same area, shooting six people dead and leaving 14 more injured. The motivations behind this incident remain unknown at the current time.

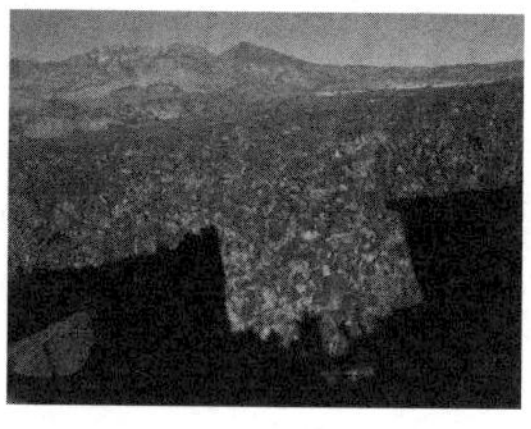

[14] We rode La Bestia with a group of migrants from Honduras, traveling from Guadalajara, Jalisco, to Tepic, Nayarit. We boarded the train early in the morning and disembarked late that evening, while the migrants continued their journey to the North and the United States. The ride was exhausting, but the landscape beautiful. We encountered some hostility as we passed through a village where locals threw stones at the train, but there were no major problems. However, the group we traveled with was assaulted when the train arrived in Sinaloa the next day.

[15] A detail of several layers of walls and fences at Yuma, Arizona, just a few miles from the official Center of the World in Felicity, California.

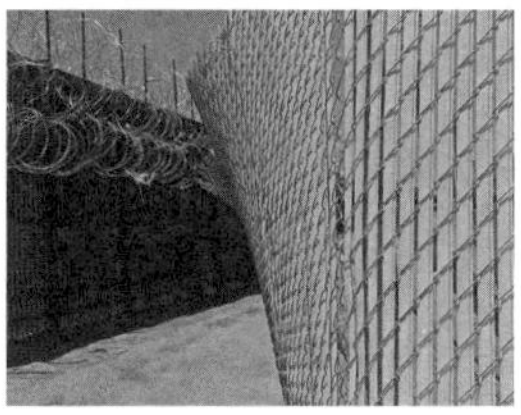

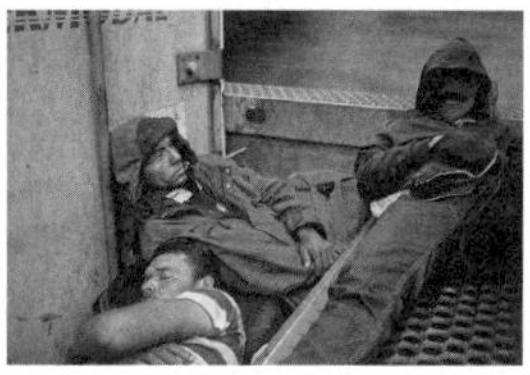

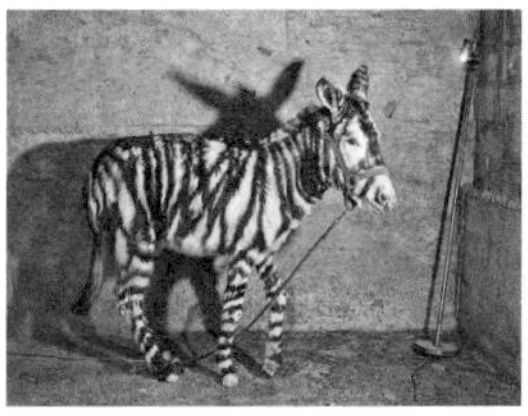

[16] Zonkeys in Tijuana, Mexico, are donkeys painted with fake zebra stripes so that tourists will pay the owner to appear in souvenir photos with them. Tijuana is both a touristic destination for North Americans and the limbo in which thousands of migrants are held, waiting for their asylum papers to be processed. It is also one of the most surveilled crossing points along the border and the place where the Trump administration tested new prototypes for the wall.

[17] The journey across Mexico on La Bestia can last several weeks. When we joined a group of Honduran migrants on the train, the operator, aware of Western press presence, changed his approach, offering advice on safe places to stand instead of the usual threats and forced removals. The migrants we traveled with on La Bestia all hailed from the same small town in the south of Honduras. They were fleeing threats from local gangs and seeking opportunities to support their families. However, their intention was not to settle in the US permanently – rather, they planned to work there for a few years, send money to their families, and return to Honduras after gaining a more comfortable and secure position.

[18] In May 2021, I joined a group of migrants preparing to cross the border near Altar, through the Sonora desert. The group consisted of 30 people, mostly men in their 20s, originating from Guatemala. I hopped on the van taking them to the starting point for their night-time walk.

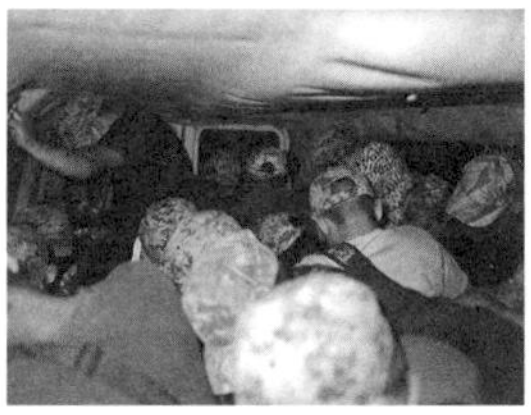

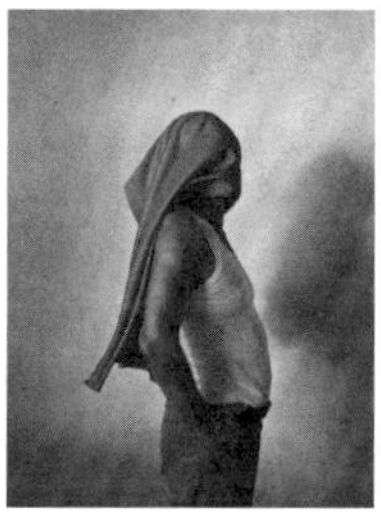

[19] The price for crossing to the US from Tapachula, Chiapas, with a people smuggler (colloquially known as a coyote) can depend on what you look like. Africans and Asians need to pay more, because migration officials require a higher bribe to overlook the traveler at the checkpoints, since they cannot pretend they are locals. This is what Marcos, an experienced coyote, shared with us, together with a comprehensive list of the checkpoints and the amounts payable to progress in the journey to the North. He said he could organize trips by plane to get to Tijuana in a few hours for $15,000, and also cheaper options traveling by road and foot for several weeks for as little as $2,500.

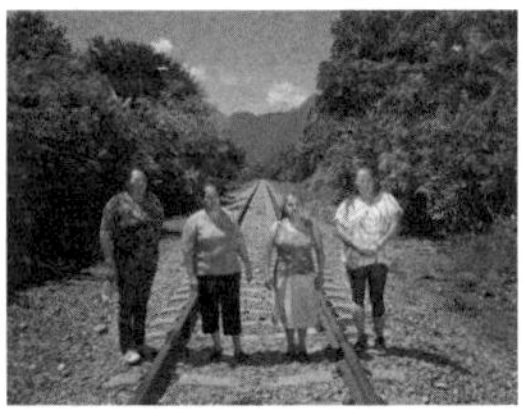

[20] Las Patronas is a group of women volunteers from Amatlán de los Reyes, Veracruz. Since 1995 they have been distributing food and water to migrants traveling on La Bestia. Led by Norma Romero, the group operates as an independent NGO, and its headquarters are sited directly alongside the railway.

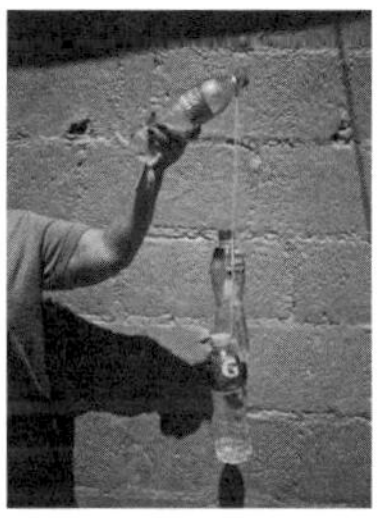

[21] To minimize the risk of accidents, Las Patronas volunteers have developed a system that makes it easier for travelers to catch hold of the food and the water from the moving train without falling off it.

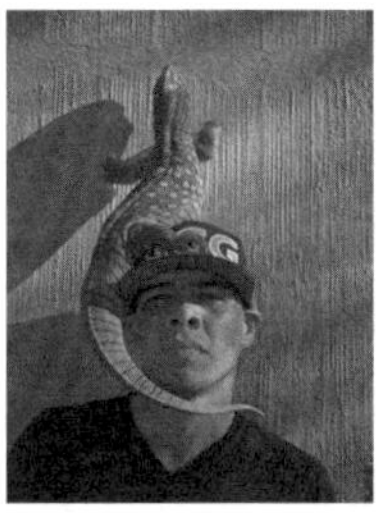

[22] As a contemporary interpretation of "Our Lady of the Iguanas" by Mexican photographer Graciela Iturbide, I've reimagined that iconic image to highlight the fascination that drug cartels have for exotic animals. The image was photographed in Hermosillo, Sonora, featuring a tegu lizard and a model whose identity I cannot disclose.

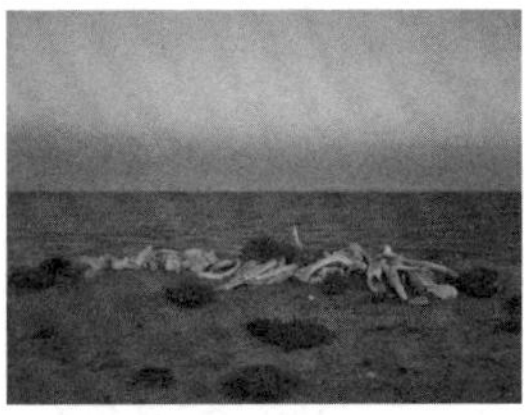

[23] The Pacific gray whale's migration route is often cited as the lengthiest known mammal migration in the animal kingdom. Commencing in the Bering and Chukchi Sea and concluding in the warm-water lagoons of Mexico's Baja Peninsula, this round-trip journey spans 12,500 miles of coastline. The image was shot in Baja California, a protected area where the whales come to breed and nurture their calves.

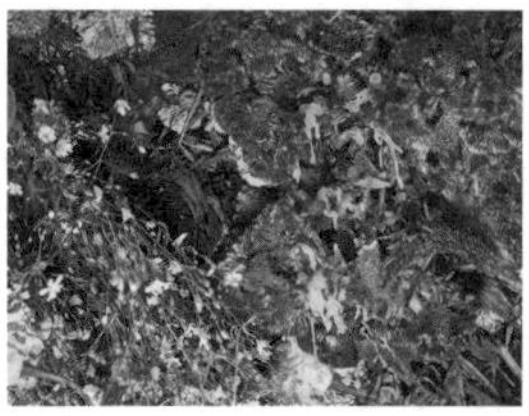

[24] Flowers at a cemetery during the Día de Muertos celebration in Michoacán.

[25] Poppy cultivation associated with the production of opium and heroin has been a significant issue in Guerrero, Mexico, particularly in the mountainous and remote regions of the state. Gaining permission and access to photograph a poppy field in this area was a challenging process, taking more than three years due to the growing wave of violence in the region, which led to several trip cancellations.

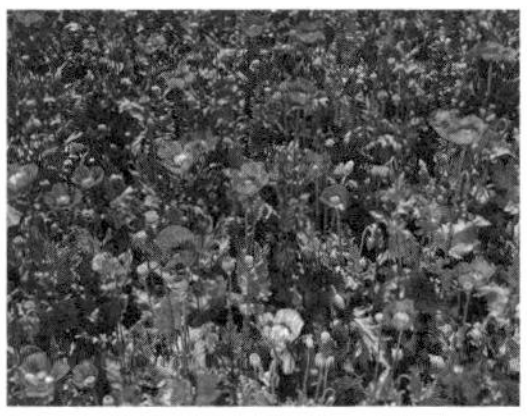

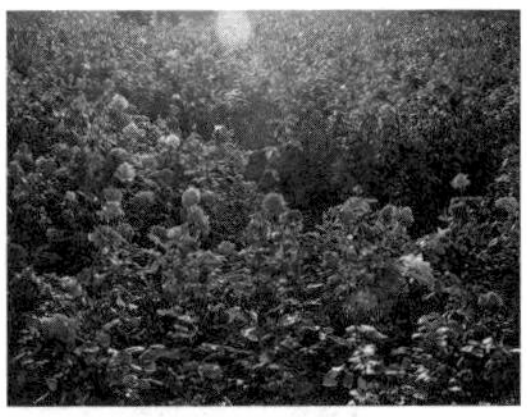

[26] Rose fields in Atlixco near the Popocatépetl volcano in the state of Puebla.

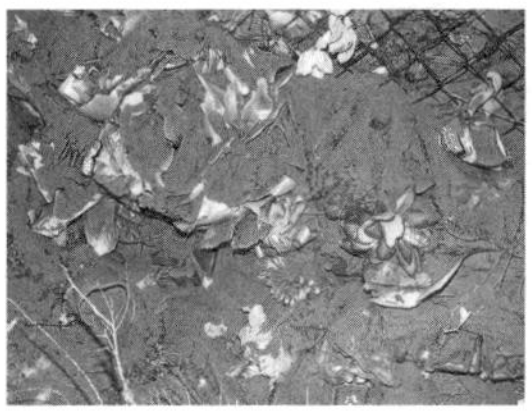

[27] Plastic flowers used to decorate tombstones pile up in the sand at a cemetery in Ciudad Juárez.

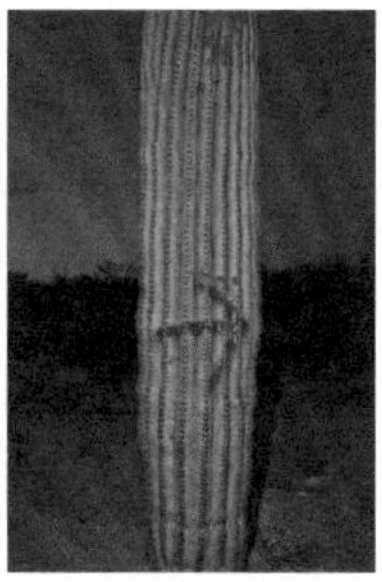

[28] "Prevention Through Deterrence" is a strategy introduced by the US Federal Government in the mid-1990s, which relies on the rugged terrain to impede the flow of people from the South. The strategy aimed to raise the risk of apprehension along traditional entry and smuggling routes by increasing the numbers of Border Patrol agents and the use of technology, thereby forcing illegal traffic over more challenging terrain. In the photo, an arrow is painted on a cactus at a crossing area near Altar, Sonora.

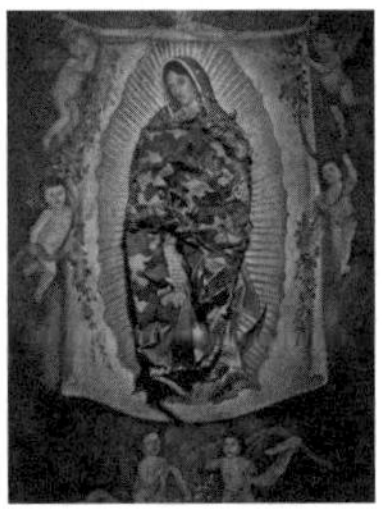

[29] When crossing the desert, migrants are asked to cover their shoes with camouflage slippers that have a furry sole, to avoid leaving traces behind them that would allow the route to be identified by the Border Patrol. The convoys often include a trace broomer, a person at the back of the line who erases the footsteps of the rest of the group. The camouflage slippers can be purchased in the makeshift supermarkets of Altar, one of the last towns in the state of Sonora before the desert border. For the picture, I used one of these slippers to camouflage the cloak of Mexico's patron saint, the Virgin of Guadalupe.

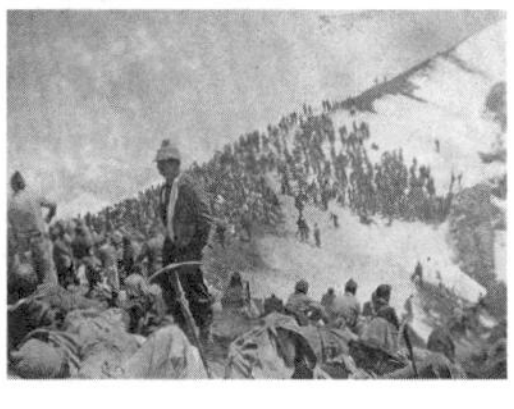

[30] I bought the album from which this image comes at the thrift market of La Lagunilla, in Mexico City. It is a compilation of photographs from various different ascents undertaken by the Alpinis Club of UNAM, the state university of Mexico City.

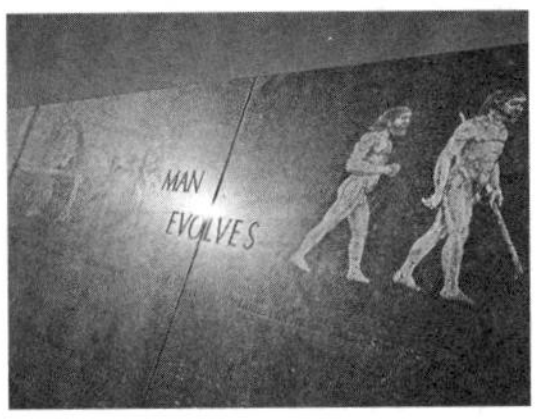

[31] Human migration has a very long history, with Homo erectus believed to have initiated early migrations out of Africa around 1.8 million years ago. This was followed around 60,000 to 70,000 years ago by significant migrations of anatomically modern humans, leading eventually to the global dispersal of human populations. The image shows a detail of a panel at the History of Humanity in Granite Museum in Felicity, California.

[32] According to official statistics, half of Mexican policemen accept bribes, but Salvador is an exception. He claims he never succumbed to that temptation during his 25 years of service in Hermosillo, Sonora. Now retired, he manages an NGO that provides alternatives to teenagers through martial arts lessons, keeping them off the streets.

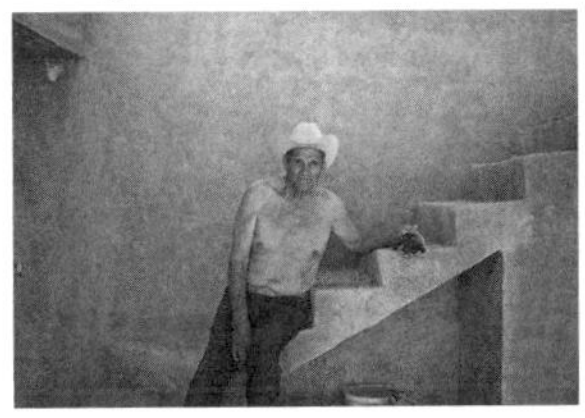

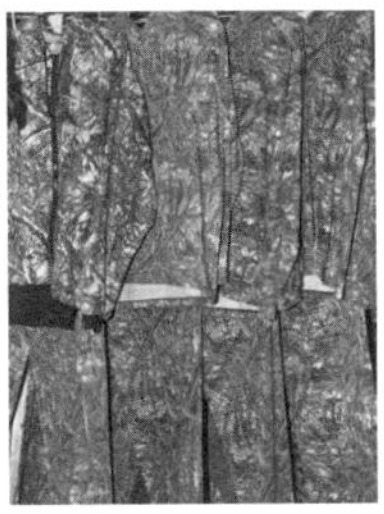

[33] Next to the church in Altar, shops offer a range of essentials for desert-crossers: camo clothes, backpacks, black water gallons, first aid kits, combs, mirrors, card decks, balaclavas, and of course, painkillers. However, these goods are of very poor quality, making the already challenging desert trek even tougher for those who have no choice but to buy them at the shops' hugely inflated prices, with basic kits often going for $200.

[34] The lowest rank in a cartel, known as gatillero, is typically filled by young recruits from the streets seeking structure and stability. Their loyalty, sense of brotherhood and willingness to follow orders can propel them through the ranks within the organization. In the picture, a gatillero in Hermosillo, controlled by the Caborca Cartel.

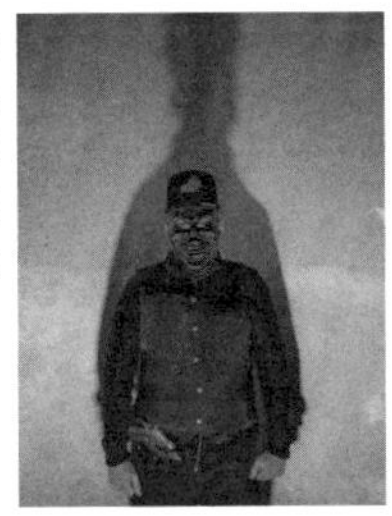

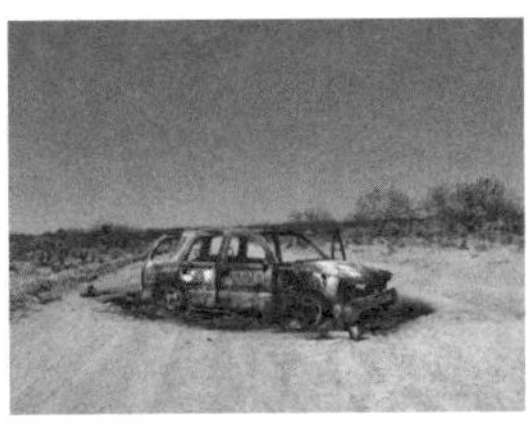

[35] The dirt road from Altar to the crossing points in the desert is controlled by the cartels, who see human trafficking as a lucrative business model that they can combine with drug trafficking. Migrants, called pollos by the coyotes, are offered a reduction in the price they pay for being smuggled into the US if they agree to carry and deliver a bale.

[36] Gregory Hess runs the Pima County Medical Examiner in Tucson, Arizona. Since a group of fourteen corpses were discovered in the Sonora desert in May 2002, the department has been investigating migrant deaths. In thirty years, it has recorded 3,356 deaths as "Unidentified Border Crossers", with approximately 64% subsequently identified.

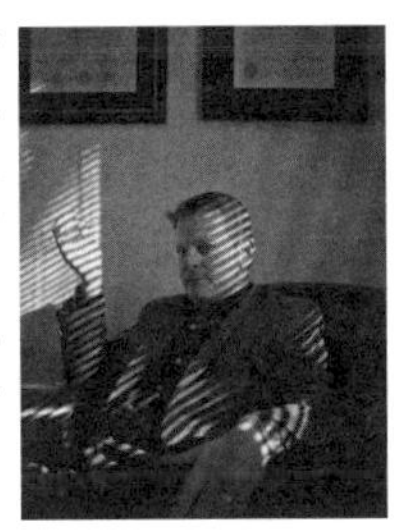

[37] The Titan missile sites near Tucson, Arizona, were part of the US Cold War strategy for nuclear deterrence, active from 1963 to the 1980s. With over 50 platforms, they aimed to showcase military strength and discourage potential adversaries, particularly the Soviet Union, from initiating nuclear conflict, contributing to the policy of mutually assured destruction.

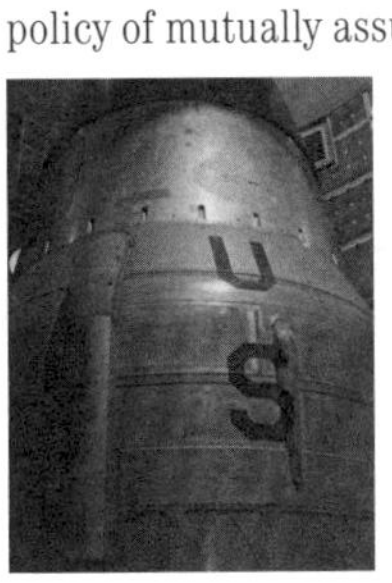

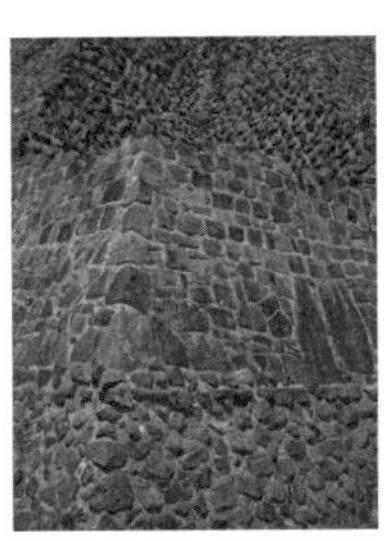

[38] Detail of the ruins of Monte Albán in Oaxaca, a remarkable example of wall construction by the Zapotecs over 2,500 years ago. The archaeological site, strategically situated at the top of a mountain for defensive purposes, features 170 tombs and underground galleries.

[39] The count of border wall miles constructed during Trump's presidency varies based on the method used. According to US Customs and Border Protection data, one tally puts it at 458 miles. However, the majority of these additions involved replacing smaller, deteriorated barriers, making minimal impact on the overall mileage. The "Trump Wall" is estimated to have cost $33 million per mile built. This picture was shot near the Nogales border point in Arizona.

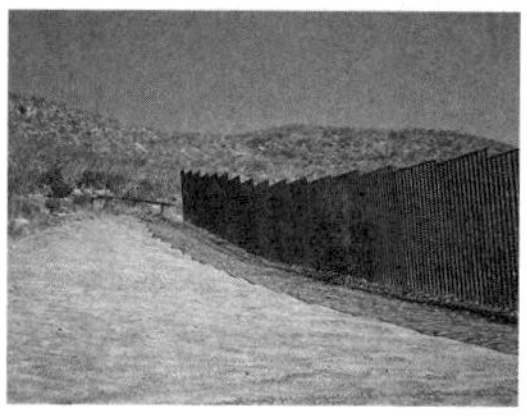

[40] Detail of the Basaltic Prisms of Santa María Regla in the state of Hidalgo. This unique geological formation consists of tall columns of basalt rock which have been shaped by centuries of volcanic activity and erosion, and was first documented geologically and graphically by the explorer Alexander von Humboldt in 1803.

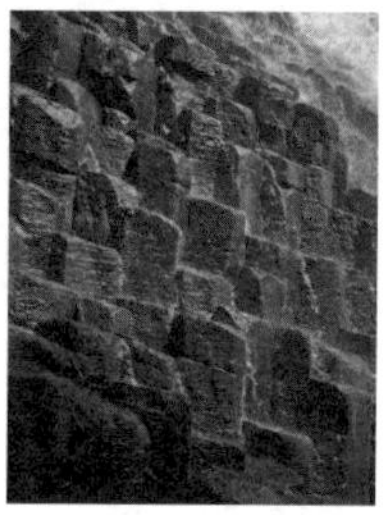

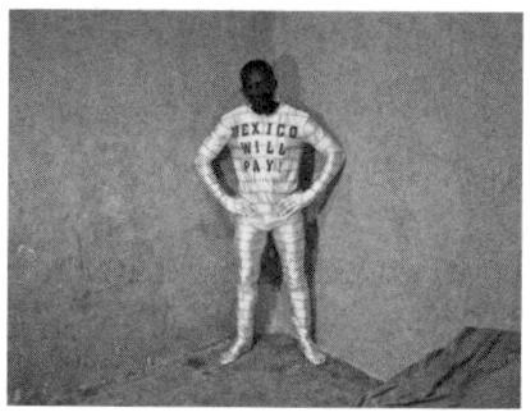

[42] One of Donald Trump's 2015 campaign slogans, along with "Make America Great Again", was "Mexico Will Pay", indicating his intention that Mexico would fund the building of a wall along the US–Mexico border. By 2020 a portion of the wall had been constructed, but Mexico had not borne the cost, and the flux of people traveling to the North was stopped only by the global pandemic. In that year I encountered migrants blocked by COVID restrictions in Tapachula, at the southern border of Mexico with Guatemala.

[41] "Zero Tolerance" and "Remain in Mexico" were the titles of two policies initiated by the Trump administration to address the increasing number of migrants arriving at the border. These policies were accompanied by an aggressive rhetoric that polarized public opinion, turning a humanitarian crisis into a political campaign. In the picture, a migrant preparing to cross that night from Tijuana wears a jumper printed with the face of Donald Trump.

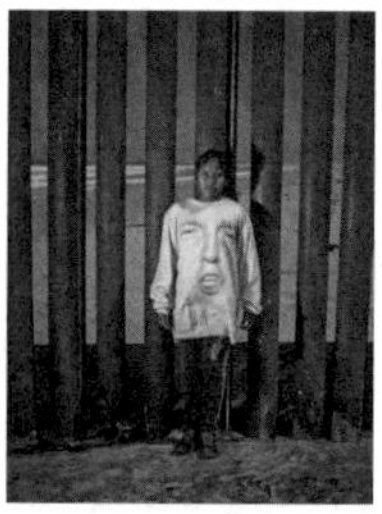

[43] Studies indicate that up to 21 percent of children in Latin America and the Caribbean live without one or both parents due to migration. Earlier research from the 2000s and 2010s showed parents migrating for extended periods, returning every two to three years. However, recent difficulties at the US–Mexican border have prompted a shift, with more parents now attempting to bring their children to the United States.

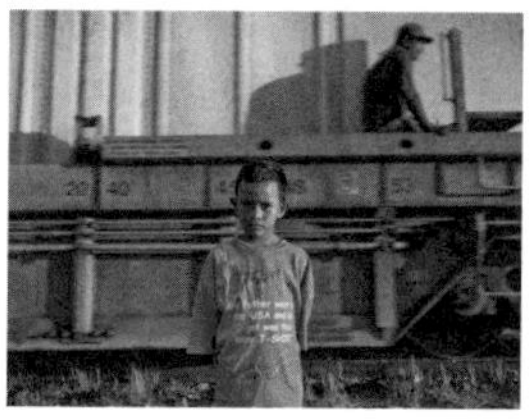

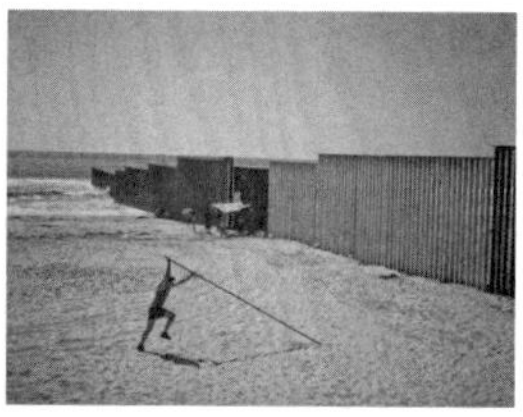

[44] The migration authority in Baja California reports that over 300,000 migrants cross illegally from Tijuana into the San Diego area annually. In 2018, I reached out to the Athletic Club of Tijuana asking for a collaboration whereby they would train beside a section of the border at Tijuana Beach known as the Tortilla Wall. The picture captures Jorge Luna attempting a jump at the point where the wall meets the sea. This crossing is particularly hazardous, due to strong currents and heightened militarization.

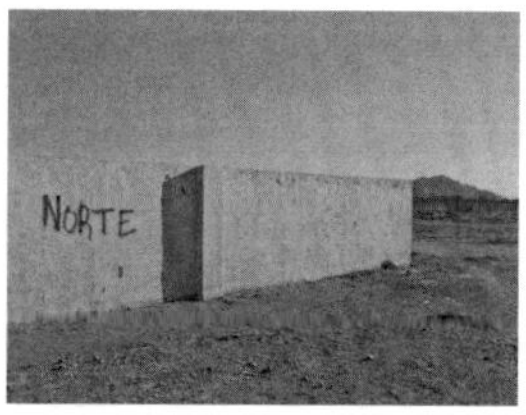

[45] Mexicans and migrants use various terms to refer to the United States, including "El Norte" (the North), "El otro lado" (the other side), and "El Gabacho", an older Spanish word historically used to refer to French people, stemming from the word "Gavach", meaning those who don't speak the language well.

[46] In a contemporary reinterpretation of "Angel Woman" by Mexican photographer Graciela Iturbide, I've reimagined that image to illustrate the control that cartels exert over the Mexican desert, transforming even the most remote places into their business playground.

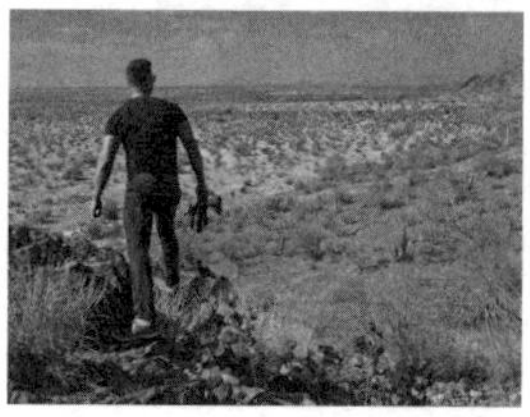

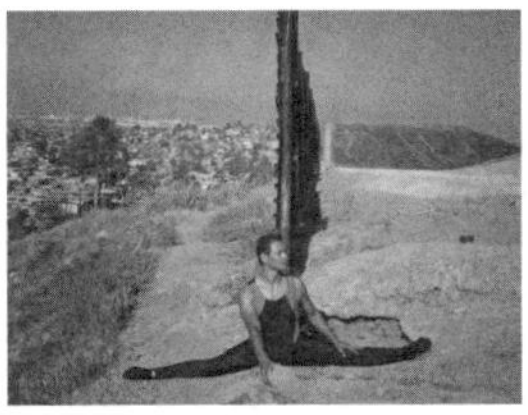

[47] A significant backlog at US immigration offices, with overall immigration court cases totaling 2.1 million in January 2023, is causing potentially decade-long delays for court dates for asylum-seekers from the Mexican border. This leaves migrants, compelled to return to Mexico after their asylum claims, in a legal limbo. In 2018, I approached the Athletic Club of Tijuana to seek collaboration for a photo shoot at various points along the wall. Here a gymnast performs the splits in Nido del Águila.

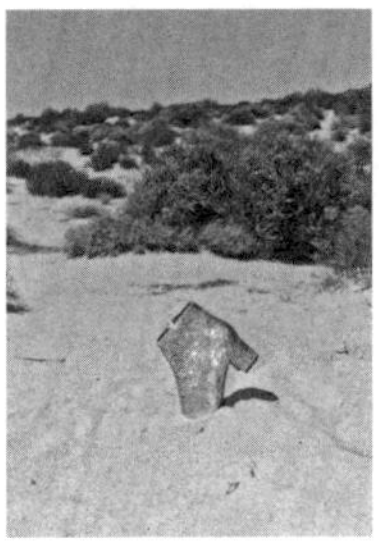

[48] In Mexico, collectives with names like Searching Mothers and Warrior Searchers have emerged nationwide to undertake the work they claim their government has neglected: locating and identifying their relatives, and laying them to rest. In the sparsely populated state of Sonora, 4,400 people are missing.

[49] The term "Unidentified Border Crossers" (UBCs) refers to foreign-born non-US citizens actively involved in crossing the US–México border without authorization from the United States government.

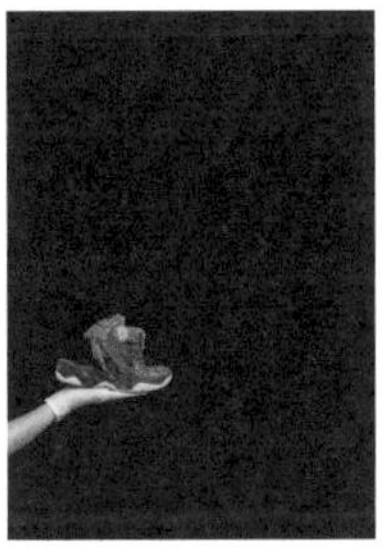

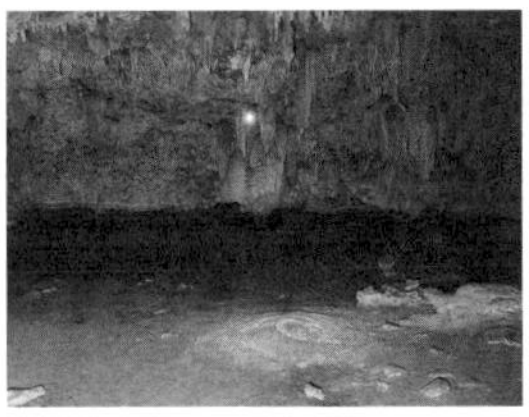

[50] Around 66 million years ago, a massive asteroid struck the Yucatán Peninsula, shaping the geological landscape and contributing to the formation of thousands of cenotes – natural sinkholes or pits, often filled with crystal-clear groundwater. In Mayan cosmology, cenotes were considered entrances to the underworld, connecting the surface world with the spiritual realm below. The image shows a cenote near the Ek Balam ruins in Yucatán.

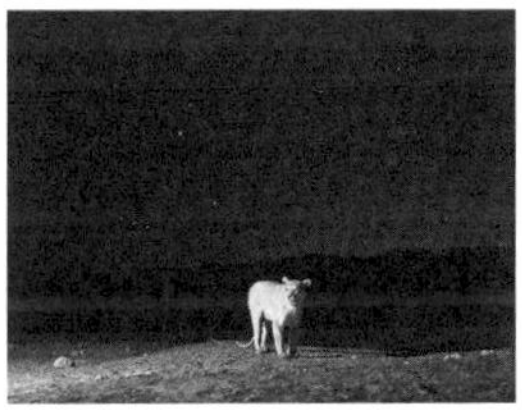

[51] The Sonoran Desert, spanning both sides of the border, serves as a hunting ground for mountain lions, mule deer, and big horn sheep. Hunting ranches, often isolated and intermittently used, provide convenient resting spots for migrants during their journey. In May 2021, I stayed at one of these farms, awaiting trucks carrying migrants to the border under the cover of night. The picture captures a stuffed mountain lion, one of several hunting trophies displayed in the house.

[52] In May 2021, I joined a group of migrants preparing to cross the border near Altar, through the Sasabe desert. The leaders of the convoy were tense and aggressive. They permitted me to stay for 16 minutes as they organized the group, breaking the silence of the night with shouted orders and emphasizing their commands with menacing rifles.

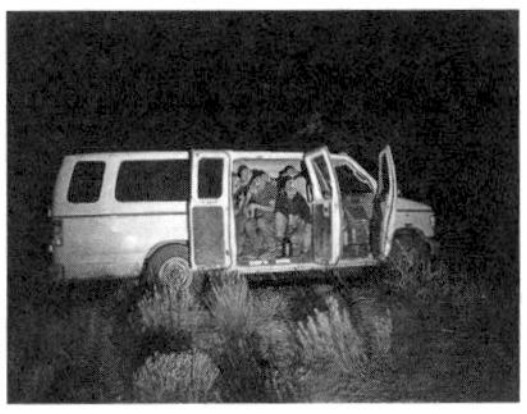

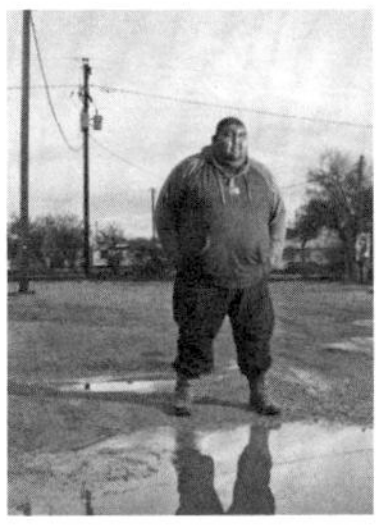

[53] Kendall M. Jose is the current tribal Vice Chairperson of the Chukut Kuk district of the Tohono O´odham nation. With a traditional territory that covers the Sonoran Desert in Mexico, Arizona and California, the tribe is alone facing the increasing numbers of migrants crossing the border by walking through their sacred land.

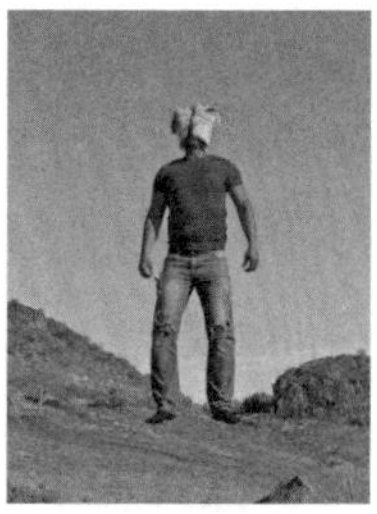

[54] President Biden's "Family Expedited Removal Management Program" imposes immigration consequences on parents crossing the US–Mexico border unlawfully with children. It requires certain families to wear ankle monitors and observe a nightly home curfew during a preliminary asylum claim review. Families passing "credible fear" interviews can stay pending a judge's decision, while those failing the interview face fast-track deportation.

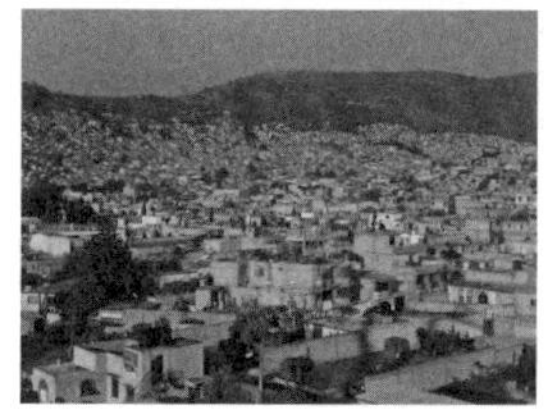

[55] In Los Bordos, a slum within Ecatepec, Mexico, lacking basic amenities like running water and electricity, limited educational and healthcare facilities, and notably, a scarcity of police presence, residents face significant challenges. Described as one of the most dangerous places to live in Mexico, Los Bordos has witnessed the murders of more than 600 women since 2012.

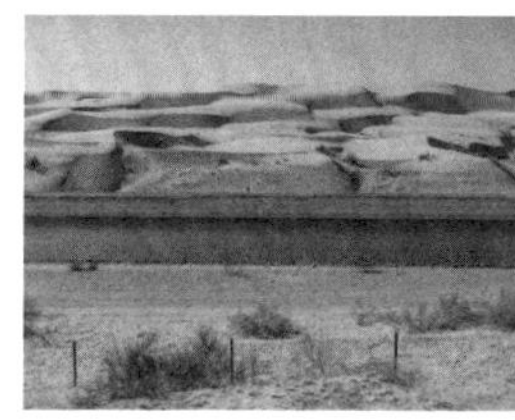

[56] The All-American canal runs parallel to the California-Mexico border for several miles and also along the Imperial Dunes (the American Sahara). With over 500 people having drowned in the canal since its completion, it has been called "the Most Dangerous Body of Water in the U.S". Fishing in the canal is also forbidden due to its elevated levels of mercury and selenium.

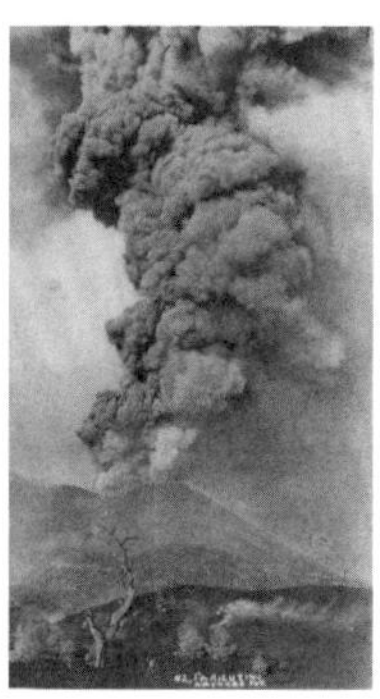

[57] Until recently, Paricutin in Michoacán held the record as the youngest volcano. It emerged suddenly in 1943 from a cornfield, growing over nine years to a cone height of 424 meters (1,391 feet), damaging over 233 square kilometers (90 square miles) by 1952. This vintage photo is part of extensive documentation of the eruption, inspiring artists like the Mexican painter Doctor Atl.

[58] Felicity, California, was founded by Jacques-André Istel and his wife Felicia in 1986. They received recognition from the state of California that the Center of the World was situated at the ceremonial granite pyramid they had constructed on their 2,900-acre land, purchased in the 1950s. In 1989, the French National Institute of Geography affirmed this decision.

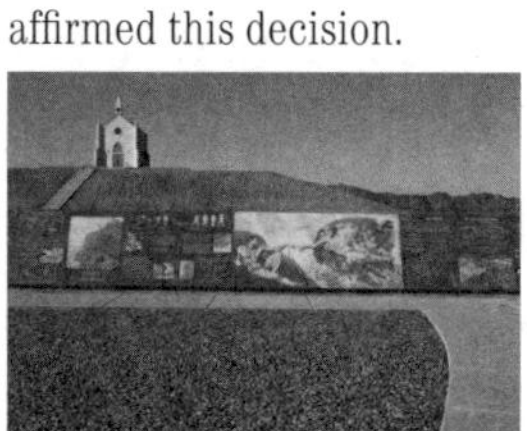

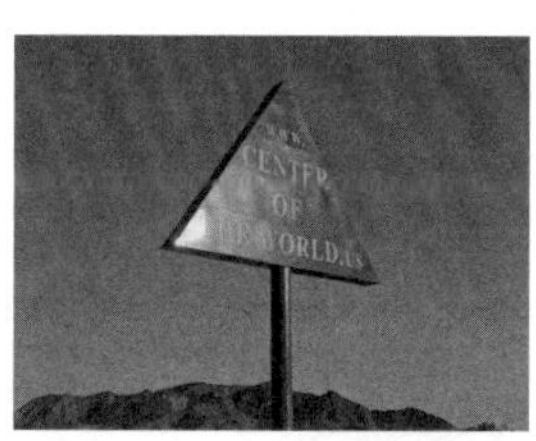

[59] I discovered Felicity by chance in 2015 while driving around the roads of southern California. Its unique history and logic, coupled with its proximity to the Imperial Sand Dunes border fence with Mexico, sparked the inspiration for this project, transforming the migrants' journey into a voyage to a hollow "Center of the World", and the travelers into the heroes of an outdated adventure book.

ACKNOWLEDGEMENTS

My respect and gratitude go to all those whose support, patience, and generosity made this book possible:

Eduardo Giralt, Magnum Photos, Jacques-André Istel, Salvador Luna, Bruno Morais, Yael Martínez, Miguel Fernández de Castro, Alicia Fernández, Pablo Allison, Luis Castillo, Astrid Rodríguez, Toño Armas, Lenin Rua Mosso, Coline Albert, Alejandro from the Tijuana athletics club, Jorge Luna, Alex Limón, Susana Vargas, Mariano Sosa, Emmanuel Massú, Sofía Cravioto, Elena Navarro, Maya Goded, Ruggiero Russo, Lynne Brower, Elías Gutiérrez Herrera, Flor de Caborca, Gregory Hess and his team from the Pima County Medical Examiner's Office, the Colibrí Foundation, Dan from Arivaca, Nahatan Navarro, the Casa del Migrante de Caborca, Nicolás Sáenz, Las Patronas, and especially the migrants I met on the road, whose stories are at the heart of this book's narrative.

Published on the occasion of Cristina de Middel's exhibition *Journey to the Center* presented at Rencontres d'Arles from July 1 to September 29, 2024.

ARLES
LES RENCONTRES
DE LA PHOTOGRAPHIE

Quotes taken from Jules Verne, *Journey to the Center of the Earth* (J. Hetzel, Paris, 1864), *A Journey into the Interior of the Earth* (translation by F. A. Malleson, Ward, Lock & Co., London, 1877), and *Viaje al centro de la Tierra* (translation by F. N., Biblioteca Universal Económica, Madrid, 1868)

Graphic design: Maricris Herrera and Israel Hernández, Estudio Herrera

Editorial RM
Editor-in-chief: Ramón Reverté
Editorial Coordination: Julieta Averbuj
English proofreading: Toni Crabb
Spanish proofreading: Julio Bueno

2, rue Rampal
75019 Paris
www.editionstextuel.com

RM Verlag, S.L.
Loreto 13-15, local B
08029, Barcelona, Spain

Editorial RM, S. A. de C. V.
Mexico City, Mexico

info@editorialrm.com
www.editorialrm.com
@editorial_rm

RM #490

ISBN: 978-84-10290-00-6
DL: B 8573-2024

Printed on Munken Polar 120 g, Creator star 115 g, and Munken Polar 90 g (interior)
as well as on Wibalin Natural (cover) in May 2024, on the presses of Musumeci S.p.A in Quart, Italy.